THE UNIVERSITY OF NORTH CAROLINA SOCIAL STUDY SERIES

SOCIAL LAWS

*The University of North Carolina Press, Chapel Hill, N. C.; The
Baker and Taylor Company, New York; Oxford University Press,
London; Maruzen-Kabushiki-Kaisha, Tokyo; Edward Evans & Sons,
Ltd., Shanghai.*

SOCIAL LAWS

A Study of the Validity of
Sociological Generalizations

BY

KYUNG DURK HAR

CHAPEL HILL
THE UNIVERSITY OF NORTH CAROLINA PRESS
1930

SOCIAL LAWS

A Study of the Validity of
Sociological Generalizations

BY

KYUNG DURK HAR

CHAPEL HILL
THE UNIVERSITY OF NORTH CAROLINA PRESS
1930

To My Friend

DR. RICHARD C. CABOT

THIS BOOK IS GRATEFULLY DEDICATED

PREFACE

In the field of social science, perhaps more than in any other field, the progress of thought depends intimately upon the interchange and comparison of ideas. The present study is in many ways tangible evidence of the dependence which those who would write in this department of knowledge have upon others. To the intellectual leadership of Professor Richard C. Cabot I owe much that I consider to be most valid in this inquiry, particularly in connection with my conception of social art. To Professors James Ford, Ralph M. Eaton, and Gordon W. Allport, I am indebted for their discussions with me as well as for their criticism of my manuscript. Mr. Hadley Cantril has kindly assisted with proofs and index. I am grateful also to Miss Ruth Carroll, Librarian of the Social Ethics Library at Harvard, for many and varied favors.

Less personal but no less genuine is my sense of obligation to all the authors whose views I have presented and presumed to criticize. If I have given unfavorable comment or unfamiliar setting to their work, it is with the hope that through such liberties as I have taken, the interweaving of thought may continue toward the gradual creation of a more valid science of society.

Several publishers have given permission for the use of quotations, and I should like especially to acknowledge the courtesy of the American Historical Association, the Century Co., Doubleday, Doran and Co., D. C. Heath and Co., Henry Holt and Co., Houghton Mifflin Co., Alfred A. Knopf, Methuen and Co., The Macmillan Co., G. P. Putnam's Sons, Charles Scribner's Sons, The Williams and Wilkins Co., the University of California Press, and the University of Chicago Press.

K. D. H.

FOREWORD

Sociological laws are dead. Long live sociology! Such is the conclusion of Dr. Har's remarkable book. Laws such as have been discovered in physics and chemistry he has not found in sociological literature, though he has examined one hundred and thirty-six generalizations called social laws by their authors or by other writers in the field of the social sciences.

There remains a small body of valid empirical correlations. These have limited validity but are nevertheless useful. Like medicine, sociology may make itself serviceable in the world even though it rests not on certain causal laws but only on probabilities and tendencies. It is idle to frown on medicine or on sociology because we may not care to call either of them "a science," or because much nonsense has been talked in the name of each. There is still wheat to be separated from the chaff. It is one of the valuable achievements of Dr. Har's book that he has shovelled together and piled up the chaff so that we can focus our attention on the small but growing heap of serviceable wheat.

In this piece of work he supplements effectively the labors of Professor Sorokin, who in his review and critique of "Contemporary Sociological Theories,"[1] arrives at conclusions with which Dr. Har's substantially agree. Both these writers face the future with confidence that by following the lead of the causal psychologists, by studying empirically the behaviour of man, valid and significant generalizations are being and will be built up. On this basis "social arts" can flourish.

Like Professor Sorokin, Dr. Har insists that we must not mix sociological observations with ethical precepts. But "Science," as Dr. Har reminds us, "may help us to get what we want by presenting us with sets of facts" about human nature. Amelioration is indeed the express interest of the book. The chief value of sociology as of all other sciences is as a vestibule to a better life for

[1] Harper & Bros., N. Y. and London, 1928.

[ix]

mankind. But so long as we are studying human nature, so long as we remain sociologists, the facts must be faced and studied with no desire more concrete than the desire to find the truth.

In this book I feel a new spirit blowing into musty corners, sweeping out rubbish, clearing the air for constructive work on the science that was christened "sociology" a hundred years ago,—a good while before it was born.

RICHARD C. CABOT.

CONTENTS

PAGE

PREFACE vii

FOREWORD ix

CHAPTER

I. IN SEARCH OF SOCIAL LAWS 3
   Purpose of the Present Study—Selection of Laws—
   Classification of Laws—Results.

II. THE IDEALS FOR SCIENTIFIC SOCIAL LAWS 11
   What is a Law?—Scientific Laws—How Scientific
   Laws are Discovered—Definitions—Science—Limitations of Science—Scientific Social Laws—Definitive
   Concepts— Measurement— Classification— Generalization—Assumptions—Causal Analysis—Psychological Illustrations—Special Social Sciences—Synthesis.

III. APRIORISMS AND METHODOLOGICAL PRESUPPOSITIONS.... 53
   Their Nature—List of Apriorisms—Comments.

IV. TELEOLOGICAL LAWS 78
   Their Nature—List of Teleological Laws—Comments.

V. STATISTICAL LAWS 95
   Their Nature—List of Statistical Laws—Comments.

VI. NEAR-CAUSAL LAWS 115
   Those Based on Inferences from the Order of Historical
   Sequences, Biological or Mechanistical Analogies—List
   of such Laws—Comments.

VII. NEAR-CAUSAL LAWS, CONTINUED 131
   Those Based on Psychological Analysis with Sympathy
   as their Central Principle—Imitation—Comments.

VIII. DIALECTICAL LAWS AS SYNTHESES 189
   Hegel's Idealistic Version of Dialectical Law—Marx's
   Materialistic Version — Croce's Criticism — Dialectical
   Social Laws—Comments.

[xi]

CONTENTS

PAGE

IX. SOCIAL ARTS 212

    Social Science or Social Art?—Necessity of Social Arts—
    Methodologies—Illustrations of Social Arts—Comments.

X. THE ARGUMENT IN REVIEW 239

    A Digest—General Results.

BIBLIOGRAPHY 247

INDEX 253

SOCIAL LAWS

CHAPTER I
IN SEARCH OF SOCIAL LAWS

THE PURPOSE OF THE PRESENT STUDY

THE PURPOSES of studying social phenomena may be said to be two: first, appreciation; second, melioration. By appreciation I mean the evaluation of human interests, the natural end of which is the reverence for personality. By melioration I mean the improvement of human relations and the conditions of living by knowledge of the order of Reality. Our appreciation will be of little significance, unless our will to appreciate is substantiated by an effort to improve things as they now are. But such effort presupposes knowledge of the laws by which social phenomena, with their manifold possibilities of transformation, are governed. The more accurate our knowledge of these laws, the better shall we be prepared for the task of improvement. The present volume is an attempt to examine, within a limited space, to what extent we have been successful in our search for such knowledge—an attempt to discover whether there are any valid scientific laws in social phenomena to justify the claim of the various social sciences to the title of positive sciences. For this purpose, I have gathered, classified, and discussed, in the following chapters, one hundred and thirty-six social laws, and in addition have mentioned in footnotes thirty-two other laws and propositions.

SELECTION OF LAWS

The first question one has to face in undertaking the task of collecting social laws, is which to select and which to leave out. It is comparatively easy to begin with a definition of social law, then to select those laws which fit the definition, and to omit all others which do not.[1] But in the present chaotic condition of sociology, which, in the words of the late Professor Small, consists of "ninety-five parts of omnium gatherum of all sorts of pertinent

[1] See, e. g., F. W. Blackmar and J. L. Gillin, *Outlines of Sociology*, Chap. XXI.

and impertinent selections from the scrap heap of h nan experience," an attempt to follow out consistently a schematic procedure, as just suggested, would lead to the arbitrary presentation of some laws and to the total neglect of others.[2]

I therefore think it prudent to select only those propositions which, either by their authors or by other writers in the field of the social sciences, have been *called* "social laws," "laws of history," or simply "laws." This delimitation of the scope of choice at one stroke excludes various sociological theories, principles, propositions, and maxims. Although theories as such are barred out, a number of the more important ones—for example, Professor Giddings' theory of "consciousness of kind"—receive incidental discussion simply because so many "social laws" are based upon them and cannot be understood without previous explanation of the theory.

Another consideration which leads me to exclude propositions and maxims is their irrelevancy to my present purpose. Since the object of my study is to find out whether any valid scientific social laws exist in social phenomena, to justify the claim of sociology to

---

[2] See A. W. Small, *Amer. Jour. of Sociol.*, *XXXII* (No. 1), 29.

Many eminent historians have been hostile to sociology. The late Professor Freeman despised what he called "the social stuff"; and Professor Emerton of Harvard went so far as to suggest that sociology was the philosophy of history, the "ancient enemy" of history itself. Professor Carver also once asserted that sociology, "instead of being a master science, comes nearer being a science of 'left-overs.' If ethics had continued to cover the ground which Aristotle laid out for it, there would never have been such separate sciences as politics and economics. But as ethics has actually developed, it covers a much narrower field. Again, politics as developed by such writers as Hobbes and Locke, left little room for economics or sociology either. When politics was narrowed down to the study of government, economics occupied the remainder of the field. But economics has also narrowed down, and sociology is inflicted upon the world for the sins of the economists. If economists had occupied the whole field laid out for them by Adam Smith, there would have been little excuse for sociologists. Therefore I am inclined to define sociology as economics broadened out. It is the study of the factors and conditions of human well-being, and thus includes a number of factors, such as selection, heredity, etc., which economists usually neglect."—T. N. Carver, *American Journal of Sociology*, VIII (No. 3), 393-94.

the title of a positive science, maxims and proverbs are out of place. I have therefore excluded from my selection such maxims as Professor Ross's five "utilitarian canons" of social control,[3] six "canons of social reconstruction,"[4] seven "maxims respecting stimulation,"[5] and his ten "propositions" on the system of social control, which he recasts as ten "laws of exploitation."[6] As the last-named also appear among Professor Giddings' laws, which I do present and discuss, it is unnecessary to repeat them. I have, however, given Mr. Brown's twenty-three "propositions" in the footnote to the discussion of Spencer's laws of evolution, for these seem to be apt illustrations of Spencer's method. Also in connection with Spencer's laws of evolution, I have given Dr. Müller-Lyer's nine "laws of economic development."

CLASSIFICATION OF LAWS

After having collected social laws, the next great question is, how to classify them. The answer to this question depends upon one's purpose in collecting these laws. If it were to write a history of social laws, it would seem best to classify them according to the chronological order of their appearance, beginning perhaps with those of Auguste Comte, and illustrate the way in which the various conceptions of each author have influenced his successors. Again, if the purpose of the present inquiry were to make a catalogue of social laws, it would seem most appropriate to classify them according to their sources in various types of subject matter. Thus, for example, one might begin with the laws of social psychology, which constitute by far the largest single class, and then might proceed to the laws of economics, of history, of government, of biology, and so forth.

But since the purpose of the present inquiry is to find out whether there are any valid scientific social laws, neither of these two methods seems to be to the point. For, although a history of

[3] *Social Control*, pp. 419-25.   [5] *Ibid.*, p. 661.
[4] *Principles of Sociology*, pp. 549-54.   [6] *Social Control*, p. 412.

social laws might tell as much or as little about what a social law ought to be, as a history of physics would tell as to what physics is, a large part of such a work would be irrelevant. Similarly, a catalogue of social laws might give some idea as to what sort of social laws the social scientists have formulated and where these originated; but it would be far from demonstrating what the inner characteristics of these laws are, and how they are related to one another. For, if there are any universally valid laws in social phenomena, all the social laws which circulate in one guise or another should be unified on some one fundamental basis. Such a fundamental basis is, to my mind, social psychology. The backbone of the social sciences is psychology and its laws, which may enable us to predict roughly future events. Human desires are the constant data of all social sciences, and the laws according to which human desires react on one another are the fundamental laws of all social phenomena; without these hardly any one of the social sciences merits the name "science."[7]

There remains a third possible method of classification, namely, classification from a special point of view. Among several alternatives I have chosen to classify the laws I have gathered from the methodological point of view which they suggest. This affords convenience in a critical examination of the laws, and an opportunity to discuss the methodologies in the various social sciences. In pursuance of this method I have grouped the various social laws into the following four classes:

1. Teleological Laws. It would seem strange that social scientists, who look for positive laws, should put forth teleological laws and assert them to be "natural laws." Between teleology and mechanism there is a world of difference. Nevertheless, social laws clearly teleological in character are found, which their authors call "natural laws." The generality of such laws varies greatly, some being as general as the Golden Rule, and others far

[7] J. Bryce, *Modern Democracies*, I, 13-23; H. M. Kallen, "Political Science as Psychology," *American Political Science Review*, XVII (No. 1), 181-203.

more specific, such as Professor Cheney's "law of moral progress." From the point of view of the naturalist, these are pious wishes rather than natural laws. However, to the naturalist, the conception of sociology as a positive science is as yet an item of faith, and not a demonstrated fact. It has on the whole seemed proper to present some of the most striking examples of teleological laws.

2. *Apriorisms and Methodological Presuppositions.* It would also seem strange that sociologists, who look for positive laws, should lay down a series of axioms and apriorisms, and call these natural laws. Nevertheless, a large number of social laws which fall into this class have been found. An apriorism may be granted as a methodological presupposition for the discovery of social laws, but is not in itself a social law. I have fully explained elsewhere what I mean by an axiom or an apriorism and my reasons for not regarding it as a social law.[8]

3. *Statistical Laws.* Approaching nearer to the ideals for scientific laws, is the large group of social laws based on statistical tendencies, of which Galton's laws of ancestral inheritance are examples. To speak accurately, these laws belong to a special social science, namely, eugenics. But they are considered so important that they are generally found in sociological textbooks and treatises. If sociology may be conceived either as a collection *of* special social sciences, or a collection *from* special social sciences, I see no reason for not admitting these laws as social laws.

4. *Near-Causal Laws.* By a near-causal law I mean a law which describes a limited amount of uniformity in social phenomena, and which therefore is valid within the limit of uniformity, but which offers no adequate causal explanation of the uniformity. This type of law is often called an "empirical law"; in sociology it is generally reducible to a psychological law. Sociological literature is full of laws of this type. Sometimes these laws are minutely schematized, and hair-splitting distinctions are

[8] See Chapter III.

made among them, as in the system of Professor Giddings, who probably is the greatest schematizer among sociologists.[9]

Sometimes solemn distinctions are made between social laws and the laws of the special social sciences, in order to demonstrate the masterhood of sociology. Thus, Professor Ross, following De Greef's distinction between simple and compound laws, says that the former express relations between phenomena of the same class; the latter, relations between phenomena of different classes. When two economic facts are joined, as in the proposition that the investment of capital varies directly with the rate of interest, we have an economic law. Similarly, when two political facts are connected, as in the proposition that as national oppositions grow party oppositions weaken, we have a law of political science. When a political and an economic fact are connected, as in the proposition that with the diffusion of economic opportunity the tension between classes lessens, we have a social law. But in general, says Professor Ross, the typical social laws are the fundamental truths underlying the special social sciences rather than the statements of relations between facts of different classes. For example, Tarde's laws of imitation, which Professor Ross calls "generalizations" in distinction from "laws," are, he thinks, applicable to linguistics, demography, and economics as well as to political science. For this reason, Professor Ross is convinced that "sociology is not so much a sister science to politics or jurisprudence as a fundamental and comprehensive discipline uniting at the base all the social sciences."[10]

With the examination of the four types of social laws just described, our major task will be completed. But before concluding the study as a whole, I shall present a chapter on certain philosophical generalizations on history—among others, those of Hegel, Marx, Spencer, and Professor Hocking. All these generalizations are "dialectical laws" in the sense explained in the

---

[9] F. H. Giddings, *Inductive Sociology*, pp. 13-14.
[10] Ross, *Foundations of Sociology*, pp. 67-70.

chapter; and all quite freely circulate as either "social laws," "laws of history," or simply "laws." They are presented here as classic examples of synthesis.

The laws presented in this volume are gathered mostly from sociological textbooks and treatises. I have extended the search, however, into the fields of the special social sciences—psychology, history, government, economics, and anthropology, especially.[11] One of these special social sciences—namely, economics—is found to be a very fruitful source of "laws." In Gide and Rist's *History of Economic Doctrines* and Palgrave's *Dictionary of Political Economy* alone, about twenty economic laws are stated.

The name of the author of a law, together with its location in his works, is given whenever he enunciates it as a "law." Whenever the author merely recognizes as "laws" certain propositions previously enunciated by another writer as something other than "laws," I have given the names of both the original projector and the rediscoverer of the laws, together with references. A large number of Professor Ross's Laws fall into this latter class, as do those proposed by Blackmar and Gillin.[12]

In order that I may not disappoint my reader overmuch, I may anticipate the results of the present inquiry. First, the attempt to discover rules of social phenomena which may be termed laws in the same sense as that in which a law of physics or chemistry is a law, has yielded a negative result. Instead, we have been able to gather a mass of empirical generalizations, that is, statements of little precision and of limited applicability. Secondly, since, as explained above, I have limited my scope of inquiry to the supposedly most certain propositions, namely, those

[11] See Bibliography.
[12] See Ross, *Foundations of Sociology*, pp. 41-70, and Blackmar and Gillin, *Outlines of Sociology*, Chap. XXI.

which are *called* "laws," excluding the less certain propositions such as "theories" and "principles," there is reason to believe that this negative result is not wholly due to my superficial observation. However, whether this negative result is correct or not, social scientists should not rest content until they have reached the goal of their scientific ideals. I have therefore discussed somewhat in detail in the next chapter the line of further research that may be profitably pursued. Thirdly, in the absence of any perfect social laws, we cannot have a science of society as precise as mathematics or physics or even physiology; and without this the control of social phenomena will indefinitely remain imperfect. But we may still have *social arts* as we have the art of healing. What the nature of such arts may be, I have discussed somewhat in detail in the chapter immediately preceding the last.

CHAPTER II
THE IDEALS FOR SCIENTIFIC SOCIAL LAWS

WHAT IS A LAW?

T HERE ARE FOUR main types of laws.[1] First, teleological laws, which describe phenomena in terms of some final causes, and which evaluate them in terms of certain moral and ideal standards, such as the divine, moral, and juridical laws. Such laws are either desirable or supposed to be desirable, and the observance of them is often accompanied by a moral emotion. Second, logical laws, which state a priori propositions concerning relations between the objects of thought, such as the laws of logic and of mathematics. By an a priori proposition I mean either a proposition which is a necessary form of thought in all processes of reasoning, or a proposition which is assumed to be necessary for the purpose of carrying out a special kind of reasoning. Such propositions are called a priori, because they are not established by the sense data of experience. Third, positive laws which state either the invariant causal relations between antecedents and consequents, or invariant associations between co-existing phenomena, such as the laws of physics and chemistry. By a cause I mean the uniform antecedent in a series of mechanical successions which is explicable by means of some generally accepted theory. It is sometimes called the efficient cause, in contradistinction to the ontological or teleological cause. Fourth, statistical laws which state the correlations between several phenomena that jointly appear and jointly disappear, or the correlations between the appearance of one set of phenomena and the disappearance of another set.

A definition of law so comprehensive as to cover all these four types may be that a law is a statement of relations. Now, not all of these four types of laws are of like origin, precision or validity.

[1] See also A. D. Ritchie's classification in *Scientific Method*, p. 17.

A divine law is supposed to have been revealed by a deity, and is observed by his devotees; but it often reads like the gibberings of a soothsayer. It has no validity outside the circle of his devotees; and its violation is sometimes highly meritorious. A law of the state may be regarded as an act of the sovereign, binding upon the members of the state. But the sovereign may impose laws upon the people without regard to their welfare. A law in such a case is declared to be immoral, and its violation a moral duty of the people concerned. A moral law is a law self-imposed by an individual, and may be agreed to, as what ought to be, by the best moral insight of his fellow human beings. It may or may not be as scrupulously observed as the laws of the state, but it can be violated only on pain of self-condemnation on the part of the law-breaker. The laws of logic and of mathematics, in so far as they are the necessary forms of knowledge, are universally valid. But they do not rest on sense experience, though they may be exemplified. This is the point of difference between the laws of logic and the laws of nature; for the latter are merely found in nature through our sense experience. Both positive and statistical laws are called scientific laws, meaning thereby that they both are discovered by means of empirical observations and quantitative measurements.

SCIENTIFIC LAWS

Scientific laws are of three kinds: those which describe invariant causal relations, those which describe invariant associations, and those which describe varying degrees of correlations. Of these three by far the most important is the causal law. For this reason, a scientific law is sometimes defined as a description of the invariant relations of cause and effect.[2] But this definition of scientific law is beset by a number of verbal pitfalls. For example, death is invariably preceded by birth; day and night invariably follow each other. Shall we say therefore that birth is

---

[2] J. S. Mill, *Logic*, p. 213; K. Pearson, *Grammar of Science*, Chap. IV.

the cause of death, or that day and night are each the cause of the other? In order to avoid such pitfalls, a scientific law is defined as a description of an invariable association, which can be explained by means of some generally accepted theory.[3]

HOW SCIENTIFIC LAWS ARE DISCOVERED

Scientific laws are discovered by empirical observations, experiments, and inductive generalizations. By an empirical observation is meant a naïve observation without either prejudice or prepossession. By experiment is meant the control of a situation and the observation of sequences. An ideal experiment should effect a complete isolation of the object of experiment and the measurement of the sequential variations. By an inductive generalization is meant the abstraction of a law from the data obtained by means of empirical observations and experiments. At any one of these three steps there is always a possibility of error, for our empirical observations are always limited to some particular time and place. Those who never heard any language but English might suppose that English is the universal language, and those who never saw a gray crow might easily believe that all crows are black. A single exception of this kind may invalidate a venerable scientific law. The control of a situation varies greatly according to the subject matter under experiment. In the social sciences the isolation of data is at present almost impossible. Even in the physical sciences where the greatest accuracy is obtainable, if the mean variation does not exceed one-thousandth or one-hundredth of a unit (as the case might be), the result is considered reliable. The degree of precision also varies according to the type of law. But, in general, scientific laws are rough approximations of quantitative relations.[4] As for inductive generalization, it is always a leap in the dark; unless it is confirmed by numerous subsequent observations and experiments, it remains a mere hypothesis.

[3] Norman Campbell, *What is Science?* (Methuen and Co.), pp. 49-50.
[4] A. D. Ritchie, *Scientific Method,* p. 56.

The history of scientific thought furnishes plenty of examples of laws which were once held to be incontrovertible, but which later turned out to be mistaken. "There are always loopholes left," says Dr. Campbell, "which enable us to reject a law, however much experimental evidence may suggest it and enable us to maintain a law (slightly modified) even when experimental evidence seems directly to contradict it. An examination of any actual science will show that the acceptance of a law is very largely determined by the possibility of explaining it by means of a theory; if it can be so explained, we are much more ready to accept it, and much more anxious to maintain it if it is the consequence of some theory. Indeed, many laws in science are termed empirical and are regarded with a certain amount of suspicion; if we inquire we find that an empirical law is simply one of which no theoretical explanation is known. In the science of physics at least, it would almost be more accurate to say that we believe our laws because they are the consequences of our theories than to say that we believe our theories because they predict and explain true laws!"[5]

<h3 style="text-align:center">DEFINITIONS</h3>

There are four cognate terms which the scientists use frequently without discrimination. They may be summarily defined as follows:

1. Scientific Fact. In popular usage the word fact is often contrasted with theory, the former meaning, it would seem, what one is pleased to believe, and the latter what one's opponent in a dispute believes. Disputants often ask each other, "what are the facts?" Then they often appeal to some established laws. This usage of the word fact is not altogether unreasonable. For the word fact as used in science means a law of little generality, capable of immediate verification. A fact is a datum generally accepted by scientists who have equal opportunity and equipment

<hr>

[5] N. Campbell, *op. cit.,* p. 91; cf. J. S. Mill, *Logic,* pp. 205-6; F. Znaniecki, *Laws of Social Psychology,* p. 47.

for experiencing it. Because it is a datum common to scientists, it cannot be coerced or denied, cannot be arbitrarily fashioned to suit their personal convenience but must be accepted as it comes to them. For this reason facts are called "real," and by real is meant something which the scientists do not make, but find. It is, for example, a scientific fact that the atomic weight of oxygen is 16, and that hydrogen is a colorless gas.[6]

2. *Scientific Law.* As already defined, a scientific law is a description of an invariant association. By an invariant association is meant an invariant association of *facts*. Both fact and law are generalities, but the former is simpler or more particular than the latter. The fact that hydrogen is a colorless gas in a generality like the proposition that benzene boils at 80° C, or the proposition that all gases expand when heated. But these latter, being a combination of facts, are called laws.

3 and 4. Theory and Hypothesis. A theory, according to Dr. Campbell, is a proposition which satisfies three conditions: *(a)* It must be such that the law which it is devised to explain can be deduced from it; *(b)* it must explain those laws in the sense of introducing ideas which are more familiar, or in some other way more acceptable, than those of the laws; *(c)* it must lead to the prediction of new laws which, on verification, must be true. Ordinarily a theory is suggested in view of the first two conditions alone, but accidentally it fulfills the third. In other words, a theory is an even greater generality than a law, but it signifies less certainty than does a law; nor is it immediately verifiable as a fact can be. An hypothesis is a theory of even less certainty. Etymologically an hypothesis is a "supposition," any proposition which is supposed because of its probability. To illustrate: "the individual and reproducible relations observed between pressures, volumes and temperatures of gases are the facts. The generalization of these into the relation $PV = RT$ is the gas law. The

[6] A. J. Thompson, *Introduction to Science*, pp. 40, 60; B. Russell, *Scientific Method in Philosophy*, Lecture II.

theory is the Kinetic Theory which is based upon a hypothesis as to the structure of the minute imperceptible parts of the gas."[7]

SCIENCE

Science, then, may be defined as an internally coherent deductive system which (1) explains phenomena, (2) provides the key to their controllability, and (3) lends itself to our esthetic contemplation. In order to emphasize their importance, I have numbered the three points mentioned in this definition. I shall explain them in the order in which they are mentioned:

1. Scientific Explanation. Science is an internally coherent system in the sense that the various terms within it mutually define one another as in any valid system of logic, once the fundamental assumptions are granted, rendering experience more readily intelligible. It explains phenomena in the sense that the lesser generalizations can be deduced from the greater. Boyle's law of gas, for example, is deducible from the kinetic theory of gas, which in turn is deducible from the molecular hypothesis. To explain is to deduce, to make the phenomena consistent with one another, and this is rendered possible by converting the temporal sequences of phenomena into logic sequences. Once the kinetic theory of gas is granted, not only does hydrogen expand when heated, but also it must do so; if not, it is not hydrogen, not even a gas, or else, the kinetic theory must be false.

2. Its Utility. Explanation of this type satisfies our curiosity, our intellectual hunger. But to explain is not enough; for, even the story of Alice in Wonderland has a certain amount of internal consistency, and explains why the Cheshire cat grinned at the king and the queen and why her majesty shouted at it: "Off with his head!" Such explanations have very little to do with real cats, real kings, and real queens. The scientists do not intend to deal with anything less than real. For, only by dealing with reality, can their learning yield some utility. Scientific explana-

[7] A. D. Ritchie, *op. cit.*, pp. 77-80; 155-57. N. Campbell, *op. cit.*, pp. 80-90.

tion, therefore, not only unifies experience, but also furnishes a key to the controllability of phenomena. It enables us to predict phenomena.

Looked at from the objective point of view, a scientific law is a pure description of a pattern of observed facts; and not a prediction of future events. The sun will rise tomorrow morning as it did countless times in the past, provided, the heavenly bodies will continue to rotate as they now do. Scientific laws do not guarantee that they will do so. Whatever predictability there is in a scientific law is not there till men read prediction into it. But none the less it enables us to predict future events, and often, therefore, to control the course of natural events. How men read prediction into scientific laws is a metaphysical question.[8] It is sufficient here to note that men, as they become accustomed to certain modes of life, acquire a disposition to believe the objects involved in those modes of life to be real, and to base their expectations upon the belief. No one is surprised at finding that a baby is born at the end of nine months of prenatal life, though in fact the birth of a baby is one of the greatest miracles; and every one will probably be surprised if he dreams the same dream three nights in succession. The reason for this difference in attitude is not in the nature of the events themselves, but in the *disposition* to anticipate events on the part of men, and the disposition to anticipate is probably a survival of the primitive instinct of adaptation.

3. Its Esthetic Value. A deductive system, as just described, which explains facts by laws, laws by theories, and theories by hypotheses, ever enlarging the scope of the conceptual unification of experience, is a fit object for esthetic contemplation. The simplicity of its concepts, the consistency of its internal relations, and the vastness of its explanatory scheme, have a strong fascination for our esthetic intuition. Strange though it may sound, a scien-

[8] See, e. g., G. Santayana, *Scepticism and Animal Faith.*

tist is also an artist to the extent that, in selecting examples, he is invariably guided by his creative imagination. As will be demonstrated later,[9] this is all the more clearly seen in the less exact sciences such as sociology, which is hardly a science except in name. A science is not an assemblage of the raw data of experience, presented helter-skelter to disillusioned eyes, but a work of fine art, remarkable alike for its faithfulness to facts and its departure therefrom. Its data are the brute facts, the a posterioris; but its points of view are not. There is always a possibility of pluralistic developments, each of which, once the fundamental assumptions are granted, may be consistent throughout its whole internal system. Like the panorama of existence its pictures may be endlessly varying, yet like a work of art the system as a whole can be comprehended in a single intuitive grasp. It is loved for its own sake, irrespective of its utility.

LIMITATIONS OF SCIENCE

The scientific method, though remarkable for its power of explanation, its usefulness, and its esthetic fascination, has certain radical limitations. Among these limitations the most conspicuous are the following two:

1. Teleology Disregarded. The scientific method of explanation consists of referring limited instances of uniformity to more general uniformities. Scientific facts are explained by referring them to a law; laws by referring them to a theory; and theories by referring them to an hypothesis. This method of explanation always leaves unexplained the last generalization in the series of its explanatory scheme. To say, for example, that all gases expand when heated, is not to explain why hydrogen expands when heated: it merely leads us to ask immediately why all gases expand when heated. An explanation which leads immediately to another question of the same kind is not an explanation; it involves *petitio principii.* Hence, the natural scientists are

[9] See below, pp. 212 ff.

charged with reasoning in a circle. Explanation in the sense of answering the questions of why or what for, is neither proved nor disproved, but is disregarded by science. Science deliberately ignores the question of final cause.

2. *Secondary Qualities and Values Unexplained.* Life is an organization of value-attitudes such as likes and dislikes, and value is a function, in part, of the secondary qualities such as color and sound. But in the natural scientists' account of the world, one finds nothing but motion and number. Again, science being a conceptual unification of experience, at the basis of it there is always to be found an irreducible residue of sense data which can be known only by immediate perception, and which are peculiar to individuals. The realm of experience which is peculiar to individuals is the world of private values and personal appreciation. The realm of experience which is common to all is the world of description, of science. The latter is an abstraction from the former,—an abstraction, moreover, from the point of view of some special interests such as classification and measurement. A scientific truth is, therefore, an abstract truth, and public property accessible to all. But the world of experience is a personal, phenomenal world; and the deepest, the most intimate part of one's experience is one's private property.

Being an abstraction from a special point of view, a scientific truth is an artificial truth—artificial as contrasted with *factual* and not with *real*. To play a game of chess according to the rules of the game, to write an essay according to the rules of grammar, or even to think in an orderly way according to the rules of logic, is not to play, to write, or to think *falsely*, but *artificially*. A scientific proposition is true by the grace of the good taste and by the canons of reasoning adopted by scientists. But the life which we live from day to day is prose and poetry of which we learn more from poets and artists than from scientists.[10]

[10] See C. I. Lewis, "The Structure of Logic and Its Relation to Other Systems," *Journal of Philosophy*, vol. XVIII, no. 19; R. M. Eaton, "The Value of

Scientific social laws cannot be discussed with any degree of precision without first defining what a scientific law is. A scientific social law, if it is genuine, must be a law modelled after the laws of the natural sciences, and must describe invariant patterns in social phenomena. Indeed, I should define *a scientific social law as a description of an invariant pattern of social phenomena, if there be any such invariant patterns, explicable by means of a generally accepted theory of social causation which in turn must be explicable by means of a plausible hypothesis concerning human nature and social relations, thus making the conceptual unification of social phenomena complete.*

There seems to be, however, not a little confusion in the discussion on social laws, owing to the fact that the writers on the subject state their propositions in loose terms. The Malthusian statements regarding population, for example, are called "principles" by some authors, "theories" by others, "hypotheses" by still others, and "laws" by many. Very little progress can be made in any discussion on scientific social laws, until systematic attempts are made to clear up the muddled terminology. Since, however, all the following chapters, except the ninth, are chiefly occupied with attempts to clarify terms, I shall merely outline, in the remaining pages of the present chapter, a method for social studies with the hope of furthering slightly the efforts of the social scientists to make sociology an exact science. In view of the fact that sociology is, at present, without either an adequate technique of study or a sufficient accumulation of data, the present outline will be occupied with a discussion of definitive concepts and methodological assumptions.

DEFINITIVE CONCEPTS

A definition is a conceptual image for a class of events throughout which a sufficient degree of uniformity prevails to

Theories," *Ibid.,* vol. XVIII, no. 25; R. B. Perry, *Present Philosophical Tendencies,* Chaps. IV-V.

mark them off from other events. All scientific inquiries should properly begin with definitive concepts. It then becomes pertinent to ask what sort of definition is most satisfactory. The best answer to this question is implied in von Böhm-Bawerk's discussion on the definition of capital. First, whatever definition we adopt, he says, must be logically unassailable. A definition is logically unassailable when it is consistent throughout the discourse. Secondly, "we must not be spendthrift in our terminology." Every definition must stand for a particular class of events, distinct by themselves. It is a vice of the scientist to call everything by the same name. Thirdly, a definition must be useful in the sense that it facilitates our efforts at the conceptual unification of our knowledge.

And finally, unless for any one of the foregoing reasons we need to adopt a new definition, it is desirable *for scientific purposes* to preserve and to make use of some generally known definitions rather than to invent new ones.[11] In the last sentence I have deliberately inserted the words *for scientific purposes* because science is interested in matters in which unanimity of opinions prevails, and this is the point I wish to emphasize. Unless we stick to some one workable definition and keep on measuring and comparing the data patiently, we shall never get beyond the stage of artistic discussion. This does not mean that we should never improve on our definitions. This only means that for the purpose of scientific measurements and comparison, it is well to make use of all that we have inherited from our predecessors and turn our inventive genius in other directions than the barren multiplication of verbal changes.

1. Mutual Definitions. A perfect science is a conceptual system in which the various terms reciprocally define one another, just as in the theory of relativity everything is determined in relation to everything else, just as "point," "moment," "motion,"

[11] E. von Böhm-Bawerk, *The Positive Theory of Capital*, translated by W. Smart, pp. 37-38.

"duration," and the like, in physics are defined in terms of one another.[12] If any one of the terms cannot be so defined, it is left isolated and unexplained, and therefore the unification of the science is incomplete. As applied to sociology, this means that society can be defined only in terms of individuals, and individuals only in terms of society; progress in terms of stagnation, and stagnation in terms of progress; and then society, individual, progress, and stagnation, each and all in terms of one another. And so the process of definition should go on till every social phenomenon is defined in terms of every other, making the circle of definitions complete. For, only by such a process can we render our experience completely intelligible and ultimately discover the causal connections between the various phenomena.

2. *Verification by Facts.* The definitive process is essentially an a priori activity of the mind. For, an absurd definition is as much a definition as a true one. A proposition true by definition is not necessarily true in fact. A good definition must be in agreement with fact. The reason that we are so vague about imitation, sympathy, and the like, is that we have not yet gathered sufficient data on which to generalize. We are prone to generalize a priori, and not patient enough to keep on gathering facts in detail. But since the gathering of facts is a tedious and seemingly an endless task, all discussions of social phenomena must inevitably begin with tentative definitions which must also be continually revised in the light of the new facts unearthed.

3. *Definition of Social Facts.* A legal fact is an overt act which can be testified either directly or circumstantially by somebody. An historical fact is an event in its unique space and time relations, and like all things unique, it cannot be reproduced. But what is a social fact? A social fact, as a scientific datum, may be defined as an historical fact shorn of its uniqueness. A fact incapable of verification is not a fact for natural science; and since an historical fact owes its beauty to its unique space and

[12] See A. N. Whitehead, *Principles of Natural Knowledge.*

time relations, it is not a scientific fact. It can be made a scientific fact, however, by isolating it from its space and time relations, and thereby making it abstract.

The task of unearthing facts is a difficult one. A novelist can invent facts to suit his plot; a poet can interpret his experience as his mood dictates; and a statesman may turn his faith into energy and work it into a fact. But a social scientist can do none of these. He can neither be so arbitrary as a novelist nor resign himself to the dictates of his mood; for every fact he puts forth a verification is demanded of him, because a scientist is a fact-finder and not a fact-maker. Hence, the only practicable, though admittedly inadequate, concept of social fact for a sociologist is, at present, that of abstract fact, namely, social facts in general— man in general, society in general, progress in general—always bearing in mind that a fact in general may be no fact in particular, just as the eugenists' concept of the normal American may be no American in particular. Until fully verified by subsequent events, a general fact remains hypothetical. Hence, Pareto's concept of sociology as an *hypothetical* science in contrast with an *actual* science such as physics, is for the time being unavoidable.[13]

4. Gradations of Social Facts. In the most proper sense of the term, a social fact is a consciously mutual relation, such as a friendly intercourse, a commercial transaction, or even a boxing match. I am aware that this usage of the term *social* is in some ways anomalous, due to the ambiguity of the term in common speech. For, social in this sense, a quarrel ending in a murder may be called a social phenomenon. Nevertheless, only in consciously mutual relations do we have moral as well as economic problems. A quarrel, a murder, or a war is unsocial when judged from its results; but they are highly social in the sense that it is only in such consciously reciprocal relations that our interest in the presence of others is keenest. I call, therefore, *all consciously reciprocal human relations the primary data in sociology.*

[13] Vilfredo Pareto, *Trattato di sociologia generale.*

There is next a much larger class of impersonal and unreciprocated human relations. As human desires are multiplied through invention and intertwined through commerce, we are increasingly aware of the mutuality of our interests. But at the same time, with most of our neighbors we have only impersonal relations. I call *all impersonal and unreciprocated human relations secondary data in sociology.* That John Jones lived in the same town with Mr. Rockefeller is a secondary social datum to both Mr. Jones and Mr. Rockefeller, even if neither of them knew of the other's existence, because as residents of the same town, as citizens of the same state, or as tax-payers to the same government, they are always impersonally related through the medium of a third party.

Finally, there is a still larger class of extra-human events. The fertility of the soil, the character of the climate, the amount of rainfall, the proximity of navigable rivers, the richness of mineral resources, and the like, are natural phenomena and not social. But they are of such great value to man's economic life that conflict over their possession or pride over their ownership is sure to arise sooner or later. They are therefore the mediating facts in social phenomena. I call them *the tertiary data in sociology.* There are also other natural phenomena for which no one will fight and which can be fully enjoyed only by sharing with others. If, for example, the winds whistle round the chimneys and the trees dance in glee, and if nobody notices either one of these events, they are not social. But as soon as someone takes an interest in them, they become social events. Whatsoever thing happens, therefore, in the universe, is either a social event or is capable of becoming so by virtue of the human interest invested in it. The task of gathering facts is as infinite as the universe itself; but some are more relevant to human relations than others, and in proportion to their proximity to human interests, they enter into the determination of social relations.

MEASUREMENT

Natural science does not regard an ideal or a wish as a fact. Both facts and ideals are events, their difference being that the former are realized events while the latter are unrealized. The task of a social scientist will be much simpler if he leaves out of consideration all ideals and hopes, but a science of society which ignores them all cannot be of much worth. If all our hopes and ideals were mere illusions, they would certainly be cruel impositions upon life. And yet all things lovely and precious are first born as ideals. And ideals are so intangible that the problem of reducing them to a quantitative basis is the despair alike of philosophers and sociologists. We cannot compare things which have no common denominator: ideals are not only intangible, but each one is also unique.

Though at present there are no adequate units for measuring social data, it is well to keep on measuring with such devices as we now have, and to improve upon them. The hedonistic calculus, the structural tests of Spencer, the dollar yard-stick, the mental age test, and other comparable devices,[14] are after all better than nothing, provided one avoids making exaggerated statements and interprets the results with a grain of common sense. To say that they are better than nothing is not a high compliment; yet one of the secrets of success is to take advantage of everything that is better than nothing. The usefulness of such tests and measurements does not lie in their adequacy, but rather in the hope that, by careful employment of such devices, we may some day discover something better.

CLASSIFICATION

If nature had made all things each in a separate compartment, they would have merely external relations with one another, and each would have constituted a class by itself. But things as they actually are imperceptibly shade into one another in an

[14] See below, pp. 96, 99.

infinite series of gradations. Hence, all classifications depend
on the points of view taken, and when the point of view is
changed, the same thing may be classified under different categories. For instance, from the ethical point of view, a man is
a moral being. From the zoölogical point of view, he is an
animal, more or less fitted or misfitted than other animals to
survive. And from the point of view of a chemist, he is a curious
synthesis of chemical properties. Once the point of view is
adopted, classification may be obtained through an abstraction of
the common characteristics of the data gathered. To classify
is to distribute the data according to their common characteristics.
When a classification is complete, it amounts to a law itself. In
sociology, however, classification is at present but a crude device
for the study of relations between social phenomena. We gather
as many facts as we can and study them from whatever different
points of view our curiosity may suggest.

GENERALIZATION

Generalization is always a leap from the particular to the
universal. That some men are liars is an empirical fact, but the
jump from this fact to the idea that all men are liars is a mysterious process. J. S. Mill spoke of an "instinct of generalization."[15] While we should be cautious about the term instinct,
it seems that all men above the moron grade have a tendency to
generalize; the more intelligent is the man, the keener is his
power to perceive types of events. It grew, probably, out of the
primitive man's necessity for adaptation to his environment.
Without the ability to perceive types of events one could learn
very little: each new experience would then be utterly incom-
prehensible, and life would be a perpetual surprise. Such a
man could hardly have survived in the primitive hostile environment. Since objects are readily identified as either favorable
or dangerous, the ability to perceive types was a likely tool for
survival.

[15] *Logic,* p. 204.

A generalization is never merely a summation of known facts, but *a summation plus an inference,* and therefore, unless it is explained by a higher generalization, its truth may be challenged. For instance, the proposition that all men are mortal was never derived from an observation of all men, and yet it is explicable by physiological facts; it is therefore a true generalization. On the other hand, the proposition that the dictatorship of proletariat is inevitable, is not explained by any valid social theory, and therefore it remains a mere catch phrase. An event is inevitable, if it is unavoidable by exercise of forethought and care, such as death which cannot be avoided, though it may be postponed. But, is there any such unavoidableness in the threat of the proletariat dictatorship?

1. Exceptions. A completely unified science has no exceptions. If there is anything which tends to disprove an existing law or any other generalization, it is the exception. Further, the exceptions to social laws are even more important than those to physical laws because of the ethical significance implied in the exception. For the importance of exceptions to sociological generalizations three reasons might be given. First, if a machine fails to produce a predicted result, it is always because some part of the machine is faulty, and the faulty part is obvious. But when an individual fails to adjust himself to his environment, it is not obvious that he alone is faulty; very frequently it is found that both he and his environment share the fault. Hence, until we have attained certainty of knowledge with regard to the intricate relations between individual and environment, we should be cautious about individual exceptions. Secondly, physical objects may be regarded as mere means to human ends, but no human being ought to be regarded merely as a means to another's end. The failure to predict the behavior of a human being is not the same as the failure to predict that of a physical object, even if he is an exception, because he is an end in himself as well as a means.

Finally, to condemn an individual as a social misfit often amounts to an injustice to society itself by depriving it of a chance to improve itself. For the misfit is an incentive to social amelioration; and once in a great while he turns out to be a creative genius, a General Clive, an Alexander Pope, or even a Socrates. The first man who proposed to break up the primitive communistic society was, in all probability, regarded as a menace to society; and the first woman who tied her neck with a string of wampum or fish bones and smeared her body with clay was, again in all probability, scorned by the respectable ladies of her day. Yet, without such primitive "Bolshevikis" mankind could neither have accumulated wealth nor developed any sense of beauty. Society owes something to freaks and misfits. For these reasons no genuine social scientist can afford to overlook individual exceptions.

2. *Novelties.* At this point it is desirable to make a distinction between exceptions and novelties. An exception is an event which does not fit in with the existing rules but which is capable of becoming a class by itself by virtue of its intrinsic value. The history of intellectual progress is the history of men who asserted exceptional propositions which later turned out to be true; and the history of moral progress is the history of the rebels who maintained heretic standards which later were accepted as more reasonable. That which enabled these exceptional propositions and heretic standards to displace their rivals was not their oddity but their value beneath the mask of their oddity.

A novelty, on the other hand, is an exception devoid of any intrinsic value; its sole value consists in its ability to capture attention. That a cat can really catch mice or that an ass can kick, is a scientific proposition, though few men are interested in it. But the proposition that the Cheshire Cat grinned, or that the Golden Ass misbehaved itself, is a novelty. It is true that men are ever hungry for novelties, especially, when their motives are governed by vanity, and if novelties do not present themselves, they readily invent some. Even in novels and short stories those with the O. Henry touch are probably far more read than those which faithfully describe actual lives. Nevertheless, mankind cannot live on novelties any more than on salt and pepper. The hunger for novelties is a sure sign of the immaturity of the sense of value. Social scientists are interested in a society of real cats and real asses and not in those of Cheshire Cats and Golden Asses.

    3. Verbal Pitfalls. In the literature of the social sciences verbal pitfalls are ever numerous because of the intangibility of the subject matter. Adam Smith and Malthus, for example, described the wage-funds as "funds *destined* for the maintenance of labour." The word "destined" became the cause of many arguments among the subsequent writers; for it suggested the idea that a certain sum of money was set aside for the payment of wages, which could not be used for any other purpose. But in J. S. Mill's interpretation of the wage-fund doctrine the myth of the *destiny* turned out to be a mere truism.[16]

    For another example, Malthus used the phrases "the tendency of population" and "the tendency of food supply," both of which have since become the household words among economists. The meaning of the term *tendency,* however, is different in each case. For the yield of a given piece of land per unit of labor and capital is a natural tendency which operates with mechanical regularity, while the increase of population is a human tendency and its regularity is partly due to the physiological and economic causes and partly due to the force of custom. Verbal pitfalls are especially dangerous to generalization. For the superficial similarity, reinforced by verbal kinship, easily misleads one. For instance, Tarde's definition of imitation as any repetitive social phenomenon greatly simplified on the surface the task of formulating social laws. But as the scope of generalization widened, the concept of imitation gradually expanded, covering

---

[16] *Principles of Political Economy,* pp. 343-44.

even invention and opposition. Yet on account of our habit of
metaphorical thinking, it is exceedingly difficult to avoid verbal
pitfalls.

Any scientific inquiry beyond rudimentary definitive concepts
invariably leads to the assumption of certain fundamental principles. Assumptions are necessary because we are ignorant. But
scientific ignorance differs from ordinary ignorance. For a man
of ordinary ignorance, though he may make fewer assumptions
than does a scientist, confounds assumptions with facts and de-
nounces his opponents as either fools or knaves. A scientist
knows what assumptions he makes; and since no assumptions
can be regarded as final, he is, further, interested in verifying his
assumptions.

1. The Principle of Least Assumption. Since a scientist always has an eye on the controllability of phenomena, he tries to
make only the fewest and most indispensable assumptions. This
ideal is known as the principle of least assumption. For instance,
the earlier philosophers assumed that man had a faculty of reason,
and by means of this assumption they explained why man is rational, why animals are irrational, why certain people become
insane, and why there must be a God. Present day psychologists
split up mentality into so many habits, instincts, and reflex activities, in an attempt to discover what is the nature of our reason,
how we come to possess a soul, and if possible, to assign specific
causes to each mental phenomenon. Thereby they hope to control the growth of the mind, and not to leave it to fate or the mal-
ice of the devil of unreason.

2. Methodological Assumptions in Causal Psychology. Assumptions are of several kinds, some being more fundamental
than others. The most fundamental assumptions in sociology are
those relating to its methodology. A methodological assumption
is a necessary presupposition for carrying out a special kind of
reasoning in view. The law of causation, sometimes called the

uniformity of nature, for example, may be, as has been suggested, merely "a vast lie"; there is no compulsion to believe it. But it is a necessary assumption in the sense that it is a logically prior assumption to the discovery of causal laws.

One of the most reasonable of the various methodological assumptions in sociology is the following, borrowed from psychology: Behavior is the Function of Stimulus and the Determining Tendencies in the Nervous System, or, $B = f(S \times D)$.

By behavior is meant all the visible manifestations through which a man expresses himself or carries on social intercourse. By a function is meant the process of covariation. By a stimulus is meant any external or internal condition which excites reactions in the behavior-mechanism within the body. By a determinant is meant any disposition of the nervous system to react in a given way to a stimulus, for example, instincts, habits, and emotional drives. The kind and complexity of both stimuli and determinants vary greatly. I shall return to this subject shortly and show its social significance.

CAUSAL ANALYSIS

To analyze is to describe internal and external relations. In saying that a book is made of ink and paper and ideas, I have analyzed the book into its constituent elements, and have stated their internal relations. And in saying that the book is on a table, I am stating its external relation to the table. Since, as remarked above, a cause in natural sciences means a uniform antecedent, a causal analysis should consist of a description of the uniform relations of antecedents and consequents—a description, moreover, as complete, simple, and consistent as possible.

Since all social phenomena are phenomena of human behavior, every social law may be resolvable into psychological law; some psychological laws, if not all, may further be resolved into the physiological, physical and chemical laws. The spread of cultural patterns, for example, is in part an imitative phenomenon which is resolvable into the learning process, into emotional drives and reflex activities, into neural transmission and chemical changes. Other familiar social phenomena such as business cycles, landslides in political elections, the solidarity of the Catholic church, and the like, may be similarly analyzed, or, at least it is the ambition of the social psychologists to carry out such a program of analysis.[17] When the description is complete by means of such a chain of causal analyses, resolving the complex into its simpler units, and then the simpler units into still simpler units, we have arrived at accurate understanding of the causal relations in social phenomena, and we can offer a key to their controllability. Men are not born with any ready-made economic motives, party loyalty or religious dogmas; they acquire these through the maturation of the conative tendencies, through the development of the code of signals, through the emergence of self-consciousness and socialization of behavior. Causal analysis traces with minute care the successive steps of these developments and describes their uniform variations, if there be any uniformities.

1. Skeptical Attitude Toward Metaphysical Dogmas. It may be objected that such a program of causal analysis as just suggested rests on a doubtful nominalistic bias. There can be no doubt that a bias, whether nominalistic or realistic, is anti-scientific. Sociology being at present in the stage of fact-finding, there is no necessity to commit itself to either one or the other of these biases. From the point of view of the emergent evolutionists, evolution may be described as a series of emergent phenomena at different levels. The simplest of these levels is supposed to be that of space and time.[18] From this level nature is supposed to have made a leap to produce a world filled with electrons and protons, atoms and molecules, which moved in perpetual whirl and dance. From such mad dances of the "in-

[17] See F. H. Allport, "The Group Fallacy in Relation to Social Science," *Journal of Abnormal Psychology and Social Psychology*, vol. XIX, no. 1.

[18] See, e. g., S. Alexander, *Space, Time, and Deity.*

animate matter" life is supposed to have mysteriously emerged on a higher level; and after life, on a still higher level, mind, with its wonderful powers of perception and conception, memory and imagination. And on a still higher level, society is supposed to have emerged from the individual psychic lives; and with society, culture and civilization.

In this view of evolution, all that we are (perhaps we can ever be) reasonably certain of is, that at each of these emergent levels, the emergent phenomena have a "plus value," something which is not found in the lower level. The emergent is sometimes called a "creative resultant," and is supposed to be characteristically something more than the sum of its component elements. Life is something more than a mass of atoms; mind is something more than a collection of neurons and synapses; and society is something more than an aggregation of individuals. If this view is true, it will be useless to attempt to analyze a given phenomenon on any one of these levels in terms of the level below. No social phenomena, for example, could be causally analyzed in terms of the psychological, no psychological phenomena in terms of the physiological.[19] But such a view suggests the idea that nature has completely shut up each of its created objects in a separate level, whereas a naïve view would suggest that this does not seem to be a faithful interpretation of one's experience.

Further, even those who hold such a view do not mean by space and time a *bare space* and an *abstract time* such as the mathematicians and physicists sometimes speak of, but a real space and a real time such as are already equipped with the potentialities of producing the emergent phenomena.[20] For instance, when an atom of oxygen combines with two atoms of hydrogen and results in one molecule of water, there is an emergent phenomenon. But the water did not come from nowhere, it was

---

[19] See, e. g., A. L. Kroeber's argument, "The Possibility of a Social Psychology," *American Journal of Sociology*, vol. XXIII, no. 5.

[20] See E. A. Burtt, Real vs. Abstract Evolution, *Proceedings of the Sixth International Congress of Philosophy*, 1926, pp. 168-77.

potentially present in oxygen and hydrogen. Until the chemists had discovered the exact proportions in which they combined, the synthetic production of water remained an unpredictable phenomenon; but as soon as they had discovered the exact proportions of the combination, the synthesis was made predictable and was reduced to a law. If the unique aspect of the whole (for example, emergents) is emphasized, no synthesis can be resolved into its component parts. If, however, the universal aspect of the whole is emphasized, they may all be resolved into their constituent elements. The causal analysis of social phenomena is concerned with the latter view, without committing itself to realism or to nominalism.

2. *Reconciliation of Teleology and Mechanism.* The adoption of the causal psychological assumption does not necessarily imply the belief that man is a machine and not a rational being; neither is this saying that the brain is the mind. From the metaphysical point of view, personality has come from apparently nowhere; while from the causal psychological point of view, it has emerged from the integration of habits, these from the integration of conditioned reflexes and simple reflex activities. The former view having started out with the mind, tries to deduce all events from it, and thereby create a metaphysical psychology. The latter view, however, having started out with mechanism, attempts to trace the successive steps in the evolution of the mind, and to correlate psychical and physical tendencies. The former view starts out with the final cause, and works backwards; the latter view starts out with the efficient cause, and works forwards. The issue, therefore, is at bottom one between idealism and naturalism: the latter is as much a faith as the former—the faith, namely, that causal explanation from the "efficient" point of view is more reliable than teleological explanation, that sober analysis and measurement will in the long run be more profitable than the attempt to sit still and to deduce everything from one's own rational consciousness.

The idea that anything has come out of nothing is anti-scientific. Even God the Creator is said to have started His creative work with "void" and "darkness" and "the waters," and these were after all something and not nothing. *Ex nihilo nihil fit.* We cannot help being naturalists any more than we can help being idealists. If we are naturalists our naturalism leads us involuntarily to look for the causes in phenomena, and a knowledge of causes brightens our prospects for amelioration. If a race of men without visions will perish, a race with nothing but visions will perish with equal certainty. We need facts in order to build our ideals upon them. Perhaps in the end we may find that mechanism and teleology coincide: the former representing the temporal, and the latter the eternal. The true view of the world may be mechanism *in* teleology, and not mechanism *or* teleology.

PSYCHOLOGICAL ILLUSTRATIONS

1. Mechanical and Chemical Stimuli as the Causes of the Baby's Behavior: A baby is born probably little more than a lump of flesh and a bundle of vaguely differentiated reflexes. What little more he is, is yet unknown. It may be a very important little. But in so far as he can be known through his behavior, he is a bundle of vaguely differentiated reflexes, and as such he is responsive only to mechanical and chemical stimuli such as heat and cold, hunger and thirst. Within the first twelve months, his muscles become slightly more differentiated and integrated in function through continual and coördinated exercise. Still his life seems to center round his belly. He reaches out for everything and leads everything to his mouth. That which gives an agreeable stimulus is pushed into his mouth, and that which gives a disagreeable stimulus is pushed out of it.

2. *Conditioning Stimuli as Cause.* The process of differentiation and integration of the muscles gives the baby an increasingly greater capacity for activity, and his activities bring him into

contact with a greater number and variety of stimuli. A puppy, for example, at first does not seem to make an impression different from any other object. But if the puppy suddenly springs up at the sight of a cat, uttering a sharp snarl, the animal and auditory stimuli are so sudden and violent that they throw the delicate mechanism of the baby's muscles temporarily out of balance, and at the same time a process, probably electro-chemical, takes place in the baby's cortex, establishing a conditioned reflex. The conditioned reflex once established, the presence of the puppy or even any other animal resembling a puppy is sufficient to reproduce the responses, namely, fear reactions.

3. Language as Cause. The process of specializing and integrating through conditioning is greatly facilitated by the development of the code of signals. For, when the ear and vocal organs of the baby are sufficiently developed to produce various sounds and to respond to them, a sound or a string of sounds attached to the stimuli, after several times of repetition, is sufficient to evoke a response, even in the absence of the original stimuli. The language of a baby is just such a code of signals. If every time the nurse wishes to convey the idea of a kitten to a baby, a kitten has to be brought to him, teaching would be cumbersome indeed. But when the sound "Miaow" becomes a surrogate for the visual and auditory stimuli of a kitten, it enables both the baby and his nurse greatly to economize labor in discourse, and thus to telescope space and time.

4. Phobias and Sentiments as Causes. The process of conditioning, differentiating, and integrating, goes on throughout the rest of life—most rapidly during the period of childhood and adolescence, and gradually slowing down after about twenty years of age. Many of the conditioned reflexes we formed during the period of our childhood and adolescence we carry throughout the rest of our lives: some as phobias, others as sentiments; many as habits. A child who has been previously frightened by a bug, may become excited by a bug in a nutshell, because the

IDEALS FOR SOCIAL LAWS 37

dead bug evokes the original creepy sensations. If this repulsion is sufficiently strong to establish a conditioned reflex, he refuses thereafter to eat the nut; sometimes he refuses to eat any kind of nut whatever, even nut cakes and anything else which has a nut flavor. This simple mechanical integration of fear is called a phobia. The emotion of fear is accompanied by the movements of withdrawal; and if the fear of the bug is generalized by integration to a fear of all creepy objects, such as eels and snakes, it becomes a sentiment of repulsion. A sentiment is an integration of conditioned reflexes accompanied by a generalized emotion.

5. *Emotional Drives as Causes.* As the child passes through adolescence and manhood, conditioned reflexes are still further integrated and generalized. For instance, the maturation of the sex reflexes tremendously increases the adolescent boy's emotional capacity, and awakens his sensibility to various stimuli. The presence of anything associated with sex may sometimes be sufficient to touch off emotional current. When the sexual emotion is sufficiently strong to overshadow other emotions, it unifies various other emotional activities with the sexual emotion as the center, just as a sharp pain centralizes them from moment to moment. Any organized emotional activity whatsoever dominated by some one emotion seeking its satisfaction is an emotional drive, also called a desire.

6. *Socialization and Habit as Causes.* An emotional drive such as that of sex seeks its outlet, and if left unsocialized, it seeks its satisfaction in the most direct and mechanical fashion. But in all societies beyond the most primitive, there is always some measure of socialization which takes various forms. Vocal exercises such as in the singing of amorous songs may temporarily relieve the excited feeling caused by the sexual emotion. A public exhibition of a stunt such as running a two-mile race may drain the superfluous energy and extinguish the emotion for a while. But oftener persons who are swayed by the same sort

of emotional drive gather together and work off their emotion in various other ways, less strenuous than doing a stunt and more quiet than the vocal exercise. With repetition the device to satisfy one's emotional drives becomes a routine work, called habit.

Emotional drives are many and are of varying degrees of intensity and permanence. Hence, they may either conflict with one another and result in an over-development of certain emotions and a total repression of others (as often they do), or under favorable conditions they become integrated. When integrated, they adjust to one another semi-automatically.

A well organized personality, gliding smoothly through its habitual groove of daily routines, is essentially a semi-automaton. If one asked our neighbor, Mr. Efficient Citizen, "How is your personality," he would in all probability answer somewhat as the Swiss mountain guide answered to the question, "How is your constitution,"—namely, "Sir, I never knew I had a constitution." Of course, even Mr. Efficient Citizen has occasions of alternate frettings and self-reproaches, rebellion and submission; but they are mere ruffles on the surface of the steady stream of his life. A sick man most frequently thinks of his constitution; a healthy man oftener forgets it. A split personality, torn between conflicting desires, is most frequently conscious of itself; a healthy personality oftener forgets itself.

7. *Interest.* On a fine Sunday morning, Mr. Efficient Citizen may wake up too early, ruminate over his routine life and ask himself: "What reason have I to go through all these routine acts?" He needs to find a justification for his life. The only rational answer he may find may be that, in the light of his past experiences, he has found that it is the best suitable kind of life; that he is tied to a wife and a string of children with whom he has either tacitly or explicitly agreed to live this kind of life; and that this is the kind of life which others live to their satisfaction. To give a rational explanation is to unify one's past and present experiences and to make them an intelligible whole. An interest is

an emotional drive with a rational explanation attached to it. And rationality is a product in part of socialization, and in part of the slow emergence of self-consciousness. To the question, how self-consciousness has emerged, one can give only an hypothetical answer somewhat like the following.

8. *The Emergence of Self-Consciousness.* · When one says aloud to oneself "fire!" one hears the signal and recognizes its meaning. This is possible, first, because one's vocal, visual and auditory muscles are integrated; if they were all disconnected from one another, one could no more understand the signal than a telephone-receiver could. Secondly, the signal has been a conditioning stimulus to one's previous responses. As explained above, *the conditioned reflexes are the rudimentary forms of intelligence,* like the animal intelligence, and the development of the conditioned reflexes is greatly facilitated by a code of signals. Children at the parrot stage apparently learn to think by talking to themselves. Even adults, when deeply absorbed in a long train of thought, frequently talk to themselves; and a long train of thought is sometimes nothing but a long train of implicit reflexes, to each of which a code of signals is attached, as for example, in the process of recalling a series of exciting events of the past. As the field of emotion expands, the various reflexes integrate into emotional attitudes, and emotional attitudes into routine habits and interests. The functional unity of all these conative tendencies I have called personality. Self-consciousness is the cognitive aspect of this functional unity.

A functional unity is not a static but a processive unity, differentiating and integrating, redifferentiating and re-integrating itself. Self-consciousness being a functional unity, like every other unity, implies a multiplicity of entities and therefore conflicts. One is most self-conscious when one is torn between several conflicting desires; or to put it in another way, one's self-consciousness heightens when one's emotional drives clash with one another. Conscience is the emotion which arises from such conflicting desires, and which is mediated by judgments of right and wrong, and is therefore a socialized emotion. One can debate with oneself or persuade oneself only when one is made up of multiple selves, which are various foci of integration for one's conative tendencies. Children are least self-conscious; they respond almost mechanically to external and internal stimuli. As they grow older they are increasingly self-conscious, and their self-consciousness acts as a mediator between stimuli and their responses, that is, as a new determining tendency.

9. *Conclusion to Causal Analysis.* Such is the technique of study in causal psychology. But there are many points of doubt, especially in the more highly integrated levels of human behavior. At the level of the reflex activities we are reasonably certain that the specific causes of behavior are the stimuli of a mechanical and chemical character. At the level of conditioned responses, there is again a reasonable degree of probability that the specific causes of behavior are the conditioning stimuli of various kinds and the code of signals. And Pavlov's and Köhler's studies of the animal psychology show that even dogs and monkeys are capable of responding appropriately to such stimuli. At the level of phobias, emotional and habitual responses, there is a large mass of empirical evidence which also suggests specific stimuli, and also a rough measure of uniformity of responses on the surface. But the behavior mechanism has become so complex at this stage of development that it is exceedingly difficult to isolate the various springs of action from one another. Some psychologists lump these springs of action into half a dozen of prepotent drives, others split them into some forty or more of instincts. Finally, with the emergence of self-consciousness and the beginning of rational activities, it is well-nigh impossible to put one's finger on the specific causes of behavior.

Imperfect though it is, psychology is the backbone of sociology because the fundamental data of all social sciences are human desires, and the causal psychological method is legitimate method of study for the realization of the ambition to make sociology a positive science. This ambition, then, can be realized, if at all through the employment of psychological methods, combined where necessary with the methods of the other special social sciences.

SPECIAL SOCIAL SCIENCES

1. Society and Social Environment. The progressive enlargement of one's social relations may be represented by a series of concentric circles, with the individual at the center, himself a social product; after the individual the family circle; after the family the educational circle; after that the circle of friends, neighbors and acquaintances; after that the occupational circle; after that the political circle; and in the outermost circle the ideational and the spiritual or religious associations. Each of these concentric circles represents a particular kind of interacting group, and the laws governing the relations between the members within the circles are social laws. Again, each of these circles may be taken as the central point of study: the special social sciences are just such studies. I shall discuss some of the most important ones, every one of which has been claimed by some author to be a master science, and at times their scope and method of study have been so extended as to warrant some justification for such claims. Indeed, there is no science which may not some day be claimed to be a master science.

The term *society* is a vague word signifying any one or all of such concentric circles as presented above. Its essence is functional unity and community of purpose. A government, for example, is not the brick and mortar with which the state house is built, nor the brass batons and the red-tape with which the governmental authority is exercised. These are merely the mediating factors in social relations, the tertiary data in sociology as defined above. The real government is the system of relationship between the governing and the governed. These relations may be studied either as they exist in concrete situations or from some abstract and arbitrarily defined point of view. For instance, most economists study all economic relations from the hypothetical point of view that all men are governed by purely pecuniary motives, and draw conclusions from it. Similarly, a Machiavellian political scientist studies all political relations from the hypothetical point of view that men are governed by the motive of domination and will dominate whenever possible, irrespective of any moral compunction. The so-called pure social sciences are just such a body of arbitrarily defined and hypothetical sciences. They owe their origin in part to a priori dogmas concerning human motives, and in part to the love of systematized knowledge as a means of control.

In the future a wholehearted coöperation among the special social scientists is desirable. A synthetic science, which sociology aspires to be, can be realized only through such coöperation. Through coöperation the psychologists, for example, may provide a more reasonable theoretical background for economists and political scientists, while the latter can supply the former with careful studies of the environment. The study of the environment is important because men never have social relations in a vacuum. They are always concerned with some objects of interest in the environment. The improvement of human relations can never be to any appreciable extent without the improvement of the environment also.

2. *Anthropology.* Anthropology is the study of the natural man from the impersonal point of view. Its ideal is to observe the evolution of human society as objectively as monkeys examine themselves. It is specially interested in primitive races, archæology, and fossils. The value of the study of origins is generally slight, simply because we do not value things by their origin. Few things have such a boastful origin as that of the Holy Catholic Church. Yet, there were times when the Catholic Church was neither Holy nor Catholic nor even worth the name Church; and in such times the origin was of little importance. So far as

sociology is concerned, the value of anthropological studies lies, not in the origin of the primitive races and their institutions, but in the possibility of discovering the causal relations in their development, just as the genetic study of children is of value in so far as it suggests the possibility of control of behavior.

And from this point of view, the study of the primitive people affords several advantages. First, the conditions of life among them are so simple that causal effects of the introduction of new social factors in their society are less difficult to trace than in a more complex civilization. The introduction of alcohol among the Central African negroes, that of gunpowder among the North American Indians, and the spread of Christianity as well as of diseases among the Pacific islanders, and the like, all seem to have had far reaching effects on the natives' health, their economic and political conditions, their moral ideas and inter-tribal relations. Secondly, primitive men are less sophisticated than more advanced peoples. Their child-like naïveté in speech and manner makes it easier to understand their motives and their reactions to stimuli. Thirdly, since primitive peoples are at various stages of cultural development, they afford an opportunity for comparative studies of the genesis of culture. To this extent primitive societies are sociological laboratories. Of course, no two primitive societies are exactly alike, nor does any one primitive society remain exactly alike at two different periods of experiment. Hence, the study of the primitive peoples, like all other sociological studies, must be supplemented by deductive generalizations. For the immediate future, however, the accumulation of data is a good program.

3. Economics. As remarked above, anything whatsoever, if an object of somebody's interest, is capable of possessing social value. Among such objects there are some which are of no economic value. Economics does not propose to solve all problems of value; it confines its study only to those objects which owe their value to scarcity as well as utility. An object of this type is said to possess an exchange value. By an exchange value is meant the power to command goods (or services) in exchange. In general, objects of high esthetic and moral value are only imperfectly treated by the economists. They are most at home when they treat with material goods which satisfy some immediate physical need such as hunger or thirst, but even here the economic order presupposes a certain moral order. For instance, in North America in 1930 pajamas are in normal demand. But in the tropical regions such as Java and Ceylon, where the natives do without pajamas, the pajama manufacturing industry is out of the question. If these natives are converted to teetotalers and prohibitionists, the geniuses in the brewing industry will also have to go out of business, as have meat packers among the Brahmins.

Given an environment, a population, and a moral order, there is also an economic order, and a rough measure of economic justice is obtained "in the long run" through the operation of the law of demand and supply. In primitive economy things could have exchange value only in so far as they were conducive to survival. For the primitive man's motive of production is consumption; and he consumed in order to survive. But with the advance of civilization, man's motive of production is creative activity or the love of display, and not the mere desire for consumption or survival. Of course, even today there are large masses of unskilled laborers who are driven to work most of the time probably by hunger. But the labor of this class of workmen is of little exchange value. The real producers of great economic value are the skilled workers, the organizers and the managing capitalists, whose motives of production are other than mere consumption or survival.

Ultimately both the producers and the consumers are men themselves, though the instruments of production are many, and the chief among them are land and capital. To economize is to balance the forces of production and consumption so as to yield a maximum amount of welfare on a given standard of living, expressed in terms of material goods. By the term "forces of production and consumption" is meant anything whatsoever that has an exchange value. From the economic point of view, even the institutions of family and religion, of government and law, of trade and international relations, are either productive forces or consumptive forces, according as they are conducive to production or to consumption. To progress economically is so to balance the forces of production and consumption as to yield a cumulatively greater amount of welfare on a progressively higher or more efficient standard of living. This is largely secured by the race between invention and population. When invention and improvement run ahead of population, there is an opportunity to lift up the standard of living. And when population runs ahead of invention and improvement, there are sure to follow stagnation, poverty and misery. The normal state of economic balance is, or should be, one in which all the productive forces are pitted against the consumptive forces, through birth-control, a maximum utilization of the natural resources, and redistribution of human talents.[21]

Economics is an *hypothetical* science as distinguished from the *actual* sciences like physics. Its point of view is narrow and its procedure is arbitrary. Dollars and cents do not measure all values, nor can welfare be expressed in terms of material goods alone. Nevertheless, it is one of the few special social sciences, which has a clear-headed program for social amelioration to offer, and a clear-cut technique of study to present. The objective correlations between the amount of food supply and the volume of population, between the industrialization of society and the migration of peoples, between the contact of races and the rise of new moral and political problems, between the elevation of the standard of living and the limitation of the size of family, and the like, are the useful data on which to base alike the causal

[21] See T. N. Carver, *Essays in Social Justice*, Chap. X.

analyses of social phenomena and the framing of meliorative policies.

4. *Politics and Jurisprudence.* Human desires are of a great variety, and the same man may have, and generally has, conflicting desires. Some live, like the economic man, primarily for the love of material wealth; others, like the Machiavellian Prince, for power; some live for the quest of beauty, and others for the pursuit of truth or the Kingdom of Heaven. Hence, organization is indispensable in order to secure survival and progress. The state is an organization of heterogeneous masses of interests, bound together by a geographical unity, a community of tradition or language, and other ties. Politics should be the study of such organizations and the processes whereby the component interests of the multifarious organizations within the state are fulfilled in harmony with one another. And the laws of the state should be the rules governing the proper relations between the groups of interests. A family or a school, a business corporation or a trade union, a church or a philanthropic association, are examples of such organizations of interests. Both politics and jurisprudence are concerned, or should concern themselves, with the realization, perpetuation and enrichment of the common good which subsumes all the lesser goods. In a perfect society, in which all such groups of interests function perfectly, no government will be needed and the state will be simply a functional unity of all such groups of interests, neither will there be any problem of law-making and law-breaking, for whatever a perfect group will do, will be a law itself.

Thus defined, the scope of politics is co-extensive with that of sociology; indeed, it is the most ancient and honorable predecessor of sociology. But at present it is largely confined to the study of the types of political organizations, their duties and functions, their customary procedures and technical tricks. And since we have only a very imperfect knowledge of the psychological laws

governing human relations, law-making is like a blind man's attempt to feel his way through. All social interests are ultimately
those of certain individuals, and since an interest is somebody's
psychological attitude toward an object, all social interests are ultimately explicable by the laws of psychology. The laws of the
state should be based on the laws of psychology. "Thou shalt"
is meaningless unless it is also "thou canst."

5. *History.* The difference between history and sociology is
that history is *not* a science while sociology is *not yet* a science.
Science deals only with repetitive phenomena. An event which
happens only once and never again is not a datum for science,
and history deals with precisely such data. The function of the
historian is interpretative and not merely descriptive. He is to
interpret the historical events as they occurred in their historical
setting, for example, in their unique space and time relations. As
soon as an historian takes these events out of their unique space
and time relations, and classifies and compares them with one
another, he ceases to be an historian and is playing the rôle of a
sociologist.

For instance, the following news was reported in the *Boston
Evening Transcript,* Saturday, December 15, 1928: "Angora.
Gazi Mustapha Kemal, iron-handed shaper of the new Turkey's
destiny, has turned to a woman for help. She is Madame Flore
Boccart, Belgian educational expert, who has come here post-
haste at the Turkish government's request to make emancipation
safe for the womanhood of Turkey. In the present stage of
transition Turkish women are at a critical crossroad, half terri-
fied by the skeleton of their imprisoned past which dangles there,
and half befuddled by the vista of the strange free future which
stretches before them. It is this transition period which finds fifty
per cent of the women throughout the land insane or neuras-
thenic, according to the estimate of Turkey's leading alienist, Dr.
Mezhar Osman, and fills the press with almost daily instances of
suicides among girls and young women. . . . Much has been

written about their gigantic progress in the last few years, but in reality among the ten per cent of literate Turkish women can be counted today only a handful who have definitely taken up professions, not more than a half-dozen each of doctors, lawyers, actresses and writers. The vast majority of the upper classes have learned nothing new except the Charleston; over ninety per cent of Turkish women still wear the veil, and practically all of them are at their wits' end to know what to do with this new freedom. Work is the panacea for the wounds of transition, decrees the Gazi, and to work the women of the land shall go under the skilled direction of the Belgian expert, Madame Boccart. . . ."

If the historian attempts to explain this bizarre phenomenon by such facts as the weakening of parental and religious authorities, the unpreparedness of the Turkish women to make use of their new opportunities, the hardships they endure to earn a decent living, their disillusions about freedom and the woes and throes that accompany such disillusions, and the like, he is far on the way to discover a sociological law out of an historical event. Recently, many historians have adopted this sociological point of view, and have been trying to make history a science. In so far as they fail, they fail as historians; and in so far as they succeed, they succeed as sociologists.

6. *Education.* From one point of view, the problem of education and that of discovering social laws are alike. If we knew precisely how one would respond to a given kind of education, we should be able to control one's education, just as we wish to control the course of other social events. From another point of view, the problem of education is somewhat more than that of discovering social laws. For we educate our young people, not merely to reproduce ourselves, but also to help them to become something better than we are. We do not wish to control them entirely; we would rather let them become whatever they are capable of becoming. There never can be any progress if each generation does nothing but reproduce its own kind. For this reason ancestor-

worship must be viewed as the least progressive of all the ways of life. For seventy or more generations since the days of Confucius ancestor-worshipers have held each other back, waiting only for the end of time to relieve them.

7. *Metaphysics and Logic.* Metaphysics is an indispensable companion of sociology for the reason that all scientific propositions ultimately rest on some fundamental assumptions, and metaphysics deals with fundamental assumptions. A cosmologist may begin his inquiry with the assumption that the earth is square and the heaven is round, and arrive at something like the Confucian cosmology. A physicist may begin with the assumption that the ultimate reality of the universe is force or energy, and by means of this assumption render a theoretical explanation of the laws of physics. As remarked above, all such assumptions are necessary because of our ignorance and curiosity. They are the a prioris of science; and like all a prioris they must be verified or corrected in the light of facts. But scientific generalizations may also be corrected in the light of the fundamental assumptions. For instance, when two plausible theories dispute for honour, as did Newton's and Huygens' theories of light, the one fitting in better with the prior assumptions, by which other scientific generalizations are also explained, is to be accepted as more plausible.

Once the fundamental assumptions are granted, the next step is to see whether the deductions really follow. To gather as many facts as are relevant is a scientific virtue, but to present them without either head or tail is a vice. Logic is the art of orderly exhibition of the relations among the facts. An orderly exhibition must be consistent with itself. To affirm and to deny a given fact or an assumption in the same breath is inconsistency.

Scientific generalizations, as remarked above, have an explanatory value. To explain a given phenomenon is to make it a part of an internally consistent whole. Or, to put it in another way, *to establish a causal relation is to convert a temporal sequence into a logical sequence:* if all men are mortal, Mr. Hale-And-Hearty, too, must be mortal. Until we have generalized the particular facts of mortality of many a Mr. Hale-And-Hearty into the proposition, "All men are mortal," we have no scientific law. But since no particular fact or proposition automatically follows from a general principle, every conversion of a temporal sequence into a logical sequence needs verification. The greater the scope of the generalization, the greater is the risk involved in the leap from the particular to the general. A perfect science is a complete deductive system in which every particular fact or proposition can be deduced from a general principle. A fact or a proposition so deduced is said to be explained. Considering what a great many facts there are, which need to be so explained, logic is a highly useful friend of sociology.

8. Ethics and Religion. Man is an evaluating being. Every thing whatsoever, which is an object of his interest, is either good or bad; the only thing which is of no value is the unknown. And every thing is capable of becoming an object of one's interest. Social problems arise out of the need to satisfy one's interest. But in problems of value we are committed to the egocentric predicament. We can make our values universal only by persuading others and thus reproducing ourselves. To this extent we are all preachers to one another.

Those who manifest this sociability most naïvely are children and savages, and those who manifest it most deeply and earnestly are the great reformers, moralists and prophets. A prophet speaks in the name of God, and a moralist appeals to man's rationality and conscience: but they are alike the creators of values and the builders of the moral order of the universe. It is through them that ideals become facts and values become universalized. The concept of normality presupposes a moral order. *The "ought" precedes the "is."* One of the chief justifications for the existence of sociology is the attempt to discover the laws of social progress.

And progress presupposes a series of progressive "oughts." The laws of progress, therefore, ultimately rest on the laws of "oughts."

SYNTHESIS

It is to be observed that every special social science has a partial solution of the social problems to offer, but none of them has a complete solution of them all. Sociology aspires to be the synthetic science. To synthesize is to integrate and to unify. The history of sociology is the history of incomplete successes of the various attempts at such a synthesis: some through biology, others through anthropology; some through economics, and others through the philosophy of history. At present causal psychology gives some promise, but its technique of study is as yet meager and its discussions are largely hypothetical. And yet the unification of the social sciences cannot be accomplished until the multifarious generalizations, which in one guise or another circulate as "social laws," are brought together on the basis of valid social psychological laws. For the fundamental data of all the social sciences are human desires, and from the attempts to satisfy these desires all social problems arise. Society is no other than a system of human relations by which the satisfaction of human desires is secured.

To use the hackneyed distinction between form and substance, the form of society is the unity of the functional relations between the groups of interests, and the substance of society is the accumulation of human values through such a unity. Hence, the nearest approximations of a synthetic social science are thus far the various philosophies of value. Since, however, the ambition of social scientists is to make sociology a positive science, their future lies in the direction of causal psychology, and their success will be measured by their ability to coöperate with the various other special social scientists. For a positive social law can be no other than a causal psychological law which explains the laws of ethics, economics, politics, and the like. The name sociology at present is a mere symbol standing for such an Herculean achievement of the future. As a science, it still remains in the stage of definitive concepts and artistic discussion, without either an adequate technique for study or a sufficient accumulation of data.

CHAPTER III
APRIORISMS AND METHODOLOGICAL PRESUPPOSITIONS

THE NATURE OF APRIORISMS AND PRESUPPOSITIONS

Economists have formulated numerous laws, some of which like the "law of self-interest" are mere apriorisms, while others like the "law of substitution" are deductions from their a priori assumptions. By an apriorism I mean a proposition which is doubtful, but which may be accepted on the ground of sheer dogmatic faith. The postulates relating to the "economic man" are apriorisms, and are probably false, because they seem untrue to our naïve experience, and are anything but proved in the light of the present day psychological discoveries. And if there is no such creature as the "economic man," the postulate of the "economic man" can be accepted only on the ground of dogmatic faith, or from pure love of system. By deductions I mean the particular inferences drawn from the general assumptions. If the general assumptions are granted, the deductions may logically follow, but a logical demonstration is not necessarily true in fact, unless the premises be true and the deduction is also verified by an inductive process. A large body of the laws in pure economics, being logical deductions, still want inductive verification,—a task with which present day economists are occupied.

I have selected for the purpose of presentation only a few from the impressive list of economic laws. These laws are interesting chiefly from two points of view. First, they illustrate the methodology of the economists, who have played a very important part in the development of the social sciences. Secondly there have not been wanting sociologists of great distinction who seem to have held that sociological laws should be developed along the line pursued by economists. The value of this type of law is, if properly developed, its systematic character. For in spite of the seeming absurdities of these laws, the method has a certain attractiveness,—its cool-headedness and its logical rigidity, the indispensable prerequisites for discovering scientific laws. It is interesting to note, however, that some sociologists of great renown, who proceeded with evident seriousness to formulate sociological laws after the model of economic laws, stopped at laying down mere axioms for sociological laws. By an axiom I mean either a proposition which is self-evident like a mathematical axiom or a necessary presupposition for the discovery of positive laws. The proposition that the whole is greater than any of its parts is self-evident needing no demonstration, while the proposition that behind every social phenomenon there is an adequate cause is not so self-evident but must be assumed if we are ever to discover valid causal laws. An axiom, therefore, is a necessary logical presupposition for social laws, which may or may not be self-evident, but is not in itself a social law. Gumplowicz's ten "universal laws" discussed below are of this character.

There are some economic laws which are beautifully clear-cut, very closely approximating the ideals for positive laws. Of this class Gresham's law is an example, the psychological foundation of which may be said to be man's desire for security, and which therefore will probably remain a valid law in catallactics (i.e., the science of exchange) so long as the present economic system, the institution of private property, will last. Others like the law of diminishing returns are of fundamental importance to economics, and a discussion on such laws may lead us far into the field of economic theory. Sociologists, however, have made apparently little use of the law of diminishing returns. This omission may at first look rather startling; but a little reflection will show that the applicability of the law of diminishing returns to sociological phenomena is very limited as compared with its applicability to economic phenomena. For all that is the gift of nature such as the fertility of soil, fishery and mineral resources, seems to yield an output per unit of labour under more or less accurate operation of the law of diminishing returns. But what men continually try to do is to counteract the tendencies of diminishing returns by invention and improvement. The large scale production in the manufacturing and transportation industries at a progressively cheaper cost per unit is a direct reversal of the law of diminishing returns.[1]

[1] A list of Economic Laws follows, which I have not discussed for the reason either that they are a priori construction like the "law of concentration of capital," or their field of application is extra-human like the "law of rent," or they want psychological explanation.

The following nine economic laws with four others discussed in this and other chapters are found in Charles Gide and Charles Rist, *A History of Economic Doctrines*:
(1) The Law of Concentration of Capital (pp. 450, 475-76).
(2) The Law of Demand and Supply (p. 359).
(3) The Law of Diminishing Returns (pp. 118, 126, 148, 153, etc.).
(4) The Law of Indifference (pp. 148, 525, 527, note).
(5) The Law of International Exchange (pp. 363-66).
(6) The Law of Rent (p. 362).
(7) The Law of Sale (p. 531 and note).
(8) The Law of Variation of Intensity of Need (p. 543 note).
(9) The Law of Wages (pp. 360-61).
The following eleven economic laws with others, which are either discussed in this study or included in the foregoing list, are found in Palgrave's *Dictionary of Political Economy*, II, 582-85 or elsewhere as specified below:
(10) The Law of Constant Return.
(11) The Law of Costs.
(12) The Law of Demand.
(13) The Law of Distribution (I, 599-602).
(14) The Law of Diminishing Utility.
(15) The Law of Increasing Returns.
(16) The Law of Indifference.
(17) The Law of Subordination of Wants.
(18) The Law of Supply.
(19) The Law of Surplus (III, 498-99).
(20) Gresham's Law (II, 262-3).
The following three economic laws, together with other eight laws which are included in the foregoing lists or discussed in this study, are found in N. H. Comish's *Standard of Living*, chap. III:
(21) The Law of Complementary Wants.
(22) The Law of Utility.
(23) The Law of Want Expansion.
Practically all these "laws" can be found also in Marshall's *Principles of Economics*, 8th ed., where they are called "tendencies" rather than "laws."

LIST OF APRIORISMS

Among the various a priori assumptions of economists and certain sociologists the following four seem to be the most fundamental:

1. "Law of Parsimony: Under any or all conceivable circumstances a sentient, and especially a rational being will always seek the greatest gain or the maximum resultant gain—his marginal advantage" (at the least cost or pain).[2]

2. "Each man will desire the largest return with the least labour—this on a purely economic ground is the only rational attitude of mind, and thus presumably the universal one. . . . This axiom expresses the law of forces which are uniformly present in human action, no matter how much they may be modified in any given case by other considerations."[3]

3. "The Law of Self-Interest: Every individual desires well-being, and so would be possessed of wealth. Similarly he would, if possible, avoid evil and escape effort."[4]

4. "Law of Individual Choice: Each individual seeks the largest return for the least sacrifice. What is meant by this is that whether we consider wealth getting or wealth using, religion or art, culture or learning, or indeed life in any of its various important phases, the individual is seeking his highest good or best interests so far as his powers or capacities will permit. The laborer seeks the highest wage he can command; the professional man strives for the position that will yield him the largest return for his efforts; and the business man enters the field which will most rapidly increase his wealth. The expression 'largest return' includes, to be sure, a number of things; it involves physical health, mental development, material welfare, and social-well-being. But the truth is a universal one and manifests itself in all our services; even a man engaged in missionary work would endeavor to seek the largest results possible for the smallest amount

[2] Lester F. Ward, *Pure Sociology*, pp. 59-62, 161-63. Quotations by permission of the Macmillan Co.

[3] John Bascom, *Sociology*, p. 59.   [4] Gide and Rist, *op. cit.*, p. 355.

of work in order that he might do the most possible for those for whom he was laboring."[5]

The foregoing four laws are four different versions of one apriorism, and are all claimed as social or economic laws. What importance has been attached to this apriorism may be seen in the following statement of the late Professor Ward who said: "There are many social or sociological laws, but they all may be grouped and generalized into one fundamental law, the law of parsimony. This has been regarded as merely an economic law, but it is much broader than this. . . . This refers not alone to pecuniary gain, or temporary or immediate gain. It allows the effectiveness of worthy as well as unworthy motives, and the 'transcendental' interests."[6] The deductions drawn from such an apriorism might run parallel with the laws in pure economics, and the result might be the creation of a "sociological man" to keep company with the old reputed "economic man."

Now, I wish to take issue with these authors on three points. First, this apriorism speaks of "the great gain" or "the largest return" as the goal of every human effort. This assumption has some plausibility in pure economics which deals with quantities alone, and which assumes as its standard of measurement the dollar yard-stick. But can sociology also disregard qualities and adopt the dollar yard-stick for its quantitative measurement? This difficulty is seen at its worst when the same apriorism is carried into ethical discussions in which the arguments proffered in support of the apriorism are often confounded with hedonism, the maximum amount of pleasure.[7] But morality and the sense of duty do not derive from any considerations of pleasure. The performance of duty generally involves conscious overcoming of one's natural inclinations, which means the sacrifice of one's pleasure.[8] Hence the terms "the largest return," "the greatest

[5] Blackmar and Gillin, *Outlines of Sociology*, pp. 368-69. Quotations by permission of the Macmillan Co.

[6] *The American Journal of Sociology*, VIII (No. 1, 1902), p. 143.

[7] See, e. g., Ward, *Dynamic Sociology*, II, 108, and *passim*.

[8] See James Martineau, *Types of Ethical Theory*, vol. II, bk. I.

gain," "the largest result," etc., have very little meaning as social concepts.

Furthermore, the very fact that the expression "largest return" is so vague precludes the possibility of applying the law to any specific cases. What we live for we do not always know; and if we do find out what it is, it turns out to be anything under the sun, from bread and butter up to the Sermon on the Mount. To be sure, we may abstract certain unitary principles out of these multitudinous and multifarious desires, such as "the greatest good for the greatest number" or "the will to power" or "the love of God," but so soon as we talk about these we cease talking about positive laws and instead we are talking metaphysics. Professors Blackmar and Gillin think that "even a man engaged in mission- ary work should endeavor to seek the largest results possible from the smallest amount of work." But what are "the largest results possible from the smallest amount of work"? Are they the counting of the heads of converts, or the measuring of the size of the missionary reports? All human relations fundamentally differ from mathematics. If you subtract five from five, you get zero. But if you have loved a person who later turns out to be a serpent, you do not get zero, instead you get an increase of value through a sharpened insight into human nature. The friend whom you have loved and lost still means something to you.

From the a priori assumption that each man desires the greatest return at the least cost, some sociologists have proceeded to construct an objective scale of choices. Professors Blackmar and Gillin, for example, say:

5. "Each individual has a schedule of choices ranging from the most desirable objects to the least desirable. This law, ob- served primarily in economic life, serves as the basis for market valuation, and furnishes the opportunity for exchange. The de- mand schedule for articles of utility is manifested in the practical

affairs of life; but the law operates with no less exactness in other departments of human activity, for individual motives vary in proportion to their valuation of various objects of life. Of two men, both laying stress on the material objects of life, one may put food first and then clothing, books, works of art, and furniture, while others may, under different circumstances, give the following order: books, works of art, food, furniture and clothing. Again, others may make schedules like this: wealth, virtue, learning, public approbation, and leisure; or like this: virtue, learning, wealth, leisure, and public approbation."[9]

This is a clear statement of what the law means, where it is originated, and of what use it is. It seems to be a reasonable axiom, for at any given time, when we are called upon to make important decisions, we generally make something like the above schedule of values. But this "law" should be considered together with several other commonplace observations among which are: first, we are not always conscious of our scale of values; second, there is no obvious and easily statable objective scale of values applicable to all men; third, even our own scale of values changes as our knowledge of values advances. If these observations are true, as they seem to me, on what ground can we call this a positive law? Is it not a mere a priori assumption? Does not the very fact that from this same axiom several scales of values can be deduced (as the authors point out) preclude its claim to being called a social law? The axiom may acquire some semblance of a social law when some one asserts that everybody conforms to some one universal scale of pleasure, but this no one seems to dare do. Further, in economics where every value is arbitrarily represented in terms of dollars and cents, the mere fact that a given article is exchanged for certain others is the sufficient reason for regarding them as being of equal values; and whatever surplus values may be derived from the exchange the

[9] Blackmar and Gillin, *op. cit.*, p. 369.

economists generally overlooked until recent times when they, under the leadership of such scholars as Marshall and others, have begun to study economic problems from the point of view of welfare rather than price-list. Thus at a time when the economists themselves recognize the inadequacy of their earlier method, it would seem strange that the sociologists should eagerly grasp it.

6. "Individual minds respond similarly to the same or like stimuli. This law is a recognition of the universality of certain characteristics of the human mind; but it must not be carried too much into detail, or it will conflict with the one previously stated [i.e., the law just discussed]. Nor is it best to presume too much upon the constancy of human nature; for while the stimulus of hunger or cold may in general affect individual minds in the same way, the actions resulting from these may be of entirely different nature."[10]

This is a modest statement of the law, but the very modesty seems to be a sufficient argument against its being called a law. If a bone is thrown at a group of hungry dogs or to one dog after another, they will all respond alike; hence we may deduce a law from this observation to the effect that all individual dog minds respond similarly to the same or like stimuli. But not all men always respond in the same way to a decoy, a handsome bribe or flattery. There are only a few conceivable situations where this law may work almost perfectly, such as, when a person tells a pleasant joke in the presence of a company. In such situations most people laugh or try to laugh because they find the joke agreeable to them, and they fear to be taken as dullards or possibly to offend the joker if they sit still like a row of Buddhas. The present law may be regarded as an axiom of causal psychology: certain environmentalists, for example, have built a whole science of mind on this axiom.[11] It is rather amusing to contrast this law with the following law of Spencer:

[10] *Ibid.*, p. 369; Giddings, *Inductive Sociology*, p. 60.
[11] E. g., J. B. Watson, *Behaviorism*.

7. "In society, as elsewhere, a single cause produces a number of unlike effects."[12] The contrast between Giddings' law and Spencer's is like that between the Golden Rule of Christ and the new Golden Rule of Mr. G. B. Shaw. The former commanded: "Do unto others as ye would have others do unto you," on the assumption that human nature is fundamentally alike everywhere; while the latter advises: "Do not do unto others as ye would have others do unto you," on the assumption that human nature is nowhere exactly alike. But this law again is an axiom which may or may not be necessary for the discovery of causal laws, but in itself it is not a social law, since it can help to predict nothing specifically.

8. Another assumption reads as follows: "That motion follows the line of least resistance is as true . . . for societies as for molecules."[13] This is Spencer's law, in support of which he instanced the congregation of men at places of abundant food supply, the lines of migration, the growth of industrial centers, the location of trade routes and many other economic facts. Professor Ross criticizes this law as follows: "This proposition can hold only in so far as men economize. If there is a play side as well as a work side to human life, if men are squanderers of energy as well as economizers of energy, they will not follow lines of least resistance. The development of games and social festivity, the self-expression of artistic and religious activity, as well as the devotion to sport, adventure and exploration, show that there is such a thing as a surplus of human energy."[14] This argument seems to miss the mark. For the point is not whether there is such a thing as "a surplus of human energy," but rather how do men spend their surplus energy. The development of games and social festivity, the self-expression of artistic and religious activity, etc., are not necessarily the squandering of the surplus energy; they are on the contrary, to a large extent, a

[12] E. A. Ross, *Foundations of Sociology*, p. 46. Quotations by permission of the Macmillan Co.
[13] E. A. Ross, *op. cit.*, p. 43.   [14] *Ibid.*, p. 43.

necessary part of life. Loafing, for example, is an irrational act, but even the loafer may economize his time in such ways as best suit his lazy temperament. Economy from the point of view of the loafers, is different from the economy of the business men or of misers. That which appears wasteful from the point of view of the former may appear economical from the point of view of the latter; and that which appears economical from the point of view of the former may appear wasteful from the point of view of the latter. Few things seem more wasteful and distressful than to sit in a foul-smelling mud-hut and to dream, to poetize and to philosophize. Yet this is considered by a great many people in certain countries as the most gentlemanly thing to do. And the point in dispute is whether the gentleman-loafer and the business man, in so far as they are conscious of what they are doing, do always economize their time and resources from their own point of view?

Professor Ross further argues: "But even economic men do not follow the line of least resistance in the same way as molecules. Compare the path of a flood with that of an army. Water will meander a score of leagues to find an outlet but a furlong away. An army clambers over an intervening ridge to reach its objective. Each moment of its course the river follows the line easiest at that moment. Man knows his goal and, having foresight, takes the line that on the whole is easiest." This looks more like an argument for Spencer's law than one against it. This argument amounts to saying that men follow the line of least resistance with the aid of their intelligence, whereas the course of water obeys the same law presumably without the aid of its intelligence. I should think the law is deliberately violated in our moral decisions. All our moral decisions are conscious decisions, and our sense of duty demands action against our natural inclinations. When two desires clearly conflict, one easier to follow, leading straight to perdition, and the other harder to obey, leading to "the strait and narrow path," our inner voice commands us to follow the latter, the line of the greatest resistance. Obedience to this command is a moral act, the following of the line of the greatest resistance, and a direct violation of Spencer's law.

There is another group of a priori assumptions, namely, the laws of competition. Of these laws the following versions are found in various economic and sociological treaties:

9. "A second fundamental assumption is that the direct, natural corrective, and within the science itself the only corrective, of exaction is competition. If one will not put forth a given amount of labour for given wages, another person must be sought who will accept the terms, and the consensus of a given community as to wages and prices is the only possible measure of values—of human desires and repugnances expressed in terms of wealth."[15]

10. "A third principle follows from these two, and is urged as a safeguard against either a selfish or a benevolent trespass on the field of economics. Each man is the rightful judge of his own desires and the appropriate protector of his own interests."[16]

11. "The law of free competition: Every restriction of competition is an evil, and every extension of it is always an ultimate good."[17]

The foregoing three laws are laws of economics, but they are broad enough to be applicable to the general field of sociology, and neat enough to serve as models for apriorisms. The root of these laws is the law of parsimony or of self-interest quoted above. As applied to economics, this law yields the economic "law of least social cost" which may be stated as follows:

12. Other things being equally favorable, people tend to con-

[15] Bascom, *Sociology*, p. 60.

[16] *Loc. cit.* These two laws were originally stated by the author together with No. 2 quoted above. The author called them "laws," "fundamental assumptions," "principles," "axioms," etc., indiscriminately.

[17] Gide and Rist, *op. cit.*, p. 358; J. S. Mill, *Principles of Political Economy*, bk. IV, chap. 7, paragraph 7.

sume goods, that are produced with the least expenditure of effort.[18] A counterpart of the law of least social cost is the "law of substitution" which reads:

13. "When there is more than one method of producing a given result, the least costly method available will be selected."[19] Since the consumers demand the least expensive articles, provided the quality be the same, it is reasonably assumed that the producers would adopt the least costly method available, in order to beat off their competitors, and to adjust the supply of goods to the demand. And since the production of a commodity, beyond the primitive savage economy, requires more ingredients than one, some of which are more important than others, the demand price for the less important will depend on that for the more important. Hence the "law of derived demand," to wit:—

14. "When a commodity is such that there exists no independent demand for it, the demand for the goods, in the production of which it is associated with a number of others, serves to determine a law of derived demand for the commodity in question. The aggregate of the price at which the appropriate supplies of the other things, which are associated with it in the production of the goods, will be forthcoming, being subtracted from the price at which the corresponding quantity of those goods can find purchasers, the remainder is the limit of the demand price for a given amount of the said commodity."[20]

So the series of deductions goes on. The two indispensable companions of all economic laws are the term "other things being equal," and the term "it tends to," even though "other things" are rarely equal, and the various tendencies continually counteract one another. Hence Marshall's definition of an economic law as "a statement of economic tendencies,"—or a set of circumstances which, if not counteracted, may come to pass, but by no

---

[18] See N. H. Comish, *The Standard of Living,* pp. 47-49.
[19] Palgrave, *Dictionary of Political Economy.* II, 582-85.
[20] *Ibid.,* p. 582. Quotations by permission of the Macmillan Co.

means inevitably.[21] These few examples, I hope, are sufficient to indicate the nature of economic laws, and to suggest the nature of social laws that might be modelled after them.

Now, after this rather lengthy illustration, what should we say about the laws of free competition? At slight acquaintance, they look extremely individualistic or even egoistic; indeed they have been used as justifications for the laissez-faire policy. And their alliance with the eighteenth century hedonistic psychology rendered them all the more impressive. J. S. Mill believed in free competition, and on that ground utterly dissented from the anti-competition doctrines of the socialists of his day. He was anything but an upholder of the status quo but he believed that much of the social evil in his day was due to imperfect competition, and that the forces which hinder free competition such as monopolies of various sorts were among the worst obstacles to social improvement. The present day apostles of free competition urge a vigorous governmental interference to minimize, if not totally to abolish, artificial restrictions to free competition. The doctrine of perfectly free competition, such as they conceive, is a highly unselfish or even a utopian ideal, not likely to be wholly realized on earth in the near future. It means the maximum possible equalization of opportunities for all, free self-expression on equal terms. It presupposes the abolition of all monopolies other than those conducive to competition. Sham titles, the odious caste system, inheritance of private property beyond a certain reasonable amount, the monopoly on land, and a number of other artificial restrictions must go. When these are got rid of, the only inequalities that are likely to remain are the various forms of natural inequalities, the differences in natural gifts. Next comes the elimination of the naturally unfit, and the speeding up of progress toward Zion. But this very idealistic conception of competition disqualifies the law of competition from being taken as a natural law. It is a teleological law if it is a law at all. It

[21] A. Marshall, *Principles of Economics*, pp. 30-36, 770-80.

presupposes the creation of an ideal society in which to compete, and the society we live in is anything but ideal.

When it is said that "each man is the rightful judge of his own desires and the appropriate protector of his interests," whom does it mean? It cannot be everybody. Even Mill excluded children, savages and the abnormals.[22] The doctrine that "the consensus of a given community as to wages and prices is the only possible measure of values" ignores the fact that all public opinions are initiated by some individuals, and that an able and enterprising employer like Henry Ford can raise or cut the wages as he sees fit in advance of all other employers, and thereby he may create a public opinion as to what a fair wage is. Furthermore, the doctrine that "every restriction of competition is an evil," and that "every extension of it is always an ultimate good," can have meaning only when competition is understood to mean fair and legal competition. The laissez-faire economists thought that free competition would result in the lowering of the price through the elimination of inferior producers, but it turned out the other way round: it enabled the inferior producers to survive by producing inferior or adulterated goods, and to drive out of business the honest producers. In conclusion, it may be said that the law of free competition is an apriorism in pure economics, has been a handy instrument for self-justification by the unscrupulous, and is an ideal which presupposes the creation of ideal societies in which to compete.

There is another apriorism which was made famous by Herbert Spencer, and which has been variously understood and misunderstood. In recent years it has found a very clear and authentic enunciation in the presidential address of Professor Edward P. Cheyney. His words are as follows:

15. "A Law of Continuity: 'There is no new thing under the sun.' All events, conditions, institutions, personalities, come from

[22] *Essay on Liberty.*

immediately preceding events, conditions, institutions, personalities. . . . It is the continuity of history that makes possible the popular and fascinating search for origins. . . . Actual origins elude us; everything is the outcome of something preceding; the immediate, sudden appearance of something, its creation by an individual or a group at some one moment of time, is unknown in history. . . . We say sometimes that a certain event came like a thunderbolt from a clear sky. But this is a mere form of speech. Thunderbolts do not come from a clear sky; they come from unobserved clouds. So the suddenness of an historical event is only the measure of our carelessness of observation. . . .

"The continuity of history is not merely a fact; it is a law. By no voluntary action can any great breach of historical continuity be accomplished. The English parliamentary leaders of 1649 might abolish the Kingship and the House of Lords and found a republic; but they could not prevent the government of England drifting back through the Protectorate and the Restoration to a monarchy but little changed from its old form and powers. The French revolutionists might attempt to make all things new; but little by little they were forced to submit to the law of continuity and restore the Church, the monarchy, the nobility, and much of the social system as it had existed before 1789. And now poor Russia, perhaps poor Germany, is finding how incapable a nation is of making any great break in historical development. Institutions have been modified, not destroyed; races have been subjugated or absorbed, not exterminated; beliefs have been altered, not ceased: human history has been an unbroken narrative."[23]

The term "law of continuity" like the term "law of causation," is capable of conflicting interpretations. Since the scientists are interested in discovering causes, it is well to understand by the term "law of continuity" a regular serial order of mechanical suc-

[23] E. P. Cheyney, "Law in History," *American Historical Review*, XXIX (No. 2, 1924) 237-38.

cession. The business of the social scientist is to describe the way in which the various events follow one another: he may be credited with having discovered a social law when he shows the necessary connection between an event and the ones preceding it.

It is a mistake to regard the law of continuity as an historical law: for the law, signifying no more than a necessary logical presupposition for all scientific laws, is true of all laws, but is not in itself a specific law, whether historical or sociological. It is a necessary logical presupposition for all scientific laws, because without it one can predict nothing; but it is so devoid of any specific content that it is applicable to no particular social phenomena. It may acquire a specific content when it is conjoined with some such phenomena as Comte's three stages of intellectual development or Gumplowicz's five stages of religious development, and then—and then only—have we anything like an historical or social law. Comte's law of three stages may or may not be a valid social law, but it has some specific content and therefore tries to be one.

Professor Cheney seems to confound the law of continuity with fatalism. I see no reason for saying "By no voluntary action can any great breach of historical continuity be accomplished." The author says in an earlier paragraph: "I think it is safe to say that the Reformation would have occurred in England at about the time it did and about in the form it did, if Henry VIII had never seen Anne Boleyn, indeed, if Henry VIII had never lived"; and "Providence, fate, destiny, law, has controlled the affairs of man, as it has of men, as it controls all things"; and he quotes with approval from the *Precepts of Ptah Hotep:* "Never hath that which men have prepared for come to pass; for what the deity hath commanded, even that thing cometh to pass"; and from Gladstone's speech in Parliament: "Those great social forces which move on in their might and majesty, and which the tumult of our debates does not for a moment impede or disturb," etc.[24]

[24] E. P. Cheyney, *op. cit.,* pp. 235-36; for other similar utterances, see *passim.*

Now it seems to me that in these utterances the author's poetic imagination has got the upper hand over his scientific sagacity. Indeed, even the author's reasoning may be questioned. If it be true, as he insists, that "everything is the outcome of something preceding," should we not say that whatever a man does leads to some necessary sequence? According to the author's view the English Reformation was the work of "economic change, political change, intellectual change," apparently all sorts of changes, but not of Henry VIII's change of heart for the black-eyed Anne. According to the scientific view Henry's change of heart in all probability had some important effect on the political and economic changes of the day and, through these changes, on the Reformation itself; and it is the business of the scientist to ascertain and describe the precise extent and the manner in which these important effects came about, so that if some day another Henry should change heart, the social scientist might warn the people: "Beware, beware, prepare ye for the evil days to come!"

The danger of the fatalistic notion is that it can justify anything or nothing. If Italian liberty is trampled upon by a political adventurer the fatalist might say with Ptah Hotep: "Verily, verily. Never hath that which men have prepared for come to pass; for what the deity hath commanded, even that thing cometh to pass." If the Italians rise up and tumble the adventurer head over heels and restore Italian liberty, the fatalist might again say with the air of profundity of a modern Ptah Hotep: "Surely surely, this is all in accordance with the law of continuity, for now the Italians are prepared for liberty."

The attentive reader in the recent philosophical literature such as Professor Lloyd Morgan's *Emergent Evolution* probably has felt a sense of uneasiness in his blind faith in the continuity of history. Now that the mid-nineteenth century tumult and excitement over evolution is over, one finds upon calm reflection, instead of a smooth seamless continuity from nature to man, a series of phenomena on different levels,—Space-Time, Matter, Life, and Mind. If anyone wishes to believe (believe! I say) in the continuity between the different levels, let him believe; but he should remember that he is all the while only believing. In a recent book by Professor Ogburn, the author gives a list of some 148 simultaneous discoveries in science.[25] These simultaneous discoveries do not prove fatalism, though they may justify a sort of scientific determinism in the sense that under similar conditions similar results may be expected within some rough limits. Determinism in this sense is a necessary logical presupposition, and is what we tacitly assume to be true in our every day reasoning,—in making appointments and keeping contracts, in enacting criminal laws and convicting offenders, and in numerous other ways. Nor is determinism in this sense incompatible with freedom, since freedom cannot be mere random movement; if an act is to be free, it must be free from something: for nothing can be free unless there is something to be free from; and this something is precisely the limiting factor of freedom.

Finally, in reply to Professor Cheney, I may quote a magnificent passage from Professor Whitehead's book, *Science and the Modern World:* "The progress of civilization is not wholly a uniform drift toward better things. It may perhaps wear this aspect if we map it on a scale which is large enough. But such broad views obscure the details on which rest our whole understanding of the process. New epochs emerge with comparative suddenness, if we have regard to the scores of thousands of years throughout which the complete history extends. Secluded races suddenly take their places in the main stream of events: technological discoveries transform the mechanism of human life: a primitive art quickly flowers into full satisfaction of some aesthetic craving: great religions in their crusading youth spread through the nations the peace of Heaven and the sword of the

[25] W. F. Ogburn, *Social Change,* pp. 90-102.

Lord."[26] That which draws along this unyielding cosmos steadily, though in a zigzag fashion, toward better conditions, is what may be called the strenuous human will guided by clear foresight, the understanding of the laws. Where men keep on by sheer force of strenuous will guided by foresight, they make some headway against the brute forces of nature. But where men sit down and reflect upon, and dream of, fantasies and say, "Never hath that which men have prepared for come to pass; for what the deity hath commanded, even that thing cometh to pass," there seems to result the Chinese stagnation and the Hindoo lethargy.

The claim of a priori assumptions to the high title of social laws is immodest enough. But some sociologists have gone even further, have laid down a series of a priori assumptions with dogmatic hardness, and have proclaimed them to be "universal laws." The following ten are Gumplowicz's "universal laws":—

16. "The Law of Causation: Every social phenomenon is the necessary effect of anterior causes. No social phenomenon originates in the nothingness of individual whims. The principle of sufficient cause is true also. Every social phenomenon whether political, juridical or economic, must have a sufficient cause in one or more social agencies. The effects must also be equal or at least proportional to the energy of the causes alike in the social, the physical and the mental domain. The deed of an individual will never create a social condition nor change it, however much appearances may deceive us."

17. "The Law of Development: Each social phenomenon is a momentary phase in a period of development; though often the end of the period may be beyond the reach of calculation. Every political organization, all rights, every economic relation suffers change. We can distinguish the beginning, the process of growth and often the decline and decay."

[26] A. N. Whitehead, *Science and The Modern World*, p. 1. Quotations by permission of the Macmillan Co.

18. "Regularity of Development: Development does not in and of itself involve the idea of regularity; the sequence of like or similar phases might or might not be uniform in all cases. But actually progress is regular; it conforms to law everywhere."

19. "The Law of Periodicity: In all domains of phenomena, regularity of development passes into periodicity. Wherever we can watch the whole process, we find a period of existence extending from the origin through the phases of growth and perfection to decline and fall."

20. "The Law of Complexity: Every state, every people, every tribe is complex in a great many respects. Every principle of right is a composite of views, conceptions, ideas and principles. Every common economic interest is made up of conditions, activities, relations. In every language there is an endless variety of philological elements."

21. "Reciprocal Action of Foreign (heterogen) Elements: Although there is an endless variety of cases in each particular domain, yet the law seems to express the first and most important impulse to development in each and every one of them. The significance of this force in social processes was surmised long ago, but it was erroneously interpreted by individualists and atomists as the reaction of man upon man and was designated as love or hate, as sociability or mutual hostility (bellum omnium contra omnes). The error in this conception will appear as we proceed. Specific reciprocal influence of man upon man can not be affirmed in a universal law. What holds true between man and man in one group is not necessarily true in another group. Here it may be love and sociability and there hate and thirst for strife. . . . Social groups exhibit reciprocal effects which are fundamentally the same always and everywhere."

22. "Adaptation to an obvious End: Every social growth, every social entity, serves a definite end, however much its worth and morality may be questioned. For the universal law of adap-

tation signifies simply that no expenditure of effort, no change of condition, is purposeless on any domain of phenomena. Hence the inherent reasonableness of all social facts and conditions must be conceded."

23. "Identity of Forces: The reciprocal action of foreign (heterogen) elements obviously proceeds from forces immanent in them or arising from their contact. These forces never change their character. They are identical, as we wish to say. Those operating in the domain of physical phenomena have always been the same that they are now. So of mental forces; thought, feeling, volition, each has moved man and controlled his actions in the same way always. Likewise the social forces, the causes which we must conclude from the effects that follow on the social domain, have ever been the same."

24. "Similarity of Events: A necessary consequence of the last law is the perpetual similarity of events on all domains of phenomena. . . . Nobody doubts that the sun's warming powers acting on moist ground age after age have produced and always will produce the same effects on vegetation that they produce now. . . . So, too, nobody doubts that man's mental faculties have produced the same effects in all times and climes. Always and everywhere men feel and think and plan; even the sensible . products of these mental processes are the same."

25. "Law of Parallelism: In every domain we find some phenomena which are similar, but we do not know the ultimate cause of their similarity. In the physical domain such phenomena are ascribed to identical forces directly. But in the mental domain, the tendency is rather to attribute the similarity to some alleged connection between them; and in social phenomena it is considered the result of consanguinity or of some historic relationship. But actually there is something fundamental at the bottom of all these similarities which we must refer temporarily to a

law of parallelism, since we do not know more precisely what it is."[27]

Professor Ross reduces these ten "universal laws" to the following seven:

26. "For every phenomenon there is an adequate cause.
27. "Phenomena run in sequences. .
28. "These sequences are law-abiding.
29. "Concrete objects have parts.
30. "A developmental process is initiated by the contact or conflict of unlike elements.
31. "Forces differ only in strength and direction.
32. "Identical forces produce similar effects."[28]

Here we find an interesting series of laws which their author, Gumplowicz, claims to be not merely social laws, but "universal laws valid for social as well as for physical and mental phenomena."[29] Nor is this all: he claims them to be proofs of his monism, although he is evidently indifferent whether it be a materialistic or a spiritualistic monism.[30] That a law so abstract as to be applicable to all phenomena whether physical, mental or social, can not be much of a social law, the author was evidently aware. For he insists that, in abstracting the general characteristics from such heterogeneous masses of phenomena, "we ought not to go too deeply into the characteristics of the species; for where the peculiarities begin, the common traits end. Where the physical nature commences the laws common to the mental and social domain cease to apply."[31] It is evident that the author lays down these laws with his eyes open.

But to push the question a step further, has the author proved his contention that these laws are "valid for social as well as for physical and mental phenomena"? No, instead he has laid down

[27] Ludwig Gumplowicz, *Outlines of Sociology*, translated by F. W. Moore, pp. 74-82.
[28] Ross, *Foundations of Sociology*, pp. 53-54.
[29] Gumplowicz, *op. cit.*, p. 75.
[30] *Ibid.*, pp. 81-82.   [31] *Ibid.*, p. 75.

a series of propositions with dogmatic hardness. Professor Ross has re-shaped these laws with a reasonable degree of fairness to the author. But neither the original nor the re-shaped propositions are worth the name "social laws." The first three propositions of Professor Ross that "for every phenomenon there is an adequate cause," that "phenomena run in sequences," and "these sequences are law-abiding,"—these may be granted as the necessary methodological presuppositions for causal laws. For, without some such assumptions I do not see how anyone can discover causal laws or even talk about them. Professor Ross's fourth proposition that "concrete objects have parts" is merely an axiom of metaphysics.

In the fifth proposition that "a developmental process is initiated by the contact or conflict of unlike elements," if the emphasis is laid on the word "developmental," it is nonsense, for what reason is there to suppose that the contact or conflict of unlike elements may not warp them both or even put an end to their developmental process instead of initiating it? But if the emphasis is laid on the words "contact or conflict," the proposition becomes too vague to mean much, signifying no more than that a contact or a conflict leads to some sequences. The last two propositions, namely that "forces differ only in strength and direction," and that "identical forces produce similar effects," are axioms in mechanics, but whether or not they are social laws is anything but certain, depending a great deal on what is meant by "forces."

COMMENTS

With regard to these apriorisms the following summary comments may be made:

1. Apriorisms not Social Laws. These apriorisms, doubtless with many others, may be granted as methodological presuppositions; but in themselves they are not social laws. Some of them like Gumplowicz's "law of causation" and "law of the regularity of development" are the necessary presuppositions, if any causal laws are to be discovered. For, the very meaning of a causal law implies causality and regularity of occurrence. Others, like Spencer's "law of social motion" that social development follows the line of least resistance, being founded on the crude analogy between a machine and a human being, are mere specimens of the unclear thinking of a past generation. If consistently developed, these assumptions may result in the creation of beautifully clear-cut logical constructions, as in pure economics. But logical constructions are not social laws.

2. *Apriorisms Indispensable.* This brief examination seems to show how helpless the social scientists are, without metaphysics, in spite of the undisguised prejudice of some of them against metaphysics. It seems that we cannot help being apriorists, unless we cease thinking altogether. At every turn the social scientists pile one apriorism upon another; and the great pity is that they "talk prose," even while violently protesting that they do not.

3. *Efficient Cause Challenged.* Another important result from the discussion of these apriorisms is the challenge to the discovery of unitary efficient causes in social phenomena. Since human motives are ethical as well as economic, no law which has resulted from the assumption that man is a mere "economic man," can be a valid social law. So also, no law which has resulted from the assumption that man is a pure moral being, can be a valid social law. Either an ethical or an economic motive may tip the balance of the scale in determining the course of conduct, according as the occasion presents itself. And if this be true, it seems to be a serious challenge to the discovery of unitary efficient causes in social phenomena.

4. *Their Value.* Since apriorisms are often the necessary methodological presuppositions for social laws, they are of value in two ways. First, they satisfy the intellectual craving of those who love pure system. The economists, for example, starting out

from some such crude assumptions as the "law of parsimony" (quoted above), have built remarkable systems. In the systems of such economists as Ricardo, Marshall and Böhm-Bawerk there is a great deal to be admired from the methodological point of view. They have demonstrated to the admiration of social scientists in other fields, with what dignity and consistency in reasoning, the economists can go about their task. Secondly, in so far as these apriorisms will ultimately lead to the discovery of true social laws, they are the indispensable equipment for the social scientists. For example, the "law" that "individual minds respond similarly to the same or like stimuli," is a very crude assumption; still, if on the basis of this assumption, psychologists succeed in discovering true causal laws, the assumption has a practical value. Or, even if these apriorisms fail to lead to the discovery of true social laws, they may suggest some schemes on which to base the framing of social policies. The apriorisms of economics, for example, may enter into the determination of practical affairs.

CHAPTER IV
TELEOLOGICAL LAWS

THE NATURE OF TELEOLOGICAL LAWS

THE POSITIVE sociologists are interested in discovering efficient causes, and not final causes. The laws based on the former are called causal laws; and the laws based on the latter, teleological. Whether or not a sociologist should confine his task to the discovery of efficient causes is a debatable question. But in no case should a teleological law be mistaken for a causal law. Since the present study is concerned with a critical examination of positive laws in sociology, teleological laws might reasonably be ignored; but since a fairly large number of teleological laws have found their way into sociological literature, it has seemed desirable to make a digest of those which are specifically called by their authors "social laws" or "natural laws." Many of them are so obviously teleological, needing no demonstration, that I shall do little more than present them.

LIST OF TELEOLOGICAL LAWS

Among the numerous teleological laws the most conspicuous from the point of view of sociologists is probably the "law of social aims" which reads:

1. "The greatest good for the greatest number or social well-being is the aim of social action."[1] In what sense should we call this a law? Certainly, not in the naturalistic sense. For the formula, the greatest good for the greatest number or social well-being, may mean a great variety of things. It originally meant the greatest amount of pleasure, but we have long since discarded the hedonistic calculus. As an expression of natural pietism, however, it is a good formula.

After the formula of the greatest good for the greatest number. the various formulas of "survival and progress" are probably the

[1] Blackmar and Gillin, *op. cit.*, pp. 370-71.

most popular. The relation, indeed, between the two is so close that the latter may be regarded as revised versions of the former—revised in accordance with the present day Social Darwinism.

2. The following "law of survival and progress" is a typical example of such formulas: "Institutions flourish or decay according to their adaptation to the circumstances of life surrounding the people which possess them." The authors of this law give an impressive account of it. "The track of social progress is strewn with the ruins of social institutions that have lost their usefulness. When a society at a given stage of progress adopts certain customs, habits or institutions, it retains these only so long as they contribute to survival; when they are no longer useful, they are cast off. The statute books are filled with laws once alive, now dead; the habits of life today are far different from those of centuries past; and as society unfolds itself in human progress, there is a constant elimination of the unfit. Old forms and functions give way to new ones; those that are ill adapted to the survival of society will pass away through non-use, just as biological forms or functions have become extinct through atrophy."[2]

This is a clear and forcible expression of a wide-spread opinion. It sounds plausible because of its analogy to the Darwinian theory. It is probable that in the early stage of biological evolution when mentality either had not yet developed or had only just begun to develop, survival was a matter of adaptation. But when this same formula of adaptation and survival is applied to the present day institutions, glaring absurdities often result. One may interpret "adaptation" in the broadest possible way so as to render the law most sensible; as, for example, to mean by adaptation meeting the needs of the people. Even thus interpreted, the law is but a circular statement. Is the objective criterion of adaptation survival? If so, a thing survives because it is adapted; it is adapted because it survives! On the other hand, if it be

---

[2] *Ibid.*, p. 378.

admitted that there are other criteria of adaptation than mere survival, then the law is obviously only a half truth.

The authors point to "the statute books filled with laws once alive, now dead," as if these were conclusive proofs. But is it evident that these laws died because they failed to adapt themselves? Is the Volstead Act, for instance, in the United States or the Fascist despotism in Italy there because it is adapted? Or is it imposed by a vigorous and well-organized minority upon the rest? In order to avoid such pitfalls, present day sociologists make a distinction between passive adaptation and active adaptation. By passive adaptation they mean the adaptation of man to his environment; and by active adaptation, the adaptation of environment to man. The former is generally mechanical or is forced upon man; the latter is purposive, and its aim is to meliorate the environment, to make it a better place in which to live. The idea of progress is therefore teleological; and in the absence of purpose there can be only motion without either progress or retrogression.

3. Another version of the "law of survival and progress" is the "law of impermanence" which Professor Cheyney expounds as follows: "Looking over the field of history, there seems to be a law of impermanence, of mutability. The fall of empires is one of the most familiar of historic phenomena." After enumerating the successive rise and fall of the great historic empires, the author goes on to say: "So persistent and infinitely repeated has been this disappearance of successive organizations of men and types of civilization that it gives every indication of being the result of a law rather than of a mere succession of chances." He intimates that the "clue to such a law may possibly be found in a biological analogy. Biologists have long observed that organic species highly specialized and suited to one environment or mode of existence tend to become extinct. They have not been adaptable, and have therefore died out, while the ever active causes of evolution have produced new spe-

cies from older and simpler stocks to take their places. Palæontology, the study of life in the geologic past, is largely occupied with species specially adapted to one set of circumstances and therefore unable to survive in another." Similarly whole races and nations have been observed, which in the course of their career have become over-differentiated from their neighbors, physically, mentally, and culturally, and over-differentiation has led them to a gradual ossification into fixed types. "They have ceased to be adaptable; politically and socially they are no longer capable of change or of conformity to a changing world. Populations insufficiently responsive to the requirements of subsistence, to the pressure of competing nations, to new inventions or new ideas, have stolidly awaited conquest or absorption or transformation. The law of mutability, of decay of nations, is a measure of man's incapacity to change his habits. Unless nations can change as the time changes, they must die."

As regards the practical applicability of this law, the author says: "Conservatism, therefore, with a curious inversion of its intention, brings about the destruction of the group of fixed institutions it wishes to preserve. One hundred per cent Americanism is more dangerous to the perpetuity of American institutions than a less percentage would be. Established formulas, traditional conceptions, fixed legal principles, dominating ideals, are the marks of a highly specialized unadaptable, unchanging, community, and however elevated and admirable, are forces tending, under this historic law, to its ultimate destruction. Fundamentalism is self-destructive. 'The letter killeth, the spirit maketh alive.' It has only been the amendment and the stretching of the Constitution of the United States that have enabled us to survive politically under it. It has only been the abandonment of the old imperial ideas that has kept the British Empire in existence. Elasticity, adaptiveness, capacity to conform to change, are the requisites for survival of a race, of a nation, of a type of civilization. The absence of these has brought about their fall. Perhaps an America scornful of a League of Nations, wedded to isolation, struggling to keep her life separate, unconformable to a world that has been made essentially one by economic and intellectual changes, may not be able to survive. Thus the law of mutability, of instability of nations, will receive one more illustration."[3]

In face of such a forcible statement, it does seem probable that mutability is everywhere encountered; but have we here a law? A social law, in order to merit the name, must not only announce that established formulas, traditional conceptions, etc., are the marks of a highly specialized and unchanging community, and that there are forces which tend to bring about the ultimate destruction of such a community; but the law must describe the concrete situations, the exact conditions, under which an "established formula" or a traditional conception of such and such type tends to bring about its own extinction. It is poetic to say that "the letter killeth, the spirit maketh alive"; or that "it has only been the amendment and the stretching of the Constitution of the United States that have enabled us to survive politically under it"; or that "an America scornful of a League of Nations, wedded to isolation, . . . may not be able to survive." The Law of Mutability, as it now stands, is an eloquent preface to, and an incomplete analysis of, an hypothetical law which still needs be discovered.

4. Survival and progress presuppose ideals and choices. Is there any law of choices of ideals? Professor Giddings announces in the following quotation that there is such a law: "In all social choice the most influential ideals are those of the forceful man, the powerful community, of virtue in the primitive sense of the word; second in influence are the ideals of the convivial man, the prosperous and pleasure-loving community, the utilitarian or hedonistic virtues; third in influence are the ideals of the austere man, the righteous or just community, the Stoic or

[3] E. P. Cheyney, "Law in History," *American Historical Review*, XXIX (No. 2, 1924), 238-39.

Puritan virtues of self-restraint; fourth in influence are the ideals of the rationally conscientious man, of the liberal and enlightened community, of the virtues of reasonableness, broadmindedness and charity: but if mental evolution continues, the higher ideals become increasingly influential."[4]

The thing which first strikes the reader in this hierarchy of ideals is the conspicuous absence of beauty. Professor Giddings labels these four ideals in order as the primitive, the Epicurean, the Stoic or Puritan, and the Humanistic; elsewhere he has labeled them as the Stoic, the Epicurean, the Puritan, and the Humanistic.[5] But it is highly doubtful whether such catalogues of historical facts represent the law of social choices, if there be any such. Professor Giddings offers, as a proof of the law, that the most influential ideal in social choice is forcefulness, the observation that "the crowd will always sacrifice utility and integrity to exult in a display of power."[6] This might be true of a great variety of crowds, but not of all; for the morality of a crowd depends largely on its leadership. More careful studies of the crowd since LeBon's and Martin's discussions on the subject[7] have made it sufficiently clear, I think, that certain crowds, such as the religious crowd, when led by a Savonarola or a Luther, are at times quite capable of rising above their own level of daily morality. Moreover, I question the legitimacy of treating society as if it were always a crowd in making its choices.

Survival and progress, ideals and choices, all have had their law. But is there any law of spirit? Professors Blackmar and Gillin announce in the following quotation a "law of spiritual development":

5. "All development in spiritual matters depends on the stimulating effects of contact with a different stage of culture

---

[4] *Inductive Sociology*, p. 178. Quotations by permission of the Macmillan Co.
[5] *Principles of Sociology*, pp. 405-7.
[6] *Ibid.*, p. 408.
[7] Gustave LeBon, *The Crowd;* E. D. Martin, *The Behavior of Crowds.*

upon the self-consciousness of a people."[8] A change of one word in the statement of this law might render it an unimpeachable truism, and that word is "development" for which might be substituted the word "change." The notion of "spiritual development" presupposes a direction of change or some ideal good, in the absence of which there can be no spiritual development. The law as it stands amounts to saying that all cultural changes depend on the interplay of different types of culture, which is an incomplete analysis of cultural development. It can be made over into a law only when "the stimulating effects of contact" are analyzed and the conditions for a deliberate control of the interstimulation of different cultural types are specified.[9]

6. Mechanisms and purposes, instincts and ideals, all have been called in to explain social phenomena; but the will of God remains to be called in. "In general," says Mr. Walthew, "all (political) systems may be classed under three heads: first, where the selection is left to God (or nature); second, where the selection is made directly by the body of the people; third, where an intermediate body of some sort is employed."[10] After discussing each one of these systems in turn, the author pronounces that "all the systems which have been devised by the ingenuity of men for the selection of the head of the state have been failures."[11] "And herein comes the question: What sort of strength must be possessed, what kind of ability is required? What manner of man is he who is entitled to the premiership by right of being the strongest and the ablest in the nation?"[12] The author answers that "under the true form of government, the premier will always be precisely the man intended by the Great Design to occupy that exalted place. He will be the efflorescence, so to speak, of his time and nation. In every nation and at every

[8] *Op. cit.*, p. 377; quoted from Tiele, *Elements of the Science of Religion*, I, 239.
[9] See discussion of dialectical laws in Chapter VIII.
[10] George W. Walthew, *The Philosophy of Government*, p. 82.
[11] *Ibid.*, p. 89.   [12] *Ibid.*, p. 93.

time there is always one man who is the sum, as it were, of that nation. In him appears all that that nation, at that particular time, is. He is the expression of the national life—the nation personified, the conglomerate mass individualized; and this man under the true form of government will certainly be premier. The law of natural selection and of the survival of the fittest [apt terms of expression for use in this connection!] will inevitably force him to the top."[13]

That the people in the long run select for their leaders men who in a general way are capable of serving the best interests of the people, is a reasonable assumption. That the people should select for their leader the kind of man who is "precisely the man intended by the Great Design to occupy that exalted place," is a political pietism too good to admit of any dispute. But that "in every nation and at every time there is always one man who is the sum, as it were, of that nation"; or that "in him appears all that that nation, at that particular time, is"; or that "the law of natural selection and of the survival of the fittest . . . will inevitably force him to the top"—these are sheer dogmas which may be true in the author's ideological world where "the true form of government" exists, whatever that be.

The appeal to the will of God as a method of explaining social phenomena being nowadays somewhat unpopular, other authors have had recourse to less presumptuous instruments of explanation, and have formulated political laws in varying degrees on a naturalistic basis. Of such laws the following is an example:

7. "There seems to be a law of democracy, a tendency for all government to come under the control of all people. . . . Every invention that makes easier the diffusion of information, every increase in the mobility and alertness of mind of the mass of the people, every rise in the standard of life, draws a larger part of the people into contact with the problems of government. Education brings a sense of power over government; moral train-

_____
[13] *Ibid.*, p. 116.

ing brings a sense of responsibility for the use to which government may be put. Printing, steam and electrical transmission, radiation, popular education, increased wages, the progress of thought, leisure, all tend to extend democracy. These are practically irresistible forms of advance and the resultant advance of democracy therefore cannot be prevented. Our own generation has seen the introduction in all progressive countries of an additional half of the population into the political sphere, and the dikes set up against the spread of popular government have been overflowed in all directions. . . .

"Again, democracy is being extended to other interests of mankind than those traditionally considered as political. The absolute control of economic life by the possessors of capital has long been recognized to be disadvantageous and has been limited in various ways. Of recent decades, in various countries, under the leadership for the most part of enlightened employers, something approaching industrial democracy has been introduced in its place. The control of trade interests has been placed in the hands of all those connected with the trade, instead of being left in the hands of one class. In other cases, the modern democratic state has drawn industry more or less within its own sphere. It would seem that the law of democracy is subjecting this group of men's interests also to its sway.

"If the argument for the existence of this historical law seems to be drawn from the phenomena of a more recent period than for the other laws[14] it may perhaps be attributed to its overwhelming interest in the immediate past and in the present. A world war to which the genius of one American President gave dignity and unity by describing it as a war to make the world safe for democracy, just as a former President had at Gettysburg declared the war he was waging to be for the preservation of democracy in the United States, has nevertheless placed in power in almost every country a dictator or a majority whose be-

[14] See below for these other laws.

lief in democracy is hesitant and incomplete. If a law of democracy exists, this condition can only be temporary: the law will soon again work with compelling force. If there is no such law, we are adrift on a sea whose winds and tides and shores are all unknown. Who would not trust, if he may, the instincts and aspirations of the mass of the people in the passage perilous of the next few years, rather than the vagaries of a Mussolini, the obstinacy of a Poincarè, the pedantry of a Lenin, or the narrow vision and restricted interests of any one class of the people?"[15]

This, I think, is an admirable suggestion that there might be a law of democracy; but I wonder whether it is enough even for the most sanguine apostles of democracy to be merely assured that there is a law of democracy. That "printing, steam and electrical transmission, radiation, popular education, increased wages, the progress of thought, leisure, all tend to extend democracy," is a presumptive empirical fact which, upon further careful observation, may yield a true law of democracy. The suggestion that the reliance on "the instincts and aspirations of the mass of the people" would lead to democracy rather than to despotism, is highly doubtful, unless we were to assume the existence of such a psychological monster as an "instinct of democracy." As for the observation that "there seems to be . . . a tendency for all government to come under the control of all the people," it is indeed merely a pious wish.

8. Democracy cannot mean much unless it is based on the free consent of all the people concerned. But is there any law of free consent? Professor Cheyney announces in the following quotation that there is "A Law of Necessity for Free Consent": "Human beings are free agents in their relations with other human beings: they cannot permanently be compelled. Not only should all government be by the consent of the governed, but all government has been by the consent of the governed. When men have not been willing to give their consent they have found

[15] E. P. Cheyney, *op. cit.*, pp. 241-43.

numberless ways to avoid acceptance. They have protested, they have refused to acknowledge authority, they have refrained from action, they have resisted, they have rebelled; as a last resort they have allowed themselves to be put to death. It is consent, not force, that has on the whole held society together, that has supported governments, that has procured services. The consent has often been reluctant, it has never been actually forced. When forced it has not been consent, but mere yielding to violence, and violence has born little fruit of achievement or permanence.

"It has lately been said in excuse for his action by one of the European dictators that freedom has failed and force is the only remedy. Making a wider survey of history I should say rather that force has failed and freedom is the only remedy. Nothing has ever been really settled till the willing consent of all concerned has been obtained. Bismarck's 'blood and iron,' as a means of settlement of the internal affairs of Germany, has already proved itself not a settlement. It could and did bring about a temporary cessation of conflict, but that was hardly a settlement which lasted less than half a century. A settlement, if this is a true historic law, requires a genuine acquiescence, however reluctant, in the arrangements being made. . . . The effects of force in history have been temporary and partial and illusory; voluntary acceptance alone has been permanent and adequate and substantial."[16]

Two things seem to me at once evident in this law: first, there is in this statement a large element of truth; second, this is good preaching inasmuch as no government which does not derive its powers from the consent of the governed can be regarded as moral. But whether it is a "natural law," as the author claims it to be, is questionable. In such statements as "It is consent, not force, that has on the whole held society together"; "Violence has borne little fruit of achievement or permanence"; "nothing

[16] *Ibid.*, pp. 243-44.

has ever been really settled till the willing consent of all concerned has been obtained"; and "Bismarck's 'blood and iron,' as a means of settlement of the internal affairs of Germany . . . could and did bring about a temporary cessation of conflict, but that was hardly a settlement which lasted less than half a century," etc.—note the cautious tone of the author. This caution plainly indicates the author's uneasiness after making such sweeping statements as "Not only should all government be by the consent of the governed but all government has been by the consent of the governed." These democratic sentiments are truly noble, but it is well to remember Carlyle's dictum that the true savior of the people is not one who is morbidly sensitive to yeas and nays and rahs and hurrahs, but one who masters the people by the force of his personality and makes them do what they ought to do.

Adaptation and survival, democracy and liberty, one and all, cannot be of much value, unless they will ultimately help man to realize greater and higher moral good. But is there any "law of moral progress"? Professor Cheyney suggests the following law:

9. "Obscurely and slowly, yet visibly and measurably, moral influences in human affairs have become stronger and more widely extended than material influences. . . . The people, always more moral than their rulers, would not at any time within the last four centuries have supported their governments in wars merely of plunder, aggression, or revenge.

"If moral ideals have become increasingly predominant in the heat and unreason of war, it will readily be believed that they have asserted themselves with still more rapidly increasing force in the realm of peace. The disappearance of slavery, of serfdom, of the whipping of soldiers and sailors, criminals, apprentices, and school children, the diminution of personal oppression, of man's physical and legal power over women, of the greater advantages granted by the law to employers over employees and to landlords over tenants, the spread of sympathy, of mercy, of helpfulness, are just so many proofs of the existence of a law of moral progress.

"Not only intensively but extensively moral forces have tended to become predominant. There was a time when fidelity to contract, justice, mercy, applied only within the family. The validity of these principles gradually extended from the family to the tribe, to the nation, and now in these later ages from the nation to international relations. . . . To Mr. Wilson and Lloyd George, mistaken though they may have been, the Treaty of Versailles was a 'peace of justice.' "[17]

The imposing array of evidence of moral progress, which the author cites, is suggestive of the existence of a law of moral progress. But he has made a mere catalogue of the instances of moral progress instead of formulating a law. There is in this catalogue neither any efficient cause nor any invariability visible; and until these are demonstrated, we have no law of moral progress.

Evolutionary theory, hedonistic formulas, ethical principles, and theological phrases, all have been called in to explain social phenomena. But the most original conception seems to be that of Mr. A. C. Hall, who presents biblical precepts in their entirety as explanations of social phenomena. Mr. Hall has presented the following three laws:

10. "The Law of Adult Life": " 'Whatsoever a man soweth, that shall he also reap.' The adult must in general take the consequences of his own character and conduct—the survival of the fittest resulting."[18]

11. "The Law of the Family." 12. "The Law of Society": " 'Do unto others as ye would they should do unto you.' "[19] The author exalts these "laws," calling them "fundamental," "great prin-

[17] *Ibid.*, pp. 244-45.
[18] *Crime in Its Relation to Social Progress*, pp. 277-78.
[19] *Ibid.*, p. 378.

ciples," "great ethical principles," indiscriminately; and in his excitement about them, he seems to have forgotten to formulate "the law of the family." Concerning this law, he says that "It is the primary law of self-sacrifice. The law of unearned benefits to offspring immature and helpless, without which the species must inevitably perish," and he goes on to say how inexorably this "law" works; but nowhere does he explicitly state just what the "law" is. I mention Mr. Hall's contribution simply to show how ideas of what *is* and what *ought to be* are sometimes hopelessly confused.

COMMENTS

With regard to these laws the following summary comments may be made:

1. Teleological Laws not Causal. From the strictly naturalistic point of view, these laws are pious wishes. By pious wishes I mean expressions of pietism, which is the reverence for the natural order of things. A wish is something other than a fact, though it is capable of becoming a fact. This is not saying that these teleological laws are false. On the contrary, they may all some day be realized. But they have little to do with causal explanations; they are not causal laws.

2. Natural Laws. Certain of the foregoing laws are called by their authors "natural laws." The term "natural" in this sense is equivalent to "teleological." Roughly, there may be said to be four different senses in which the term "natural" is used. First, *"natural" in the teleological sense* as just noted. To Ricardo the "natural price of labor" was an amount barely enough to keep the workmen body and soul together, and to enable them to perpetuate their race. To Malthus and many others this seemed to be a most unnatural price for labor, for they thought that the natural price of labor should include a compensation over and above the bare physical minimum. The conception of the "natural" in this sense is always an evaluating process. Second, *"natural" in the sense of normal.* What is natural in this sense is what generally happens with numerous exceptions. Natural, in this sense, in one place or at one time may be unnatural in another place or at another time. Patricide is unnatural here and now, and so is incest. But a tribe of Fijians buried alive their aged parents as a filial duty, and the Ptolemies of ancient Egypt took their daughters and nieces for their wives. Almost every anti-social practice which we now regard as unnatural in this sense was at some time regarded as natural: murder, theft, slavery, prostitution, lying, loafing, etc. Third, *"natural" in the fatalistic sense.* In this sense, whatever is, is natural. If there is any natural law in this sense, it can never be violated. To love one's neighbor is natural, and to rob him or even to murder him is also natural. Such a view is to make a hodge-podge of nature. Lastly, *"natural" in the sense of being consonant with the immi-nent principles in the universe.* Scientific laws are a body of gen-eralizations of such principles. This view dangerously borders upon the fatalistic view, especially, in the form in which Spinoza taught it. But in a more liberal sense in which the neo-Spinozists use the term naturalism, it may be reconciled with the doctrine of emergent evolution. It may be that both human and infra-human phenomena are subject to natural laws, but each to a dif-ferent variety of natural laws. This is the view assumed by those who approach social studies from the naturalistic standpoint. The aim of such a study is to describe completely and consistently the conditions under which social phenomena arise, to discover if possible the causal relations between them, and to make it possible to control them.[20]

Bearing these distinctions in mind, let us examine the formula of the "survival of the fittest." "Survival of the fittest" is a mis-leading formula. It is, for example, a well known phenomenon in catallactics that where two kinds of specie circulate side by

[20] *Cf.* A. D. Ritchie's fivefold distinctions in the use of the term "natural," *Natural Rights,* chap. IV.

side, the over-valued metal rapidly drives out the under-valued. The inferior metal as a medium of exchange thus survives, and the superior is exterminated. But the fitness of the metal to survive in this instance does not rest on its desirability as a medium of exchange. Similarly, where two races of different standards of living compete with each other, so long as either one of the standards is not so low as to cause deterioration of the racial vigor, the race with a lower standard survives in greater abundance than the one with a higher. In fact, the antagonism in the United States against the Oriental and the South European immigrants is based on the assumption that, with their lower standards of living which they have brought with them, they might survive in cumulatively greater abundance than the Anglo-American natives, and might some day challenge the latter's supremacy. Such a result might be desirable to the immigrants themselves; but from the point of view of the world at large, it would be a distinct loss and not a gain. For, those who will survive in greater numbers at a lower standard of living, will survive only by repressing the qualitative development of the human race. The fitness to survive in one way is opposed to the fitness to survive in another.

Many so-called "natural" laws are in this way readily reducible to ambiguity when they are applied to social phenomena. At best they are teleological statements, replete with unanalyzed assumptions concerning the value of a process, and often covering but thinly the pious wishes of their authors.

3. *Their Merit.* The foregoing laws, however, are of value in several ways: as expressions of social ideals, of moral aspirations, and frequently of poetic inspiration. They are also of value in so far as they may serve as preliminary surveys of the problems and lead to the discovery of causal laws. For example, in Professor Cheyney's "law of moral progress" a closer examination and catalogue of the instances of moral progress may indeed

suggest interrelations between various instances, in such a way as to bring us ultimately a discovery of the true forces at work in them. In its present form the "law" merely points out the road for investigation.

CHAPTER V
STATISTICAL LAWS

THE NATURE OF STATISTICAL LAWS

THE OBJECT of the statistical method is to lift up sociology to the dignity of a science by subjecting social data to quantitative measurement and thus to enable us to deduce from the correlations obtained what are presumably causal operations. As a method of approach, however, the statistical process has several serious limitations; and the obstacles to applying it to social investigation are great and many. I may briefly summarize these limitations and difficulties as follows:

1. The Difficulty in Defining Data. Measurement presupposes some sort of classification, and classification presupposes some sort of definition of the data. When the measurement is completed, and the causal relations are discovered, the original definitions and classifications of the data can be revised in the light of these discoveries. And the process may be repeated till a reasonable degree of precision and certainty is attained. In the physical sciences a given datum such as hydrogen is defined as a gas of a certain color or absence of color, of a certain atomic weight, of certain characteristics in combination and reaction. Each of these several properties can be verified by experiment and measurement. There is therefore no room for disagreement as to the proper definition of a chemical element. But in sociology almost every one of the familiar terms such as democracy, justice and progress, is disputed by someone. One author may write a volume or two on democracy, declaiming its merits and predicting its future. Another author may write another volume or two, criticizing its defects and exaggerating its failures. A third writer may write several more volumes, saying that both these writers are mistaken, and that democracy is nothing more or less than what each man conceives it to be. Much of the wrangling about definitions is a clash in the dark. But what is more important, these disagreements are not due to mere accident. For if they were merely accidental, it would be desirable to do away with disagreements entirely. These disagreements are, however, the necessary parts of life and progress, in so far as they have value. The only way to do away with such disagreements is to give up all social ideals. Children and savages have no such disagreements, and it is only persons of a high degree of development who enter into disputes about democracy, justice and progress. Progress presupposes selection, and selection presupposes variation; therefore most disagreements, even in matters of definition, are necessary to progress.

2. *Impossibility of Qualitative Measurements.* Even if we can arrive at a tolerable agreement on a given definition, there are many things which cannot be reduced to quantity. Height, weight and the circumference of the head can be measured, but not character, honesty, tact and humor. The mental testers and psychiatrists, of course, have devised various ingenious tests to measure quality, but as yet their attempt has not been successful; they can hope at the most to get some expression of quality from indirect quantitative scores; but actually they often get something which is neither the quality itself nor any recognizable quantitative scores. Similarly some economists try to express everything in terms of dollars and cents, but dollars and cents are arbitrary representations of quality, and not quality itself.

3. *The Difficulty of Experiment.* In physics and chemistry when any dispute arises it can be settled by experiment, and this is possible because a chemical element, for example, is capable of isolation. But social phenomena are well-nigh impossible to isolate. J. S. Mill pointed out this difficulty toward the end of his *System of Logic* by saying that two social groups having everything exactly alike in every respect except in one is nonsense. For if two social groups were exactly alike in every respect ex-

cept in one, why should they not be alike in that one particular respect also? There are no such two social groups. Every social group is more or less different from every other social group as well as like it. And the control of the situation for the purpose of deliberate experiment is always incomplete.

4. *The Difficulty of Classification.* All classifications depend on abstraction, and abstraction depends on the special point of view taken. If all social data can be reduced to quantitative expressions, they can be classified according to their number. But since this is impossible, classification always remains imperfect; for overlapping through imperceptible gradation is normal. And the transfer of one datum from one class to another might lead to an entirely different interpretation of the experimental results. This is especially the case in delicate psychological tests. It was said that for a long period at a prison in The Hague, Holland, the Catholic prisoners were found greatly to outnumber the Protestant. Upon investigation it was found that the Catholics were given fish on Fridays, while the Protestants were subjected to the same monotonous diet week in and week out, and that for this reason many Protestants registered themselves as Catholics. It is not merely measuring which is important, but also finding out what to measure and what to exclude. Bad sampling will ruin the whole business of counting.

5. *Correlation not Causal Relation.* In the physical sciences the purpose of isolation and measurement is to find out the relations of cause and effect, always understanding by cause uniformity of antecedence. In the social sciences, however, since isolation of any given datum is always incomplete, the attempts to discover causal relations are unsuccessful, and the statistical method can yield at the most only the correlations among the several factors present in the situation. If, for example, two social phenomena such as crime and unemployment are observed for a sufficiently long period to appear and to disappear jointly, it may be inferred that they are somehow related to each other,

but it is not certain which is the cause and which the effect. Of course, it may be said that since unemployment preceded the increase of crime, the former was the cause, and the latter the effect. But in reality it may be that unemployment merely furnished the occasion for the increase of crime through prolonged economic distress. Hence, there are no efficient causes visible in statistical findings, especially in the social field, and, instead, rough correlations among the several phenomena are revealed, the value of which depends on the way in which they are interpreted.

6. *Probability and Not Certainty.* Because statistics yield, not causal relations, but only correlations, and these correlations are *post hoc* rather than *propter hoc,* we can reach by this method some degree of probability—a high degree in some cases—but not certainty of knowledge. And probability is credibility which varies according to the gullibility of the person. To a single-tax enthusiast the single tax scheme is the sovereign remedy for all social evils. To a dogmatic eugenist, eugenic mating is certain to produce a race of Apollos. But the true social scientists smile at such naïveté and confidence, for they see that their statistics may prove too much.

7. *Deceptive Averages.* Statistics yield averages, such as the average height or the average weight of a nation. These averages are styled "the normal tendency in the long run." If a sufficiently large number of the averages are taken into consideration, they may give some idea about the general tendency. But those who use the statistical method have not always had enough patience to keep on measuring a sufficiently large number of cases to yield a reliable datum, nor have they always exercised enough caution in interpreting their findings. Even the most famous among them such as Lombrozo and Galton sometimes took a hundred or even fewer measurements and from such meager data they jumped to startling conclusions. If the number of measurements is sufficiently small, and if the sampling is influenced by prejudice,

the average may represent neither any particular individual instance, nor the general tendency, but merely an imaginary figure.

In spite of these shortcomings, the statistical method properly used is one of the most useful instruments, if sociology is ever to be made a science. And the proper way of using it is frankly to recognize its limitations, to use it with caution and patience, and to supplement its findings with deductive reasoning. It is only during the last hundred years that the application of the statistical method has come into vogue to any considerable extent. Probably its technique still needs improvement, and many ingenious devices wait to be invented, before we can represent quality by its quantitative expression. The statistical method has nothing to do with fatalism as Buckle erroneously thought it had, nor does it urge pessimistic views upon prophets of regeneration. For, all that statistics reveal are the regularities of occurrence in the long run. Some of these regularities such as the constant excess of boys over girls among the new-born have not yet been explained, while others like the constant predominance of male criminals over the female are explicable. The marvelous constancy of these and many other phenomena give us the impression of the universality of the reign of law. And these laws furnish the best hope for any program of social amelioration, for they are a measure of the dependability of human nature. If we can only get at the exact causal relations by patient research and improved methods, we shall be able to unlock the secret of the "social organism."[1]

LIST OF STATISTICAL LAWS

Among the laws based on statistical tendencies I have selected only some of the most conspicuous ones which are generally found in sociological treatises. These I hope are fair examples illustrating the usefulness as well as the defects of the statistical method.

[1] See R. Mayo-Smith, *Economics*.

One of the most important social phenomena is the growth of human population. For even the increase of the mere numbers makes social processes more complex. If men were merely biological organisms, their increase in numbers would be governed by the general laws of biology. But the fact that man is something over and above a biological organism renders it difficult to formulate any laws governing the growth of their number. From ancient times there have been kept crude census records, chiefly to meet military necessity; for the glory of the sovereign was measured by the number of his subjects. And it was not until modern times that any careful statistical studies of population have been made for the purpose of improving the conditions of life of the people themselves. Of such studies one of the most recent and notable results is Professor Pearl's curve which, he thinks, is "at least a first approximation to a descriptive law of population growth."[2]

1. Pearl's Equation. His equation is the result of a complicated series of mathematical calculations, for the details of which I can refer the reader to the author's book, Chapter XXIV. It takes into consideration several important variables in the growth of population. First, every statistical comparison of the population of one area with that of another, or of the population of a given area at one time with that at another, must base the calculation on some definite units of area. When a nation continually expands its boundaries as the United States has done, or when a large and loosely organized empire is split up like the Austro-Hungarian Empire in 1919, the volume of its population appearing in statistics says nothing as to the change of areas. For every nation at any given time there is a definite area on which it can grow, and which in the long run limits (in the physical sense) its growth. For the human race as a whole the upper limit of this area is at present the whole inhabitable portion of the earth.

[2] R. Pearl, *Studies in Human Biology*, chap. XXIV, and p. 637.

If there is an upper limit to the area upon which population can grow, then there must be an upper limit to population itself at any given stage of culture. An acre of land, for example, may be made by improved arts to yield a successively larger amount of food in the future than at present, but at any given time it has a definite limit. This upper limit to the growth of population is designated as the "upper asymptote." Third, the lower limit to population is zero. Fourth, the growth of population in any given area is roughly cyclical, each cycle superimposing itself upon the last. What bring about these cycles are the dynamic movements, such as inventions and improvements, which make it possible for the people to live in larger numbers in any given area than before. And thus each cycle roughly corresponds with a cultural epoch. The degree of accuracy of prediction for the growth of any population varies according to the degree of constancy of the dynamic movements; in fact, the prediction is most accurate where the social conditions are essentially static, while it is least accurate where catastrophic changes are frequent. And, finally, within each cultural epoch the growth of population is at first slow, but gradually faster till it reaches a point where presumably a balance is struck between the number of people and the means of subsistence. "This point of maximum rate of growth is the point of inflection of the population growth curve. After that point is passed, the rate of growth becomes progressively slower till finally the curve stretches along nearly horizontally, in close approach to the upper asymptote which belongs to particular cultural epoch and area involved."[3]

By means of his equation Professor Pearl has calculated with a remarkable degree of precision the growth of population of sixteen countries and two cities.[4] With regard to the limitations of this equation, the author says: "It seems to us fairly to correspond, in a modest way, to Kepler's law of motion of the planets in elliptic orbits, but to lack the heuristic element which

[3] *Ibid.*, p. 568-69.   [4] *Ibid.*, chap. XXV.

Newton added in showing that gravitation would account for elliptic orbits; or, to Boyle's law prior to Clark Maxwell's kinetic theory." For, nothing in the mathematics on which the present law is based, "gives the slightest inkling of the nature of the causes lying behind" the cyclical growth of population. Professor Pearl immediately adds: "The one real step in the direction of the discovery of the causes which has so far been made, is the demonstration that these causes are not things peculiar to human beings, such as the economic or social structure or organization of human society. This is proved by the experimental demonstration that the same curve describes with precision the growth of population of the fruit fly Drosophila Melanogaster. This means that the search must be thrown back to more fundamental natural causes, biological, physical or chemical. It seems probable that the hopeful direction of further research in this field is not along the statistical pathway with human population as material, but along the experimental, where populations of lower animals can be studied under controlled conditions."[5]

The two statements contained in the foregoing quotations deserve different evaluations. The statement that the causes lying behind the cyclical growth of population are "not things peculiar to human beings, such as the economic or social structure," and that this is proved by the experimental demonstration that "the same curve describes with precision the growth of population of the fruit fly," seems to need modification. For, even if the growth of human population and that of the number of fruit flies conform to the same curve, in the absence of other evidence, this fact alone does not prove that the same causes are operating in both cases. Very likely, biological, physical, and chemical causes are at work in both instances, and the study of lower organisms under controlled conditions will throw much light on the question. But it seems also probable that economic, moral, and other social factors ("things peculiar to human beings"), do enter into

[5] *Ibid.*, p. 585.

the determination of the population curve, and that the reason that they have apparently had no influence upon it may be that these causes in their endless variety of combinations counteract one another. The increase of food supply through improvement, invention and commerce encourages the multiplication; while the spread of moral ideas discourages it; certain religious dogmas encourage it, while the neglect of hygiene and the spread of contagious diseases may counteract this influence; military adventurers stimulate it, while the consequent wars undo the work of years of reckless multiplication; and so on and so forth.

In view of the statement that the present equation being a description of empirical facts, needs a valid theory to explain it, as Kepler's law waited Newton's explanation, and in view of the great importance of the problem of population, I shall present three leading theories of population, every one of which has been called a law, but not one of which can accurately be designated as a statistical law.

Among these three theories Spencer's is by far the most sweeping. According to it the reproduction of the species diminishes in proportion to the evolution of individuality. This "law" is applicable not merely to human beings, but to all species of animals and even to vegetables. Its defect is that it fails to explain the differential ratio of multiplication within the same species. Granted that the ratio of multiplication of the human race, man being the highest of all animals, is smaller and its rate is slower than those of lower animals, why is it that some races multiply faster than others? and why even within the same society do some couples multiply faster than others? To the latter of these two questions, Dumont's law of capillarity is the answer, according to which "Population varies inversely with social capillarity, for example, the tendency to rise in the social scale."[6] To the former of these questions, the Malthusian "laws" are the answers, which may be stated in three parts as follows:

[6] F. A. Bushee, *Principles of Sociology*, p. 293.

(*a*) "Population is limited by the food supply.

(*b*) "Population tends to outrun the means of subsistence, for, under favorable circumstances population increases in a geometrical ratio, doubling itself every twenty-five years, while the food supply at best can increase only in an arithmetical ratio."

(*c*) "Population is kept within the limits of the food supply either by positive checks which resolve themselves into vice and misery, or by preventive checks, that is, by moral restraint."[7]

It is a long observed phenomenon that even vegetables, such as weeds, once they get rooted in a vacant lot and are plentifully supplied with moisture and fertilizer, tend to multiply with a mighty speed until the whole vacant lot is thickly filled up, and the fertilizer is exhausted. In the animal world the single-celled animals such as infusoria, which have the least possible individuality, multiply by simple periodic fission at an incredible speed, and by geometrical progression. Given enough food, a favorable climate, and no accident to cause them injury and death, they might cover with their own species the whole surface of the earth within a short period. The two-celled animals multiply much more slowly, the three-celled animals still more slowly, and so the series extends to the human species where the embryonic period is longest and infancy is most prolonged, though the instinctive activities for nutrition and multiplication are none the less strong. As Mr. Hall puts it, "The minutest organisms multiply in their millions; the small-compound types next above them in their thousands, while larger and more compound types multiply but in their hundreds or their tens; and the largest and most highly developed types only by twos or units."[8]

The most primitive savages spend most of their time in quest of food, and whatever time is left is wasted generally in promiscuous indulgences. Their incessant wars are the devices whereby they keep up their supply of "beauty and booty." Moreover,

[7] *Ibid.*, p. 287.
[8] A. C. Hall, *Crime in Its Relation to Social Progress*, pp. 3-4.

among the savages the individual is nothing and society is every-thing. The individual exists for no other purpose than to per-petuate the fruitless round of birth, growth, multiplication, de-cay and death. Among races a little advanced beyond primitive savagery such as those in certain parts of the Orient, multiplica-tion goes on unchecked or checked only by the brutal forces of nature. It is even encouraged by military adventurers, sancti-fied by pernicious religions, and made a necessity in order to in-sure against the rainy days of old age. In certain parts of China banditry has become more profitable than the normal occupa-tions, and with this all security and opportunity for saving are blown to dust. Under such circumstances the bringing up of numerous children is one of the easiest and most anciently known devices of insuring oneself against the poverty and dan-gers of old age. Their religion sanctions inordinate multiplica-tion, not only sanctions but demands it. Success in bringing up numerous male children is regarded by them as one of the five greatest blessings. The main, if not the sole, end for which the individual exists is to keep alive and nourish his family tree, to offer up prayers for his ancestors, to admire and to worship them.

Among the Japanese the phrase "teeming millions" is con-ventionalized. In justification of the Japanese annexation of Korea, a Japanese writer said: "The Japanese people must either die a saintly death in righteous starvation, or expand into the neighbor's backyard,—and Japan is not that much of a saint." Another Japanese writer says: "How shall we dispose of our surplus millions? Our small country can hardly find room within its narrow boundaries to accommodate its yearly increase of half a million people. We cannot kill them wholesale, nor can we fill up the sea of Japan and make dry land for them to settle on. We would like to go to Kansas or anywhere but Hades where we could escape starvation; but however hospitable America may be, she refuses to receive so many new-comers all at once."[9]

It is only in the most advanced classes in the most advanced nations where the people are least fettered by conventions and priest-craft, and where the development of individuality is most encouraged and admired, that the Malthusian laws of population are transcended to any considerable extent. Further, even in the most advanced nations, the birth-rate of the ghetto-dwellers and slum-inhabitants,—in general of the class of underdogs among whom individuality counts for little,—still very largely conforms to the Malthusian laws. Exhaustive statistical investigations since the original statement of the Malthusian laws seem to confirm these laws rather than contradict them.[10]

The various criticisms heaped on Malthus are due mainly to two varieties of defects in his laws. First, Malthus put his propositions rather too violently, especially in his first edition, and thus too plainly gave the impression that he had no high opinion either of the eighteenth century sentimentalists, the followers of Rousseau, the admirers of the French Revolution, the upholders of the status quo, or the ministers of archaic theology. Those who held rosy views on social amelioration were offended, because Malthus seemed to make fools of them by pointing out the difficulty, if not the impossibility, of perfecting human nature. Those, who were all for things-as-they-were at any cost, were offended, because Malthus seemed to undermine their sense of dignity and self-importance by contradicting their expansionist doctrine. Like many another man who publicly dishonored popular idols, he met his natural fate. Secondly, Malthus took many things for granted, and these may be briefly reviewed as follows:

(a) *Tendencies not Iron-Clad Laws.* The three laws are statements of tendencies, and not iron-clad laws like the laws of the physical sciences. They seem to apply most accurately to the

---

[9] Quoted from E. M. East, *Mankind at the Crossroads,* p. 93.
[10] See E. M. East, *op. cit.,* A very illuminating book if read with caution.

primitive and backward races, and even more accurately to a colony of fruit-flies, than to the advanced races. In all societies beyond the stage of primitive savagery, these tendencies seem to have been more or less counteracted, except where they have been deliberately maintained under the influence of pernicious priest-craft and military adventurers. The geometrical and arithmetical ratios are metaphorical expressions to which the present day Malthusians do not attach much importance.

(b) *Increase of Productivity.* As population increases, the total productivity also may and does generally increase, though at progressively diminishing rates after a certain stage. And where invention and industrial development proceed fast, the increase of productivity may even overtake the increase of population, as was seen during the first period of the Industrial Revolution. Hence in some exceptional cases the population problem is not so much in the nature of a dilemma between an excess of number and the shortage of food supply, as it is rather in the nature of a race between invention and population. If a mechanical and industrial genius like Henry Ford can take care of a hundred thousand mouths or more, about a dozen Henry Fords may solve the whole problem of unemployment and food shortage in small struggling nations such as the Balkan states. This is, of course, a rather fantastic suggestion; even the genius of a Henry Ford is subject to natural limitations. But the point is that man's command of the forces counteracting the tendencies of increase in population is considerable; the more intelligent and industrious is the race, and the less fettered by pernicious social ideals, the greater the command of the counteracting forces.

(c) *Standard of Living, Not Mere Food Supply.* As the human race rises in the scale of civilization, the size of the family is governed by certain notions of decency such as an efficient standard of living, and not by the bare amount of the means of subsistence. A healthful home, a handy library, an autocar, and a certain amount of leisure and amusement, become the indis-

pensable equipment for life and the main determining factors
of the size of the family. The consideration of these factors is
more and more emphasized with the increase of the amount of
regular income, as is evidenced by Engel's Laws of Consumption.
In many instances the notion of decency is so exaggerated that
the motive of social display rather than that of comfort and decency determines the standard of living. The men of this class
marry late, rather too late in some cases, and when married their
wives seem to serve as a sort of emblem of sociability rather
than as family-builders. With opulence, the fear of the "slum-
savour" seems to increase, while fertility diminishes.

(*d*) *Ideals for Life.* It is obvious that unless the term "the
means of subsistence" is stretched so far as to include the most
up-to-date notions about the standard of living, the volume of
population is determined only indirectly and imperfectly by the
means of subsistence. We should rather say that ideals for life
are the determining factor not only of the size of a population,
but also of the amount of the food supply itself. Some people,
like the upper class of the native whites of America, prefer activity to other things. They like to get more in order to spend
more; more getting, more spending, and more activity. Their
great financiers and captains of industry show marvelous capacities for activity. Other people, like the Hindoos, prefer to sit
down and reflect, to poetize and philosophize. Their minds dwell
in the misty past and their hearts with the dead. Hence their
stagnation and misery, which they can only disguise by affecting
airs of spiritual superiority. Others, like the Chinese, prefer to
have as many children as they can, to offer up prayers and praises
to their ancestors. The more mouths, the louder is their prayer
and the more generous their praises. Others, like the French,
prefer to make garish display. One of the oftenest used words
in their vocabulary is said to be *"brilliance"—la gloire*—a certain
sign of vanity. Still others, like the Southern Negroes and Mexi-
cans, care neither for activity nor fantastic dreams, but would

have plenty of leisure to loaf and gossip. They get what they want. It is the spiritual outlook of the individual, of the nation, of the race, which mainly determines not only the volume of population, but also the amount of the food supply and the standard of living.

There are several other criticisms, some of which, like Henry George's, are founded on ignorance of the law of diminishing returns, while others are positively silly, such as the argument that "God created every mouth with two hands to feed it," or that "the human animal has a pretty good top-piece and when real problems arise, the solution will come!"—a poor piece of Micawberian optimism.

After these considerations and criticisms, what is left of the laws of population? I should say that a great deal is still left, that they are the statements of a primitive tendency, which holds more accurately when applied to the more backward races than to the more advanced, more accurately when applied to the retarded classes than to the dominant even in the same society; a tendency, moreover, expressed in terms of material goods for the sake of simplicity of reasoning in economics. Such a simplification of the subject matter is tolerable as a methodological assumption in pure economics: the systems of Ricardo and Böhm-Bawerk are full of such simplifications; but it invites misunderstanding and furnishes occasion for the multiplication of gratuitous assumptions.[11]

Less accurately statistical in the sense of mathematical, but

[11] Sociologists have not been slow in recognizing the importance of the Malthusian "laws," and even in imitating the economists' method of multiplying assumptions with those laws as their premises. Professor Ross, for example, announced a "law of the evolution of colonies," which reads as follows:

"For colony as well as for mother country the increase of population relative to resources is a prime cause of social evolution." *Foundations of Sociology*, p. 52. Although this law is evidently modeled after the laws of population, just discussed, it is much cruder than they, for Professor Ross is speaking of "*a prime cause of social evolution*," not merely the amount of the food supply or the number of the people.

not less faithful as descriptions of facts than is Professor Pearl's law, are Engel's laws of consumption, which read as follows:

2. "As the income of the family increased, a smaller percentage of it was expended for food."

3. "As the income of the family increased, the percentage of expenditure for clothing remained approximately the same."

4. "With all the incomes investigated, the percentage of expenditure for rent, fuel and light remained invariably the same."

5. "As the income increased in amount a constantly increasing percentage was expended for education, health, recreation, amusement, etc."

Professor Streightoff says that these laws need considerable modification before they can be applied to the American workmen of the present day, and that they may be modified as follows. "As the income increases:

6. "The proportionate expenditure for food (a) decreases for the country at large from 50 per cent to 37 per cent; but (b) in New York City it amounts to almost 45 per cent of the total outlay until an income of $1,000 is attained.

7. "There is a strong tendency for the percentage for clothing to increase.

8. "Relative expenditures for housing
    (a) remain about constant for the country at large, falling very slightly after $400 income have been reached, but
    (b) decrease rapidly from 30 per cent or more to 16 per cent in New York City.

9. "Proportionate expenditures for fuel and light decrease.

10. "Expenditures for culture wants increase absolutely and relatively."[12]

Both the laws and their restatements are based on patient statistical researches, and both approach closely the ideals for positive laws. The figures in terms of dollars need to be reinterpreted in

[12] See Ford, *Social Problems and Social Policy*, pp. 558-59.

terms of purchasing power, since the purchasing power of dollars fluctuates with the price of the medium of exchange. The significant thing about these laws is the steady rise in the expenditure for culture-wants with the rise in income. How far will it go on rising? Why don't they squander their surplus income in loafing or in raising a great many more children rather than spend it for the improvement of their health and education? These questions cannot be answered without taking into consideration what people think most worth living for. What they think most worth living for determines their standard of living, the amount of expenditure for health, education, amusement. The difference between Engel's and Professor Streightoff's findings is in itself an indication of the difference between the outlook on life of the German industrial population nearly a century ago and that of the American today.

In a stagnant society the proportions of expenditure on the several items, once determined, may remain constant until the balance is upset by some catastrophic changes; but in a progressive society the proportions of expenditure necessarily fluctuate with the change of standards, with the multiplication of desires and opportunities for earning and spending; hence, there is at the most an unstable equilibrium. The limit of any attempt to formulate a positive law on such matters is the extent to which these fluctuations are likely to occur at any given period. The value of such laws is that if used with discrimination, they may furnish data on which to base the adjustment of wages. If at any given period the schedule of wages is too low in comparison with the purchasing power of dollars, and if an advance in wages is likely to result in the improvement of the health and efficiency of the industrial population, it will be highly desirable to raise the wages within proper limits. But if an advance in wages will merely serve as a spur to more reckless procreative activity, as among the backward races whose number is actually kept down almost solely by famine, war and plague, there is no point in raising wages. Before raising the wages of this latter class of people, the wise thing to do is to teach them how to make use of their surplus income.

Another variety of statistical laws of considerable importance is the group of biological laws of which the following are typical examples:

11. *Galton's Law of Ancestral Inheritance.* The ancestral contributions to the biological make-up of an individual diminishes in the geometrical ratio with each generation backwards; thus, for example, approximately half the character is derived from the two parents, and a quarter from the four grandparents. Galton tentatively extended the series to the more remote ancestry, but his data were too meagre to lead to any reliable conclusion. Professor Pearson followed up Galton's data, measured a greater number of individuals, and reached the conclusion that the contributions of the parents are greater than Galton thought, while the contributions of the grandparents and great grandparents diminish much more rapidly. Pearson's own figures are as follows:

Parents	0.6284
Grandparents	0.1988
Great Grandparents	0.0603
Great great Grandparents	0.0202

12. *Galton's Law of Filial Regression.* The sons of parents having exceptional traits are not so exceptional on the average as their parents, but tend to revert to the mean; conversely parents of exceptional sons are less exceptional than their sons.[13]

COMMENTS

The foregoing two laws are, strictly speaking, laws in biology rather than social laws, however loosely one may use the term "social law." Yet they are found in sociological textbooks.[14] They have been given chiefly to illustrate the use of the statis-

[13] Popenoe and Johnson, *Applied Eugenics,* chaps. IV, V.
[14] F. A. Bushee, *Principles of Sociology,* pp. 329-31, as an example.

tical method in social research and the difficulties going along with its use. The first of the difficulties these laws illustrate is the difficulty of securing sufficient data to enable the investigator to draw reliable conclusions. Galton, for example, made an inquiry into about 150 families. He had to assume, to start with, that these 150 families were representative families. Next, he probably knew sufficient about the parents and the children, but he knew less about the grandparents, still less about the great-great-grandparents. So the series extends in diminishing scale in any investigations of this kind. There is no way of applying the biometric methods to the people of past generations, and there is always the possibility of error in reliance on family traditions, biographies, and even autobiographies.

The second of these difficulties is that even when sufficient data are securable, the biometric method establishes a coefficient of correlation, not a causal relation; a degree of similarity in a great many cases, not an invariable association in each individual case. A great many men may resemble their parents more than they do their grandparents. But there are individuals who resemble their grandparents more than they do their parents. The third of these difficulties is that these laws being laws of averages of a comparatively small number of selected families, I should not be surprised to find some day that they represent neither any particular individual instance nor the general tendency of the nation as a whole.

It is interesting to note the varying degrees of probability which the statistical method yields in the various branches of investigation. When applied to economic questions, the statistical method, as has just been discussed, seems to be most dependable. When it is applied to biological phenomena, the result is less satisfactory. When it is applied to psychological traits, the result is still less satisfactory. Physical traits are tangible things, such as weight and height, but psychological traits are intangible.

Honesty, intelligence, and loyalty are easy to talk about, but there is no definite agreement as to exactly what they are. Indeed, even the word "trait" itself is ambiguous and has at present no definite standing in psychology.[15]

[15] See, for example, G. W. Allport, "Concepts of Trait and Personality," *Psychological Bulletin*, vol. XXIV (No. 5).

CHAPTER VI
NEAR-CAUSAL LAWS

THOSE BASED ON INFERENCES FROM THE ORDER OF HISTORICAL SE-
QUENCES AND THOSE BASED ON INFERENCES FROM BIOLOGICAL
AND MECHANISTIC ANALOGIES

To Comte, "the father of the modern sociology," the very name of sociology meant "social physics." He held, in common with Saint-Simon, that sociology should be a positive science, and that as the physicist describes empirical facts and reduces them to exact quantitative formulae, so the social scientist should collect sociological data and create a manual of practical politics. Such a program was commendable, provided it could be carried out. But it was intended to be not only a program, but also an assertion of a theory of knowledge. For he believed that the limits of our knowledge extend no further than the observable finite contents of space and time. So far as objects and events in that field awaken in us perceptions of sense, they constitute the material of cognition; they can be classified according to their similarities and differences, or related according to the order of their occurrence. But there our knowledge of them is said to stop, though imagination may in vain try to penetrate the phenomena and ascertain their causes.

All attempts to discover causes are therefore declared to be fruitless. Even verbal expressions which imply causality such as the word "force" are interpreted in terms of a phenomenalistic philosophy. "Every proposition," says Comte, "which is not reducible, in the last resort, to the simple statement of a fact, particular or general, must be without real and intelligible sense."[1] And one must guard oneself against making mysterious the only thing which one can apprehend about phenomena, namely, their laws. For the word "law" is to be understood to mean the in-

[1] *Positive Philosophy*, VI, 703.

variable relations of succession and resemblance of phenomena, and no more.[2] How does one know even the external phenomena? Comte naïvely answers that "By an invincible necessity the human mind can directly observe all phenomena except its own."[3] The knowledge of the external phenomena Comte called positive, in contradistinction to the knowledge of the "thing in itself," which knowledge he called absolute. The word "absolute" was his favorite object of abuse. "There is only one absolute principle," he cautioned his disciples, "that there is nothing absolute."[4]

Comte's philosophy had a practical end in view, namely, the reconstruction of society. But could there be any faith in a universe which, according to his philosophy, is nothing but a system of mechanical forces? Do machines improve themselves? In order to meet these difficulties, Comte, in his later writings, more and more introduced metaphysical principles into his system. He regarded humanity as a developing organism, the impelling force of which, he said, was the affectional nature.[5] He assumed that there is in human society an inherent tendency toward orderly development, which he called the "General Mind," and regarded as prior to the individual mind. He asserted, further, that not only is the General Mind prior to the individual mind, but through the General Mind alone can the individual mind be understood; and that the individual mind is merely an abstraction from the General Mind. And he conceived it his mission, as the High Priest of Humanity, to help transform the world into an ideal humanity. For the world was by this time no longer a mere system of mechanical forces, but one endowed with an inherent tendency toward orderly development, with a heart to feel the priority of the social claims upon the individual, and with a mind which, in spite of Comte's earlier denial of all self-knowledge, was capable of knowing itself.[6]

---

[2] *Ibid.*, I, 5.   [3] *Ibid.*, I, 35.   [4] *Discourse*, p. 56.
[5] *Positive Philosophy*, II, 77, 92, 128-30.   [6] *Discourse*, pp. 36-37, 95-96.

It is evident that his doctrines are entangled with disputable theories, epistemological and psychological, and that they even flatly contradict one another. What right had he to assume that there is a General Mind apart from the individual minds? Is it consistent to repudiate all hypotheses not capable of verification (such as that of the luminiferous ether), as being metaphysical and then to bring in the assumption of a General Mind? Is not the assumption that there is a tendency toward orderly development in man a bit of metaphysics?[7] Nor was he unaware of this inconsistency, for, speaking of his biological classification, he said:

"In forming the animal series, it (our encyclopedia) takes as its continual guide the true object of that formation,—a logical rather than a scientific object. As we study the animals to gain a sounder knowledge of man by tracing through them his connections with plants, we are fully authorized to exclude from our hierarchy all the species which disturb it"![8] Again: "Not merely is it true that no organic existence ever sprang from inorganic nature, but further, no species of any kind can spring from a different kind, either inferior or superior. The limits of the exceptions to this rule are very narrow, and are as yet but little known. There is then a really impassable gulf between the worlds of life and of matter, and even though less broad, between different forms of vitality. This view strengthens our position that any simple objective synthesis is impossible. But it in no way impairs the subjective synthesis, in every case the result of a very gradual ascent towards the type of man."[9]

LIST OF LAWS

One of the most famous contributions of Comte to the study of the social sciences is his theory of the development of knowledge, to wit:

[7] *Positive Philosophy*, I, 225, 301; II, 83, 88.
[8] *Ibid.*, II, 520-21.
[9] *The Catechism of Positivism*, p. 224

1. The history of society is the history of the human mind. "The natural law by which the advance of the human mind proceeds" is the law of the succession of the three states: the primitive theological state in which the human mind endeavors to explain natural phenomena in terms of the activities of deities; the metaphysical state in which the mind refers natural phenomena to abstract entities as their causes; and finally the positive state in which the natural phenomena are explained in terms of law or the regularity of the order of succession. In saying that the three states succeed one another, it is not intended that when one state gives way to the next, the preceding state entirely disappears. On the contrary, these three states generally coexist "in the same mind in regard to different sciences." "The same mind may be in the positive state with regard to the most simple and general sciences, in the metaphysical with regard to the more complex and special, and in the theological with regard to social science, which is so complex and special as to have hitherto taken no scientific form at all."[10]

This law the author called variously "the natural law," "the scientific principle of the theory" (of intellectual development), "the great philosophical law," etc. Of these various designations the last seems most appropriate, for it certainly is a great philosophical generalization. Several writers, following the example of Comte, have laid down various laws which are chiefly based on the order of historical sequences. The following selections are examples:

2. "There is a strictly regular development from fetishism through anthropomorphism, polytheism and monotheism, to the atheism of free-thinkers."[11]

3. "Politically human societies evolve regularly by successive stages which are anarchy, the communal clan, the tribe, at first

[10] *Positive Philosophy*, II, 156-80.
[11] Ross, *Foundations of Sociology*, p. 56; Gumplowicz, *Outlines of Sociology*, p. 108.

republican, later aristocratic, then monarchy, at first elective and later hereditary. Finally certain élite peoples repudiate monarchy and return to a régime republican but very unlike that of the primitive tribe."[12]

4. "To every type of economy there corresponds a particular type of family. Thus polygamy thrives most where men control the source of the food supply; monogamy where woman has a certain food-getting capacity. The family is strictly patriarchal with the pastoral nomads; the matriarchate appears only when the woman disposes over economic resources of her own. Among hunters and pastoralists the clan will be paternal."[13]

5. "The law of aesthetic development: Architecture always precedes sculpture, and sculpture precedes painting."[14]

6. "The law of the development of exchange: Merchandise money gives way to weighed metallic money, this to coined metallic money, this in turn to the bank note, and the bank note to the clearinghouse set off."[15]

7. "The law of diffusion: Every local civilization is in certain respects like all civilizations; in certain others like all primitive civilizations; then it is like the civilizations of certain very large geographical areas, continental in their sweep; it is further like the civilization of a more restricted area; and finally it is like unto itself, in certain local peculiarities, individual and unique."[16]

With regard to these laws the following summary comments may be made:

(a) *Contradicted by Inductive Studies.* The claim that these laws are causal laws rests on two assumptions. First, every historical process must have had an efficient cause behind it, which

---

[12] Ross, *op. cit.*, p. 56; Letourneau, *L'evolution politique dans les diverses races humaines*, p. 7.

[13] Ross, *op. cit.*, p. 58; Grosse, *Die Formen der Familie und die Formen der Wirthschaft*, chap. I.

[14] Ross, *op. cit.*, p. 56; De Greef, *Les Lois Sociologiques*, p. 120.

[15] *Ross, op. cit.*, p. 62; De Greef, *op. cit.*, p. 103.

[16] E. C. Hayes, ed., *Recent Developments in the Social Sciences*, quoted from A. A. Goldenweiser, *Early Civilization*, p. 123.

may be granted at once if we hope to discover causal laws at all. Second, the order of the historical sequences described in these laws must be the invariable order. What is the ground upon which this second assumption is based? It is not based on experimental results, for historical events can not be reproduced. Its only claim to validity rests on the supposition that if a sufficiently large number of empirical observations all corroborate one another, pointing to the same regularity, there must be an invariability in the order of succession. If this assumption be granted, it follows immediately that if more careful and extensive observations show that the order of succession is reversed in any part of the historical process, this is a sufficient ground to invalidate the law. Recent studies in anthropology led several of the eminent authorities in that department of research, such as Professors A. L. Kroeber and A. A. Goldenweiser, categorically to deny Spencer's theories of evolution, namely, that evolution is uniform, that evolution is gradual, and that evolution is progressive.[17] This denial means either that the order of the historical sequences found in any cultural area is reversed in some other cultural area, or that some of the intermediate stages in the order of succession have been skipped; and therefore no social law which describes the order of historical sequences found in any one or more cultural areas, can be necessarily true of all other cultural areas.

(b) Intermediate Stages Skipped. The rôle of intelligence in social evolution is to telescope the distance traversed by the past generations: the higher the intelligence of the race, the greater is the distance telescoped. Hence discontinuity or the skipping of the intermediate stages should be the normal phenomenon in the social evolution of the progressive races. The "strictly regular development"[18] from fetishism to atheism is a logical construction and not an inductive discovery. Indeed the author himself says:

[17] See A. A. Goldenweiser, *op. cit.,* pp. 20-27.
[18] In Gumplowicz's law quoted above.

"The philosophizing human mind finds a logical and strictly regular development from fetishism" to atheism. In other words, it is "the philosophizing human mind," not the raw data found in history, which suggests this law. He then continues: "But scarcely would any one group illustrate the whole series; and how many groups still pray to fetishes, conceive their god in human form, people their heaven with throngs of deities or recognize only one Jahve as they did thousands of years ago, while on the other hand, there were occasional free-thinkers and atheists even in antiquity."[19] The same might be said with regard to the process of political evolution. The progress from anarchy through the communal clan, the tribe, republic, aristocracy, and monarchy, then back to the republic, is a fanciful reconstruction of historical processes, and presumably a true one in a great many cases. But there are exceptions like the Japanese monarchy which has lasted over twenty-five centuries without going through these regular series of mechanical ups and downs. These laws, like Morgan's generalization upon the five successive forms of the family, have only historical interest without yielding any causal connections.[20]

(c) The Assumption of Finality. The laws of the foregoing group vary in the range of their generalization. De Greef's law of the development of exchange is a minute description of the order of procession, while Comte's law of three states is a sweeping generalization. In order to regard these laws as invariable, we need to make the mechanistic assumption that social evolution is a process of "Eternal Recurrences," eternally repeating the same old things and nothing new. But this is too large an assumption. In concrete instances such as the development of exchange, it is as yet too early to say that the development is complete; we shall probably go on adding (in the list which De Greef presents in the law quoted above) the "index number" and the communist labour-coupons, and whatever else we shall find later.

[19] Gumplowicz, op. cit., p. 108.
[20] L. H. Morgan, Ancient Society, pt. III, chap. I.

(d) The Vicious Circle in Positivist Epistemology. The intellectual development does not end with the positive state. For the positivistic explanation consists in referring the lesser and particular regularities to a greater: hence the most comprehensive laws, the last in the order of generalizations, have nothing to refer themselves to, and are thus left unexplained. By what law shall we explain, for instance, the law of gravitation? If the universe rests on the horns of a snail, as the story goes in the fable, on what does the snail rest? The positivistic explanation is comparable to the answer that the snail rests on the horns of another and bigger snail, and that snail in turn on the horns of a still bigger snail, and that the series in this pyramid of snails extends to infinity. But human speculation always tends to transcend its own imaginative limitations. It is in vain to set up a fence round the door of knowledge and to say: "Thus far and no farther." Hence those of the positivist school who dogmatically assert that their method is all that is necessary do err greatly. An explanation which consists merely in referring to a larger generality is saying no more than that something is like something else, or that it happens like something else,—a mode of explanation which immediately begs the question, why does the other thing referred to happen that way. Unless we know why the other thing referred to happens that way, we are not any more enlightened by the explanation, and instead, where formerly we had only one phenomenon to explain, we now have two to explain.

(e) Coexistence as well as Succession. A common failing of all laws of historical progression is that the earlier or primitive forms, types or stages (as the case might be) tend to coexist with the later. This fact was recognized by Comte as is evidenced by his statement that he does not imply that when one stage gives way to the next, the preceding state entirely disappears, but that they generally coexist even "in the same mind in regard to different sciences."

(f) The Value of Historical Studies. History may be said to arise from memory, and to be perpetuated by the reaction of each succeeding generation to the total past. There is therefore a rough measure of superficial repetition, biological and psychological. But each historical event has a certain unique aspect which can not be reproduced at will. This unique aspect is what gives each historical event a melancholy beauty. Historical institutions are the emblems of value-attitudes, the things for which people have lived. And since the things for which people live consist partly in facts and partly in visions, there is probably no invariable order of procession in historical institutions, which does not in some measure represent mere superficial coincidences. If there be no invariable order in historical events, the attempt to deduce positive laws from the order of historical sequences, is futile. Historical studies therefore will probably yield, at the most, some philosophical generalizations, such as Comte's law of three states and Hegel's idealistic version of the dialectical progress.

The true value of historical studies, then, is that they may help us to impersonate the characters of the past, and thereby to build our interest. Every man is fit for something. Yet one of the greatest difficulties of life is to discover for oneself for what one is best fitted. The retirement into historical scenes enlarges one's circle of acquaintance and lifts up one's mental horizon. Since no two historical epochs are exactly alike, the men of the past, of course, can not tell one precisely what to do; they do not enunciate any social laws, of which they probably knew even less than we now do. But they do tell us how they interpreted the signs of their times, and what they lived for. And the thing for which they lived might be precisely the kind of thing which one has been seeking.

To impersonate is to place oneself by imagination in the historical scenes and to act as the heroes did. One may rise with Giovanni Giolitti amidst a Fascist-packed national assembly, and in spite of the forlornness of the cause of liberalism, with all his serenity and eloquence, protest in the name of the Italian Liberal Party against the dictatorial abrogation of the constitutional rights of the king and of the people. One may re-sail with Columbus, daring a mutinous crew, over the "dreadful shoreless sea" from which God Himself seemed to have fled, to open up a new world before them and to teach mankind a grand lesson, "Sail on and on!" And if one does not care for such exciting scenes, one may still retire with Darwin into a biological museum and retrace the origin of species, or one may explore with Pasteur the world of microscopic organisms. If by means of such impersonations they have become one's daily companions, their interests may become one's vocation, and their victories the cause of one's joy. The study of historical progression is better suited to the building of interests than to the revelation of necessary law.

Herbert Spencer inherited from Comte and various other earlier writers the metaphor of "social organism," and led an exhaustive discussion on it. He pointed out that society resembles a biological organism in point of continuous growth, increasing complexity, mutual dependence of the parts, and possible independence of life as an organism. He also demonstrated four dissimilarities between society and a biological organism; namely, that society lacks any specific external form, that social units are discreet and dispersed instead of being continuous; that social units possess a greater mobility than do the parts of a biological organism; and that society has no sensorium corresponding to the brain of a biological organism. He concluded that the defining character of the social organism was the permanence of the relations among component parts, which constitutes the individuality of a whole as distinguished from that of its parts.[21] He went still further and pointed out the analogies among the three levels of evolution, cosmological, biological and social; and on the bases of these analogies he set up the stupendous thesis that "evolution is

[21] *Principles of Sociology,* I, 447-48.

the change from an indefinite, incoherent homogeneity to a definite, coherent heterogeneity through continuous differentiation and integration."[22]

To all these analogies he attached varying degrees of importance at various times. Such admirable analogies and sweeping generalizations naturally gave impetus to various imitators who pushed the analogies further and based upon them numerous social laws. The following selections are some of the conspicuous examples:

8. "The individual in his development from childhood passes through the culture epochs traversed by human society."[23]

9. "Within any social group can be found coexisting all the types of culture traversed by man in his ascent from savagery."[24]

10. "Up to the point in the growth of a colony when it ceases to be dependent on its metropolis, the political and social evolution recapitulates in a few years the entire evolution which the mother country may have taken centuries to accomplish."[25]

The foregoing group of laws are based on the biological analogy that the individual from the embryonic period up to his birth recapitulates in rapid succession the whole history of evolution. In Haeckel's language, "the rapid and brief ontogeny (the life history of the individual) is a condensed synopsis of the long and slow history of the stem (phylogeny): This synopsis is the more faithful and complete in proportion as palingenesis (the reappearance or repetition of old, ancestral traits) has been preserved by heredity, and cenogenesis (deviation from the phylogeny of the group) has not been introduced by adaptation."[26] The late Professor Ward collected over forty-six such biological metaphors. I present a few of the examples from his collection:

[22] *Data of Ethics*, V, 65.

[23] Ross, *Foundations of Sociology*, p. 49, quoted from von Lilienfeld, *Gedanken über die Socialwissenschaft der Zukunft*, II, 113, 198.

[24] Ross, *op. cit.*, p. 48.

[25] Ross, *op. cit.*, p. 51, quoted from Collier, *Popular Science Monthly*, LIV, 807.

[26] Ernst Haeckel, *The Evolution of Man*, translated by Joseph Macabe, II, 357.

The social unit or cell is the individual. (Spencer, Lilienfeld, etc.)

The social unit or cell is the reproductive couple, man and woman. (Worms)

The social unit or cell is the trio, man, woman, and child.

The social unit is the clan.

The social tissues are settlements, roads, buildings, etc. (locative); facilities of exchange, commerce, trade, production (commercial); civil and military appliances and technique (administrative). (De Greef)

Social tissues consist of the simpler voluntary organizations of society. (Lilienfeld)

The social ectoderm or mucous layer is the governing class; the social endoderm or serous layer is the governed class (proletariat); the social mesoderm or vascular layer is the bourgeoisie. (Spencer)

The circulating mass of commodities in society constitutes its blood. (Spencer)

Merchandise in transit is unassimilated nutriment. (Lilienfeld)

Money is the homologue of the blood corpuscles. (Spencer)

Roads, railroads, water ways, etc. constitute the blood vessels of society. (Spencer)

The bourse is the social heart. (Worms)

The substance or matter of society consist of territory and population, of which the first is its bony framework and the second its muscular and fleshy portion. (De Greef)

Trade unions and guilds are the ganglia of the sympathetic nervous system of society . (Durkheim) etc., etc.[27]

Ward, who was so wise in pointing out the ludicrousness of biological analogies, was in turn guilty of using mechanistic analogies. Not content with Comte's designation of sociology as "Social Physics" and with his division of it into "Social Dynamics and Social Statics," Ward called sociology the "Mechanics of Society."[28] The same author treated the psychic factors as so many "social forces." He described the processes of imitation and

[27] L. F. Ward, "Contemporary Sociology," *American Journal of Sociology*, VII (No. 4), 484-86.

[28] "The Social Forces," *American Journal of Sociology*, II (No. 1 and 2), 82-95, 234-54.

suggestion in terms of "difference of potential." He improved upon Darwin's formula of "struggle for existence" as a "struggle for structure."[29] He characterized feeling as "the propelling agent in animals and in man."[30] He asserted that the only rational or thinkable idea of creation is that of "putting previously existing things into new forms."[31] He declared that the dilemma of determinism is a "fool's puzzle."[32] His *Pure Sociology* fairly bristles with these and many other mechanistic concepts such as "the dynamic agent" and "equilibrium of social forces."

The mechanistic analogies have had great vogue since Comte and Spencer, and many laws are based on them, of which the following are examples:

11. "Those traits and institutions most special, complex and recently acquired are the first to disappear when social decadence sets in."[33]

12. "The attraction of cities is directly as the mass and inversely as the distance."[34]

13. "Incident forces tend to collect the like and to separate the unlike."[35]

[29] *Pure Sociology*, p. 184.
[30] *Ibid.*, p. 99.
[31] *Ibid.*, p. 81.
[35] *Ibid.*, p. 46, quoted from Spencer:
[32] *Ibid.*, p. 21.
[33] Ross, *op. cit.*, p. 52.
[34] *Ibid.*, p. 48, quoted from Spencer.

NOTE: Spencer's laws of social evolution and Mr. Brown's twenty-three "propositions" discussed below with the dialectical laws may also come under this analogical group, as well as Dr. Müller-Lyer's following nine "economic laws of development," which he has laid down with considerable dogmatism, as follows:

(1) "The law of size: In every social body there exists the desire to extend. In the same way as men tend to unite into groups, so these groups have the tendency to combine in increasingly greater social and economic forms."

(2) "The law of form: The development of labor organization is caused by the continual entry of new elements, and with every new element there arises a new phase."

(3) "The law of organoplastic groups": There are said to be two main types of these groups; and "with the increasing activity of the social union, the economic importance of the family union must decline," while that of the social union rises.

(4) "The law of coöperation: Simple coöperation . . . always merges into division of labour."

COMMENTS

With regard to these laws the following series of comments
may be made:

1. Fundamental Limitations in Analogies. There are at least
two fundamental defects in analogical reasoning. First, no
analogy is complete; all analogies, if pushed far enough, may lead
to false conclusions. Spencer pointed out the four well-known
dissimilarities between society and a biological organism. Ward
himself pointed out four such dissimilarities.[36] Secondly, there
may be outward similarity without either functional or causal
similarity. As Ward wisely pointed out, though he failed to heed
his own warning, "the eyes of mollusks and of vertebrates,
though serving the same purpose, are altogether different structures; the wings of insects, of bats, and of birds, all enable their
possessors to fly, but all three are distinct organs anatomically;
the proboscis of a hawk-moth greatly resembles the long beak of
some humming birds, and both are used to penetrate tubular
flowers, but of course they have not structural resemblance; the

(5) "The law of differentiation: In every economic body there exists the
tendency to differentiate more and more between the various forces contained in it. As a rule, internal differentiation precedes external."

(6) "The law of integration: Differentiation and integration stand in a
reciprocal relationship. Every advance in the systematic division of occupations involves an advance in trade and intercourse, and vice versa."

(7) "The law of centralization: Every economic body has a desire for centralization, i. e., uniformity of production."

(8) "The law of concentration: Every economic body makes an effort to
concentrate in forces, and thus to save labour."

(9) "The law of association: All these laws can be summarized into one
general formula as follows: In every economic body there is an increasing tendency to associate in matters of labour. Step by step non-
organized individual production is undermined by organized labour,
which will eventually supplant it completely by higher and more perfect forms. The economic phase in which we are at the moment is
speeding swiftly away, and the coming phase must lie in the direction
indicated by the law of evolution" (i. e. the law of differentiation and integration?).—*The History of Social Development,* pp. 254-57.

[36] "Contemporary Sociology," *American Journal of Sociology,* VII (No. 4),
p. 492.

horse-shoe crab chews with its legs, and the various sexual calls of insects (crickets, cicadas, grasshoppers, etc.) corresponding in purpose to the notes of birds, are made by various parts of the body, but not in the mouth or throat."[37]

2. *Not Causal Laws.* To say that the bigger and nearer cities attract more people than do the smaller and remoter ones, is to put the matter in an impressionistic way, overlooking the real cause of attraction. The same is true with the laws of recapitulation. Even during the period of embryonic development, there are deviations from the normal course. The development of children depends very largely on the amount of intelligence used by their parents and nurses, and later their friends and teachers: the more intelligence is applied the greater generally are the "leaps" or "discontinuities" from one stage to another. The rôle of intelligence in education is to "short-circuit" the normal process to the advantage of the pupil as well as of the educator. That within any social group all the types of culture traversed by man in his ascent from savagery are found to co-exist, is another empirical observation without any statement of causal necessity. Various types of culture seem to co-exist almost eternally among the stagnant and lethargic races, while among the vigorous and progressive races they rapidly disappear; the more vigorous and progressive is the race, the more rapid their disappearance, except for a few dry specimens carefully preserved in ethnic museums as a reminder to posterity.

3. *Their Value.* What is the value of such laws? First, the value of analogy is poetic. The poet's imagination is fed on analogies. There may or may not be any relation between Plato's Dialogues and Lindberg's airplane. But the poets try hard to see something common between the two, and if they succeed in discovering any analogy, they build metaphors upon it. It seems that every one is to some extent a poet, for, our language is full

[37] *Ibid.*, p. 487.

of metaphor. In general, the less developed minds seem to guide their thinking by analogical reasoning rather than by causal reasoning. Hence the greater poetic charm of the primitive languages, the language of children and of the ignorant. Secondly, analogy often suggests what to look for. A partial similarity is in general a provocation to the search for further similarity or even identity. In some cases analogical reasoning has led the scientists to discover highly useful hypotheses to work upon. Mendel's laws of inheritance are fair examples. The laws governing the heredity of garden peas have not yet been found to operate with absolute accuracy on the heredity of human beings, but they have served as an encouragement to many careful experiments.

4. *Their Inherent Vagueness.* The favorite device of the Spencerians to cover up disparities within analogies, is to adorn their arguments with such phrases as "in the long run," "by and large," "on the whole," "almost certainly." What do these phrases mean? Let us take, for example, "the long run." The "long run" can not be a short run; the "long run" can not be eternity; for eternity can only be thought of, but not lived through. The "long run" is not a period of time which can be marked off with any degree of precision. For, if we were so certain as to be able to mark off "the long run" with any degree of precision, we would not find it necessary to take refuge in such a vague phrase, "in the long run." There remains only one possible meaning which might render the expression sensible; namely, that "the long run" is such a length of time as is just sufficient to fulfil the conditions implied in the expression. Any social law, which contains the phrase "in the long run" in this sense, may be a circular statement. The same might be said of the other phrases such as "on the whole," "by and large," and "other things being equal."

CHAPTER VII

NEAR-CAUSAL LAWS, CONTINUED

THE ATTEMPTS to discover causal laws by inferences from the order of succession of events in history, and from biological and mechanistic analogies, having failed, other social scientists transferred their interest to the field of psychological phenomena. Instead of dealing with man through analogies, they dealt directly with man himself; instead of philosophizing concerning society, they attempted to analyse it scientifically. Among the psychological sociologists, one of the earliest as well as the most methodical is Professor Giddings. One of his most fruitful conceptions is the theory of the "consciousness of kind," which has been made the basis of many social laws. The following is an example of such a law:

1. "The Law of Conscious Resemblance. The consciousness of resemblance and of sympathy causes people to be mutually attracted."[1] Since the authors explicitly admit that they have derived it from Professor Giddings who "named this principle consciousness of kind," it seems appropriate to examine what the latter means by it. Perhaps the best definition of "consciousness of kind" he has given is the one in his *Inductive Sociology,* to wit: "that pleasurable state of mind which includes organic sympathy, the perception of resemblance, conscious or reflective sympathy, affection, and the desire for recognition."[2] Note the words "pleasurable," "sympathy," and "includes." The first indicates a hedonistic assumption; the second shows that the source of the idea of "consciousness of kind," as Professor Giddings admitted, was Adam Smith's *Theory of the Moral Sentiment;* while the

[1] Blackmar and Gillin, *Outlines of Sociology,* p. 373.
[2] P. 99.

[131]

third is an incontestable proof of the incompleteness of the definition.[3] To say that the United States is a great nation, which
"includes" Boston, New York, Chicago, and San Francisco, is
not defining what the United States is, but is making a catalogue
of the cities in the United States, but these (one or all) do not
make up a nation.

The author's meaning, however, seems to be somewhat as follows: The mind of a baby at birth consists of nothing but vague
feelings of attraction toward certain things and of repulsion to
certain others. These vague feelings of attraction and repulsion
he calls "organic sympathy." As the baby grows older, organic
sympathy expands into "perceptions of resemblances and differences," and these later into "reflective sympathy" or deliberate
control of feelings. Reflective sympathy in the next stage is said
to develop into "affection" or the friendly feeling between persons
either actually alike or potentially alike; and this "affection" still
later into a "desire for recognition" which is said to "include"
(again include!) "a return of sympathy and affection." These
"five modes of consciousness" are said to be "pleasurable," "including (!) the feeling that we wish to maintain it and expand
it."[4] But elsewhere he seems to identify the "consciousness of
kind" with "the awareness of resemblances and differences."[5]

The weight of importance which the author attached to this
"principle of consciousness of kind" may be surmised from the
following utterances: "the sociological postulate can be no other
than this, namely: the original and elementary subjective fact in
society is the consciousness of kind."[6] "In its widest extension
the consciousness of kind marks off the animate from the inani-
mate. Within the wide class of the animate it next marks off

[3] Preface to the third edition of the *Principles of Sociology*, p. x.
[4] *Principles of Sociology*, pp. 91-99.
[5] "The consciousness of kind—the awareness of resemblances and differences—
is, in so far as we have any means of knowing, the only social consciousness."
Ibid., p. 66. Quotations by permission of the Macmillan Co.
[6] *Ibid.*, p. 17.

species and races. Within racial lines the consciousness of kind underlies the more definite ethnical and political groupings, it is the basis of class distinctions, of innumerable forms of alliance, of rules of intercourse, and of peculiarities of policy. Our conduct towards those whom we feel to be most like ourselves is instinctively and rationally different from our conduct towards others, whom we believe to be less like ourselves. Again, it is the consciousness of kind, and nothing else which distinguishes social conduct as such from purely economic, purely political, or purely religious conduct; for it is precisely the consciousness of kind that, in actual life, continually interferes with the theoretically perfect operation of the economic, the political, or the religious motive."[7]

The principle of consciousness of kind, thus interpreted and elevated, has some resemblance to the Fichtean Ego, the conscious knower, who conquers the world by the process of continual overcoming the unconscious, and the consequent expansion of the realm of consciousness. To be sure, Professor Giddings has apparently taken pains to explain it in the most unmetaphysical terms possible; and its popularity during the last thirty years seems to have been due to its resemblance to what Professor McDougall calls "social instinct" or "gregarious instinct." The late Professor Ward who held, in contrast with Professor Giddings' view that man is social by nature, the view that man is unsocial by nature, in a comprehensive survey of the development of the theory of sociability, contrasted the "consciousness of kind" with Kant's "unsocial sociability of man."[8] By the "unsocial sociability of man" Kant meant "a tendency to enter the social state combined with a perpetual resistance to that tendency which is continually threatening to dissolve it. Man has gregarious inclinations, feeling himself in the social state more than man by means of the development thus given to his natural tendencies. But he has also strong anti-gregarious inclinations prompting him

---

[7] *Ibid.*, p. 18.
[8] F. H. Giddings, *Elements of Sociology*, p. 241; Ward, *Textbook*, p. 1.

to insulate himself, which arise out of the unsocial desire (existing concurrently with his social propensities) to force all things
into compliance with his own humour."[9]

But the greatest objection to the theory of "consciousness of
kind" as a unitary principle seems to be that it makes assimilation
impossible. All growth implies the absorption of foreign elements in order to enrich the central element which thereby grows.
Without active contact with foreign elements and assimilation of
them, there can be no growth. But if the consciousness of kind is
the unitary principle, the only "sociological postulate," as Professor Giddings contends it is, how is the assimilation of foreign
elements possible? Can there be any attraction or even repulsion
between two beings which have absolutely nothing whatsoever
in common? It may, however, be said that the theory of consciousness of kind ultimately rests on a monistic hypothesis,
according to which the universe with all its multifarious and
multitudinous contents is ultimately through and through made
of some one fundamental and all-pervading substance, be it matter, spirit, or energy. But the discussion pushed so far loses its
original positive scientific interest, and the "law of conscious
resemblance" disappears in the mist of metaphysical speculations.

With the ascendency of behaviorism, the prestige of "consciousness of kind" has been completely eclipsed by the chimpan-
zee and the reflex arc. Professor Giddings evidently felt this
change of fortune, and attempted to repair the loss by revamping
the "principle of consciousness of kind" with behavioristic colora-
tion.[10] But this attempt in turn brought upon itself disfavor
with the Instinct psychologists like Professor McDougall.[11] At

[9] "Contemporary Sociology," *American Journal of Sociology*, VIII (No. 5),
656, quoted from Kant's *Idee zu einer allegemeinen Geschichte in weltbürgerlichen
Absicht*, 1784.
[10] See *Studies in the Theory of Human Society*.
[11] See W. McDougall's polemical article on "Can Sociology and Psychology
Dispense with Instincts?" *Journal of Abnormal Psychology and Social Psychology*,
vol. XIX, (no. 1, 1924), 13-41.

present "the principle of consciousness of kind" remains a hypothesis, not without some element of plausibility. Its plausibility consists in the empirical evidence in our daily social experience that like tends to draw like, and vice versa. But the same naïve empirical experience shows that we also like variety, something different or even antithetical.

Having started out with the unitary principle of consciousness of kind, Professor Giddings has deduced from it various theories of association to account for the hypothetical continuity of evolution from the stage of "zoögenic association" of animals, through the "anthropogenic association" of ape-men and the "ethnogenic association" of the primitive hordes and tribes, to the "demogenic association" of the builders of cities and creators of civilizations.[12] Among these interesting theories there are several which Professor Giddings has proclaimed to be laws. Of these the "law of development of the social composition," is an example:

2. "The social composition develops in proportion to the intensity and scope of the passion for homogeneity."[13] By "social composition" the author means "the plan of organization." By the "development of the social composition" he means the process of assimilation, or of expansion and integration, proceeding from a lonely potential socius to a family, from a family to a village, from a village to a town, to a city, and to a nation.[14] The social composition is said to develop through the mental attraction of the like and the repulsion of the unlike, except to the extent that the unlike are so far potentially alike as to render them assimilable. As the integration of the like proceeds, the "social mind" is said to recognize the process and deliberately to promote it, because "it [i.e. social mind?] develops within itself a passion for homogeneity of type, and a judgment of the usefulness of integration or federation, as a defensive and offensive measure."

[12] *Principles of Sociology,* pp. 199-362.
[13] *Inductive Sociology,* p. 198.
[14] *Ibid.,* p. 185.

The author explicitly states that by a "social mind" he means no other than a collective name for the minds of the individuals who constitute a society; and by "passion for homogeneity," he means the "desire to maintain a general homogeneity of blood, or at least, to assimilate the different elements of nationality and speech to a common kind, and to mould the traditional belief to a common type."[15] "We therefore may say," says the author, "that the social composition is produced by the reciprocal attractiveness of like for like, and is developed by the passion for homogeneity and integration, through an effort to combine the potentially with the actually alike, and to create a common type."[16] Let us examine this law more carefully. The imposing phrase "the development of the social composition" simply means assimilation; and since the author means by "the passion for homogeneity" the "desire to maintain a general homogeneity of blood, or at least [the desire] to assimilate the different elements of nationality and speech to a common kind"; the law that "the social composition develops in proportion to the intensity and scope of the passion for homogeneity" is equivalent to the statement that assimilation proceeds "in proportion to the intensity and scope of" the desire to assimilate!

3. Professor Giddings has another law which runs parallel with the one just discussed, to wit: "The development of the social constitution is proportional to the growth of an appreciation of the value of variety or unlikeness in society."[17] By "social constitution" the author means "an organization of the individual members of the community into associations or groups; for carrying on special forms of activity or for maintaining particular interests," such as a business corporation, a political party, a philanthropic society, a church, or a school.[18] The author's interpretation of the law is as follows: "The supreme end of society in general is the protection and perfecting of sentient life. The

[15] *Inductive Sociology*, pp. 65, 200. [17] *Ibid.*, p. 224.
[16] *Ibid.*, pp. 197-198. [18] *Ibid.*, p. 186.

end of human society is the development of the rational and spiritual personality of its members. . . . For both [these] ends specialization and a division of labour are necessary. Therefore, while society maintains the homogeneity of its composition, it is obliged to tolerate and to promote differentiation in its constitution."[19]

This seems to be another partial truth in a pseudo-scientific garb. For, what the author means by the formidable phrase "the growth of an appreciation of the value of variety or unlikeness in society" is nothing but the commonplace notion of specialization, division, and coördination of labour. Therefore, if the author means by "the development of the social constitution" the increasing specialization, division, and coördination of labour, the law is but a tautological statement, equivalent to saying that the increase of specialization, division, and coördination of labour is proportional to the increase of specialization, division, and coördination of labour! If, however, he means by "the development of the social constitution" the progressive realization of the "supreme end of society," he is making the mistake of tacitly assuming that there is a quantitative correlation between the mechanical, and to some extent incidental, aspect of progress with the substance of progress itself. For, it is now a well-recognized fact that even in the department of economic activity alone the mere extension of specialization and division of labour does not pay beyond a certain stage at any given time.[20] Much less can it be said that the whole social development in general is proportional to the specialization and division of labour. Hence, the "law of development of the social constitution," in so far as it is true, is a tautology; and in so far as it is not a tautology, it is not true.

4. Professor Giddings has two other laws which run in the same strain, namely, the "laws of tradition": "Tradition is authoritative and coercive in proportion to its antiquity."

[19] *Ibid.*, p. 223.
[20] See, e. g., F. W. Taussig's *Principles of Economics*, vol. II, chap. XXXVIII.

5. "Tradition is authoritative and coercive in proportion as its subject matter consists of belief rather than of critically established knowledge."[21]

Taking the second law first, we have here another tautological formula. For, a tradition may be defined as an uncritically accepted belief, owing to its actual or supposed utility. That this definition is substantially what the author had in mind is evidenced by his description of tradition. He says that "through the intimate association between tradition and the everyday activities of life, the child insensibly associates the practical activities with its traditional background. . . . Daily life thus becomes a ceaseless discipline and drill in activities which openly or tacitly assume the truth and sufficiency of tradition."[22] Professors Blackmar and Gillin, in their explanation of this law, contrast tradition with "rational deductions." "The chief service of science," say they, "to the modern world consists, therefore, in bringing people to accept things which can be demonstrated to be true either by rational deductions or by a formidable array of facts."[23] It is evident, then, that the substance of the second law of tradition amounts to this: An uncritically accepted belief is authoritative and coercive in proportion as its subject matter is not critically established knowledge!

Now, why is tradition said to be "authoritative and coercive"? The answer is that Professor Giddings has conceived tradition as something necessarily authoritative and coercive. Thus, for example, "Tradition is imposed upon the child by his parents and elder acquaintances. He is directly taught that the traditional beliefs are true, and that it is even wrong to doubt their truth and authority. Disbelief is often punished, and disobedience of traditional precept is punished usually."[24] The notions of authority and coercion are therefore initially predicated in the author's

[21] *Inductive Sociology*, p. 177.   [22] *Ibid.*, p. 151.
[23] Blackmar and Gillin, *Outlines of Sociology*, p. 375.
[24] *Inductive Sociology*, pp. 150-51.

definition of tradition. As to the first law that tradition is authoritative and coercive "in proportion to its antiquity," the author's explanation is as follows: "Where the social mind assumes the mode of belief, it becomes an active social force tending to compel acceptance and conformity. This control by belief is reënforced by the influence of antiquity, chiefly because mere venerableness is impressive and has much of the effectiveness of emblem and shibboleth."[25] I do not see how this argument proves the law. If the coercive influence of tradition is "reënforced by the influence of antiquity," antiquity evidently is not the sole coercive influence behind tradition, nor even the main coercive influence. What, then, makes tradition authoritative and coercive "in proportion to antiquity"? To my mind there are other and more important factors, such as utility, which enable tradition to survive. What made, for example, the Apostolic tradition, appear "authoritative and coercive" to the medieval people? Was it "chiefly because mere venerableness is impressive"? or did it appear "venerable" and "impressive," because it was useful to somebody such as the Catholic clergy? Of course, it is easy to retort that, other things being equal, antiquity counts. But the "other things" are exceedingly difficult to discover, whatever they are; and when discovered they are rarely equal.

Two other laws which Professor Giddings has formulated are worth noticing, namely, the "laws of liberty":

6. "Social organization is coercive in those communities in which sympathetic and formal like-mindedness strongly predominate over deliberative like-mindedness. Conversely, social institutions are liberal, allowing the utmost freedom of thought and action to the individual only in those communities in which there is a high development of deliberative like-mindedness."

7. "The forms of social organization, whether political or other, in their relation to the individual, are necessarily coercive if, in their membership, there is great diversity of kind and great

[25] *Ibid.*, p. 177.

inequality. Conversely, institutions or other forms of social organization can be liberal, conceding the utmost freedom to the individual if, in the population, there is fraternity, and back of fraternity, an approximate mental and moral equality."[26]

The first of these two laws needs some explanation, since it contains several technical terms which Professor Giddings has invented. By "like-mindedness" he means "the total phenomenon of resemblance" which occurs "when the simultaneous like-responses of a plural number of individuals have developed through the consciousness of kind into concerted volition." He distinguishes four kinds of like-mindedness, of which only three concern us at present. By "sympathetic like-mindedness" he means a "complex like-mindedness" which is said to be "predominantly sympathetic and imitative." "The basis of all sympathetic like-mindedness is found in a predominance of the ideo-emotional type of mind, with its prompt response to stimulus, its emotionalism, imaginativeness, suggestibility, and habit of reasoning from analogy. Other factors are a reciprocal consciousness of kind which is rapidly formed, a great susceptibility to emblem and shibboleth, great imitativeness, and contagious imitation" such as are evidenced in revivals, panics, strikes, and riots. Again: "Examples of the sympathetic type of coöperator are the religious shouter, the striker, the 'heeler,' and the revolutionist."[27]

By "formal like-mindedness" Professor Giddings means a still more complex like-mindness which is said to be "dogmatically radical or dogmatic and formal—traditional, customary and conservative," impatient of criticism and little disposed to be conciliatory. "A further subjective factor of dogmatic like-mindedness is the habit of deductive reasoning, without criticism of premises." Further: "The dogmatic mode of like-mindedness is found in gentile society that is sufficiently developed to be organized by clans and tribes, and in civil society wherever dog-

[26] *Inductive Sociology*, pp. 226-28.
[27] *Ibid.*, pp. 133, 144-45.

matic emotional masses or parties are found. True examples of the dogmatic type of coöperator are found in the reformer and the political partisan."[28] By "deliberative like-mindedness" Professor Giddings means "The highest and most complex mode of concerted volition," which is said to be characterized by critical thinking, constructive reasoning, moderate and well-coördinated action. Further: "The evidences of deliberative like-mindedness on a large scale as affecting the life of great communities, the sociologist must look for in a free criticism applied to religion and theology, in the development of inductive science, in the existence of a scientific system of political economy, in the substitution of objective evidence for oaths and ordeals in legal procedure, and in the unmolested criticism of governments by the body of citizens who organize and obey them."[29]

A preliminary assumption seems to be necessary in order to render these laws of liberty either plausible or possible. Professor Giddings nowhere states what he means by "liberty," we therefore assume it to mean civil liberty. By civil liberty is meant the sum total of rights and privileges which are legally sanctioned and protected. These formidable terms thus explained, the laws of liberty seem to be either commonplace observations dressed in unwieldly vocabulary, or arbitrary constructions which need verification. They are commonplace observations in so far as they mean that in societies where the individual members are more intelligent and better behaved, where a rough homogeneity in blood, backed up by good will, prevails, there is likely to be a greater measure of liberty than in others where the conditions are reversed. Like all other empirical observations, these laws would then want causal explanation. It may probably be true that in many instances, a rough homogeneity in blood and an approximate uniformity in moral and intellectual standards are coexistent with a large measure of liberty. But, unless it is proved that with

[28] *Inductive Sociology*, pp. 145, 154.
[29] *Ibid.*, pp. 154, 162.

every increase in the homogeneity in blood and with every advance toward uniformity in moral and intellectual standards, there will be a greater measure of liberty, we have no scientific social law.

If, however, the three psychological types, "sympathetic like-mindedness," "formal like-mindedness," and "deliberative like-mindedness," are offered as causal explanations of the types of social institutions, they seem to be arbitrary constructions. Beyond empirical observations, which are always here and there contradicted by other empirical observations, it is very doubtful whether there are really such psychological types. Professor Giddings has begun his theory of "like-mindedness" with the "instinctive" or "motor-muscular like-mindedness," which according to his theory, develops and differentiates into the other three types. Hence, even if it is granted that there might be psychological types, is there any reason that there should be only three such types? Are they merely three of the high-spots in the history of psycho-physical development? Again, Professor Giddings characterizes each succeeding type as being more complex than the preceding type. Thus, he says, that "formal like-mindedness" is a "more complex like-mindedness" (than the "sympathetic"); and that the "deliberative like-mindedness" is "the highest and most complex mode of concerted volition" (i.e., like-mindedness.) Are, then, the differences among the three psychological types necessarily those of greater and lesser complexity? Shall we say that the mind of every "revolutionist" is less complex than that of every "political partisan" (whom Professor Giddings gives as examples of the "sympathetic" and the "formal like-mindedness" respectively)? These seem to be some of the moot points in Professor Giddings' theory of psychological types; and until these points are settled the "laws of liberty" will remain nebulous hypotheses.

Sympathy is a process of expanding the self. To sympathize is literally to feel with. Such a feeling may be as divine as the compassion of the deity, or as tender as the tenderest sentiments of a young mother toward her baby. Its antithesis is antipathy which also takes various forms, such as the mechanical aversion to shocking objects, distaste for foreign manners and customs, and deliberate antagonism to threatening objects. In the last instance, it is often accompanied by self-deception or rationalization. Perfect sympathy requires a high degree of intelligence as well as a large emotional capacity. Morons, then, can not be very sympathetic, because of their inability to see beyond their noses, while villains deliberately limit their sympathy.

Professor Giddings has said that consciousness of kind is the basis of class distinctions. A pernicious form of class distinction is the caste system, and the most outrageous feature of it is exploitation of various kinds. The following laws of exploitation, quoted from Professor Ross, describe in a vivid style many of the common types of exploitation. He defines exploitation as using others "as means to one's own ends." He distinguishes four kinds of exploitation, namely, sexual, or the enslavement of women among backward races; religious, or the exaction of a tribute of youths from a vanquished tribe to be sacrificed to the victors' gods, and a tribute of maidens to be dedicated to their services; egotic, or the exaction of fealty and homage from the underlings; and economic, or the exaction of personal services without due compensation. Professor Ross, further, describes with lucidity ten "lines of exploitation," to wit: exploitation of offspring by parent, women by men, poor by rich, the few by the many, the industrious by the leisured, the ignorant by the intelligent, the unorganized by the organized, the laity by priests, conquered by conquerors, and the governed by the rulers. He then proceeds to lay down the following ten "laws of exploitation":

8. "Social elements differ in original disposition to exploit." For example, those who are bred to leisure are more resolute to

live off others than those who are brought up in humbler circumstances. They have learned from childhood to despise work, and are so habituated to the parasitic life that they, in order to avoid self-support by labour, frequently sacrifice morals, religion, popular liberty and national independence. "No political movement is so bloody, sordid and unpatriotic as a White Terror."

9. "Exploitation is more open, ruthless and stubborn between the unlike than between the like." To illustrate: It has long been observed that even among the primitive races the members of the same kin group do not prey upon one another, because of the strong tribal consciousness which firmly binds them together. Among the advanced races the members of the same social group are held together by national, sectarian, and other consciousnesses. But where there is no such consciousness of kind, exploitation of one individual or group by another is the normal phenomenon. Hence, "exploitation is worst just after conquest and every step in the assimilation of conquerors and conquered is followed by a let-up." When the exploiters are intelligent enough to perceive the likeness between themselves and the objects of their exploitation, they often exaggerate or even invent the unlikeness in order to justify themselves. "The Southern master insisted the negro had no soul or made out his bondage to be God's punishment laid upon the descendants of Ham, who failed in respect to Father Noah. Aristotle justifies slavery by imagining a difference in the natures of masters and slaves. For centuries the English have striven to convince the world that the Irish are incapable of governing themselves."

10. "An element is ready and whole-hearted in exploitation in the degree that it constitutes a self-conscious group." For example, the Moslem conquerors were more ready and whole-hearted in exploiting the Spanish natives than others because of the strong antithesis between their racial and religious consciousness. The Christians' exploitation of the Jews in the Middle Ages was another illustration of the same law.

11. "The will to exploit lasts as long as the power to exploit. Exploiters never tire of exploitation. A kept class never loses its taste for consuming the fruits of other men's toil, nor does it ever give up exploiting out of conviction of sin. Its manner of life becomes completely adjusted to its parasitism, and it never fails to develop moral standards, theories, and ideals which chime with the economic basis of its life. Individual members of a kept class may come to feel that their exploitation is indefensible, but the class merely disowns them, dresses its ranks, and moves on."

12. "Foreign domination is likely to suppress infra-social exploitation. If the foreign masters exploit the dependency they will be jealous of the native exploiting groups, and if they do not they will be disgusted by them. The Romans followed the principle of *parcere subjectis, debellare superbos,* in order to create in the dependency an interest loyal to their rule. In India the British have either done away with the insatiable native princes or else curbed their rapacity."

13. "A new element menaces the continuance of an exploitation unless that element be made a sharer of its benefits. Outsiders spoil the game. In the seventeenth and eighteenth centuries negro slavery was more inhuman in the self-governing English colonies in the West Indies than in the Spanish and the French West Indies, which were governed from Europe. Lay churches, like the Protestant denominations, were more complaisant about slavery than the Roman Catholic Church. In Virginia, Jamaica and Barbados, where the masters controlled both state and church, the slaves had the fewest rights."

14. "Masked exploitation outlasts open exploitation. In an enlightened democratic society the only considerable exploitations that can survive are clandestine. Jobbery in municipal contracts is secret. The white slave traffic is furtive. Peonage is remote and wears an innocent air. Monopoly endures not in virtue of royal grants or favoring law as in olden times, but by

reason of hidden rebates from carriers or secret understandings among commercial rivals. . . . Hence, what latter-day exploitation most dreads is—being unmasked! What it fights most desperately is investigation or publicity. It centers its pressure on newspaper men, newspapers, magazines, prosecuting attorneys, legislative committees, professors of the social sciences, clergymen, agitators—in a word, on those who may expose it or direct public attention its way."

15. "The favorite mask of an exploitation is a counter service or return which falls far short of being an equivalent. The virtual slavery of the indebted peon is camouflaged by crediting him with wages for his labor and charging him outrageous prices for the scanty supplies he obtains from the planter's store. His laboring like a slave for mere food and clothes appears as a double transaction of purchase and sale."

16. "Opportunities for masked exploitation multiply as social relations become involved and social interdependence more extended. Once every man offered his sacrifice himself, but the custom of letting the priest do it opens the door to sacerdotal abuses. Once every man might conduct his own cause, but the custom of appearing in court only by attorney delivers the litigant to the legal profession. Reliance upon bought food or milk gives the adulterator his chance. In the South a too-commercial farming has often enslaved the cultivator to the store-keeper with his mortage and crop liens."

17. "Whatever equalizes social elements in respect to intelligence, courage, organization, discipline or situation narrows the power of the one to exploit the other. Gunpowder levelled up the townsmen with the barons and knights of the Middle Ages. The appearance of intelligence and capacity in the French commoners before the Revolution made the privileges of the nobles and clergy an anachronism. Many negro leaders believe that if the Southern negroes gain industrial skill and accumulate property, they will not for long be kept out of their rights. Popular

education is an anti-exploitation policy. Organization among farmers causes a prompt change of attitude in exploiting middlemen and carriers. . . . The doctrine that all are equally sons of God undermines the conviction that 'God will think twice before he damns a person of quality.' "[30]

I am sorry for having shortened Professor Ross's illustrations of these laws, which like all his illustrations are as enjoyable as they are lucid and picturesque. Professor Ross should be admired for his ability to present his views in such a vivid style as to drive home even academic jargon to the plain reader. These laws certainly do tell something about exploitation, what it is, how it occurs, and what might be done about it. All these laws are true as empirical generalizations are; and like the latter, too, every one of them has only a limited truth.

The first law says that "the social elements differ in original disposition to exploit." It is not clear whether Professor Ross means by "original disposition to exploit" a disposition innate or rather one acquired and cultivated through upbringing. It is clear, however, on empirical grounds, that persons who have been brought up in luxury and idleness, and who have been taught to despise labour, whether they have acquired their disposition to exploit from nature or nurture or both, in general tend to live on the fruit of other men's labour, obtaining their end by wit if they may, by force and even by treachery if they must. Even the handworkers, if brought up in the parasitic class, would for the most part probably behave like the people of that class. The reason for this might be explained in terms of habit-formation, of the habitual assumption of the ascendency and domination attitudes of the patricians over the plebeians, and of the archaic ideals of how a lady and a gentleman ought to live. This method might yield a psychological theory of explanation. The present law is simply a preface to a class of laws that are to follow.

[30] E. A. Ross, *Principles of Sociology*, pp. 135-56. By permission of the Century Co.

The second and third laws are evidently based on numerous ancient adages which have been made famous by Professor Giddings, namely, the "consciousness of kind." Empirical observations seem to confirm by and large the hypothesis that exploitation between the unlike is more ruthless than one within any one homogeneous or "self-conscious" group. But the question may be raised, what is a self-conscious group? It may be a racial group such as the negro slave traffickers. It may be a doctrinal group such as the Russian Bolsheviki. It may be an occupational group such as the trade unions. It may be, in short, any group of men, which is excited about some idea and is out for something. Further, it may be noted that the lines of demarcation between the groups cross one another. In the Communist Internationale racial antagonism is subordinated to class struggle. At the end of the Great War the German Social Democratic Party preferred the triumph of social democracy at the cost of a national humiliation, in place of military glory with probably worse Kaiserism. Few social groups can be said, from the objective point of view, to be more self-conscious than a family; yet a depraved husband exploits his wife, and a depraved father his daughter, even when he might never have exploited, or never have even dared exploit any person outside his family group. There are no objective boundary lines between groups, which can not be transcended in some way in the long run. Hence, the problem is how to make people lift up their mental horizon, see far and think deeply. The more clearly they see the connections among the several groups, and the more deeply they feel for the community of interests, the less will they exploit one another. Further, if the process of expanding self-consciousness is carried, as the German monists have preached, to its legitimate limit, it may coincide with the whole universe, and there may be no room for exploitation.

The fourth law may be more plainly stated by saying that the exploiters tend to continue exploiting as long as they can, due to the difficulty of readjusting their habits, customs, institutions, and moral standards, even when they are made conscious of the injustice of their exploitation. But the question, how long is "as long as they can," is as difficult to answer as the question, how long is "the long run." A law of this type, as it stands, is always characteristically too vague to be much of a law; and if it be made a little more explicit, it frequently turns out to be a circular statement.

The fifth law, that "foreign domination is likely to suppress infra-social exploitation" works both ways. Some foreign dominators like the Romans gave peace to the oppressed and waged war on the oppressors, because it was to their interest to do so. It was a display of justice. But their sense of justice was no better than that of the man in the fable who stole the bell with his ears stuffed. Other foreign dominators like the Americans in the Philippines suppressed the infra-social exploitation partly out of humanitarian motive. Still other foreign dominators like the English in India are indifferent to many forms of infra-social exploitation.

The sixth law, that "a new element menaces the continuance of an exploitation unless that element be made a sharer of its benefits," is a feeble echo of the fifth. It may be regarded as a law, provided we can accept two unsafe assumptions: first, every new element or social group is bent on exploiting another; second, every social group must be large enough to disturb the balance of power between exploiting and exploited classes. The first of these assumptions is a caricature of human nature, while the second is too vague, begging the question, how large a social group is large enough to disturb the balance of power?

The seventh law, that "masked exploitation outlasts open exploitation," the eighth law, that "the favorite mask of exploitation is a counter service or return which falls far short of being an equivalent," and the ninth law, that "opportunities for masked exploitation multiply as social relations become involved and

social interdependence more extended," are confessions of failure
of a civilization which attempts to reform human nature and to
improve social conditions through the instrument of legislative
assemblies. So long as the indiscriminate admiration for the men
of big bank accounts lasts, so long as moral progress lags behind
intellectual and material progress, so long as the slum populace
and the backward races continue to over-supply mal-equipped
workers, so long will there probably be exploitation. Legal
prohibitions frequently lead to a mere refinement of the method
of exploitation; and a refined method may be less brutal, but even
more sinful. The slave master of a century or two ago, who was
born into that system, who was taught from childhood to regard
slavery as natural, and whose moral sense was dulled through
habituation, was less immoral than the unscrupulous adventurers
of today who deliberately violate the spirit of the laws. Like all
confessions of sin and failure, these three social laws carry their
own answer: Sin no more and do better.

   Will equalization of intelligence, courage, organization, discipline and situation, lessen exploitation? Professor Ross's tenth
law says, yes. But modern civilization moves in the direction of
specialization as well as of integration; and a specialist turned
criminal can do to-day a great deal more harm than did his
predecessors. For, the present generation relies on the specialists
much more than did the past. As for courage, the kind of
courage which will enable one to knock out a champion prize
fighter is not of much use to-day, nor is the courage of the Hyde
Park orators. We need the kind of courage which will help men
to live up to their ideals of life. But is there any scientific law
about this kind of courage? As for organization, discipline and
situation, the British Labour Party seems to be a model of all
these ideals; and yet the British Labour Party stands against the
British bourgeoisie like an armed camp against another, each
trying to outwit the other and to appropriate the largest possible
slice of the produce of their industry. The frequent strikes on

gigantic scales and the inordinate demands of the British laborers look more like a retrogression to the primitive form of exploitation than a progress away from it.

In a previous quotation Professor Giddings said that the consciousness of kind is the basis of innumerable forms of alliances, of rules of intercourse, and of peculiarities of policy. This view is brilliantly developed also by Professor Ross, and is embodied in the following ten laws of social control, quoted from his famous book *Social Control*. Since these laws are less well knit together than the laws of exploitation just discussed, I shall present them singly or in a group as seems suitable, with a concise evaluation of each.

18. "Public morality is lower than private morality." To illustrate: "International dealings are more unprincipled than domestic dealings. The Christian nation surpasses the heathen nation less than the Christian man surpasses the heathen man. The state is more rapacious and perfidious than it will allow its citizens to be. Hence diplomats, statesmen, warriors, ecclesiastics, and public men continually do in their official capacity that which they will not stoop to in their private life. Society authorizes, nay, even expects of its agent practices which it forbids them to use in their own behalf. It bids the statesman steal for it, the diplomat lie for it, the spy betray for it, the soldier kill for it; yet it will condemn them if they do such things for themselves. Statesmen have always sought exemption from the moral code and pleaded the need of a special standard. We now see that they simply reflect the morality of the master they serve.

"The fact is, every group of men exhibits a morality corresponding to its place in the hierarchy of groups. The more big groups there are above it the more obligations it recognizes. The nearer it is to the top the purer its egoism. Many nepotists, sectaries, and partisans are simply victims of one of these unscrupulous group moralities. Adherents of sects—anarchists, Jesuits, Jacobins, émigrés—are induced by the sect ego to commit

crimes they would not commit for themselves. Now society is
the all-inclusive association. It limits the self-assertion of the
minor groups, but is not limited in turn. Accordingly, its egoism
is the more perfect, and in its preaching as in its practices, it is
likely to keep in view its own interest."[31]

19. "A Social Ego emerges in the degree to which collective
opinion is elaborated and organized." To illustrate: "It is
democracies that are the most active in humanitarian legislation.
'The people' are the readiest to respond to a generous proposal.
In every organization of national opinion the bottom is more
radical on purely moral questions than the top. If we would
mark the moral plane of an age, we look to the common people
and not to the hierarchies. For progressive views as to the rights
of slaves, foreigners, enemies, or the lower races, we appeal to the
intuitions of common men, and not to the spokesmen of highly
organized bodies of sentiment, such as Church, Army, Trade,
State, or 'Society.' It is to the masses, and not to the classes, that
one must protest against national wrongdoing."[32]

The foregoing two laws seem to present the type of laws
which we are now discussing, in their characteristic fashion, the
vividness of their descriptions and the looseness of their terminology, the commonplaceness of their observations and the
weakness of their analyses. They present sets of facts with an
attempt at unification. But the phrasing of the laws is very
ambiguous. What is meant, for example, by "public morality"
and "private morality"? Do they mean the morality of the
public, and that of the individual respectively? Is there any such
thing as the public apart from the individuals who compose it?
No. Does the law mean that individuals in public, or to put it
more plainly, in the presence of others, behave always less morally
than they do when alone? No. Even crowds often rise above
the level of individual morality, when properly guided by men of
quality. There seem to be many persons who privately violate
the Volstead Act, who yet put on airs of decency in public.

[31] *Social Control*, p. 71-72. Quotations by permission of the Macmillan Co.
[32] *Ibid.*, p. 75.

Prostitution and gambling are legally abolished in the United States, yet they seem to go on clandestinely.

After discounting these considerations, we may rephrase the law somewhat as follows: The moral standard (objectively, at least) in the dealings between two or more social groups is lower than the moral standard of the members within any one social group. There is, in inter-group relations, what Professor Ross calls "ethical dualism" or double standard of morality, the one applying to the members of other groups being generally lower than the one applying to the members of the same group. But this law, even so moderately expressed, is contradicted by many exceptions, as illustrated by the frequent invitations of foreign powers to the ruling classes to suppress civil wars. The Court of Queen Antoinette invited the Austrians and Prussians to overrun the Jacobin-ridden France with the sword. The government of the Russian Czarist reactionaries eagerly sought the friendship of France and England, while sending away the flower of the nation's youth to the Siberian snow-fields.

An easy verbal victory may be gained by retorting that these are diseased types of group morality, and that the Court of Queen Antoinette and the government of the Czarist reactionaries dug their own graves. But still, disease is about as common as health. Does one find many examples of perfect health? Professor Ross's law is therefore a rough approximation to a general tendency which has been on the whole steadily undermined by men in their progress from primitive savagery, when each tribal community was a sovereign group and a law unto itself, up to now when the enthusiasts for the League of Nations see a nobler vision, work to lift up the international moral standard and to place it on a securer basis.

The group morality is none other than the morality built up and maintained by some members of the group. The statesman and the clergy are the natural leaders in building up a new morality and in improving upon the old ones. Hence the states-

man who steals and lies and plunders a neighboring nation on
the plea that he is bidden to do so by "Society" is fooling himself.
It is nobody's "manifest destiny" to rob his neighbor. Hence, too,
when Professor Ross says that "society authorizes, nay, even expects of its agents practices which it forbids them to use in their
own behalf," and that "it [i.e. society] bids the statesman steal
for it, the diplomat lie for it, the spy betray for it, the soldier
kill for it," he is talking about a mythical monster rather than a
real society such as we live in. He has personified society, en-
shrouded it with myth, and placed it beyond the reach of laws.
An international scoundrel such as Professor Ross describes fills
his heart with unholy ambitions, and his head with rapacious
imagery; and he hears the voices say Murder! Lie! Plunder!
But these voices are none other than his own voice. When he
talks about society, society is but the cloak for his sins.

Is there any way of keeping the group perpetually alert? Professor Ross's second law of social control quoted above is an
answer to this question, namely, "a Social Ego emerges in the
degree to which collective opinion is elaborated and organized."
It may be more plainly stated by saying that a social group is self-
conscious in proportion to the diffusion of knowledge, community of interests and efficiency of organization. The ignorant
mass is a fit object for exploitation by intelligent crooks; heterogeneity of interests divides the attention of the group; and inef-
ficiency or absence of organization makes the group unwieldy.
But none of these three things alone is sufficient to keep the group
perpetually awake; nor am I sure that they all together can
always do so. A thoroughly organized group is easier to manipu-
late by the unscrupulous than is the less organized. Wide diffusion of knowledge also multiplies interests and weakens loyalty
to the group organization. At present by far the best organized
and the most egoistic groups are the sovereign groups, next to
them probably the religious and the economic groups. A belated
jingoist may see in the state nothing but the Absolute made

manifest, but when he is imbued with cosmopolitan ideals, his enthusiasm for jingoism may grow lukewarm. A loud communist may see in the Marxian orthodoxy nothing but the triumph of the proletariat and the regeneration of humanity, but when he is brought to witness the outrages of a Trotzky or of a Stalin, he may grow skeptical about the sanity of some of Marx's utterances. This short discussion seems to point to the conclusion that the members of any social group are in general capable of being aroused to self-consciousness by means of popular education and of efficient organization; that they are occasionally capable of performing heroic feats if properly guided by judicious leaders; but that as to the exact limits and proportions in the use of these instruments there is nothing as yet that can be said definitely; too little is known of leadership.

20. "If any class finds itself leading the march at the head of the social procession, it is only because the other classes have more confidence in it than they have in themselves. Social power is concentrated or diffused in proportion as men do or do not feel themselves in need of guidance or protection. When it is concentrated it lodges in that class of men in which the people feel the most confidence. The many transfer their allegiance from one class to another—from elders to priests, or from priests to savants —when their supreme need changes, or when they have lost confidence in the old guidance. When they begin to feel secure and able to cope with evils in their own strength and wisdom, the many resume self-direction and the monopoly of social power by the few ceases.

"Such is the underlying law of the transformations and displacements of power. The immediate cause of the location of power is prestige. The class that has the most prestige will have the most power. The prestige of numbers gives ascendancy to the crowd. The prestige of age gives it to the elders. The prestige of prowess gives it to the war chief, or to the military caste. The prestige of sanctity gives it to the priestly caste. The prestige of

inspiration gives it to the prophet. The prestige of place gives
it to the official class. The prestige of money gives it to the
capitalists. The prestige of ideas gives it to the élite. The prestige
of learning gives it to the mandarins. The absence of prestige
and the faith of each man in himself gives weight to the individual and reduces social control to a minimum."[33]

21. "As the social environment becomes rich and varied we
can distinguish a development of man's feelings, judgments, and
choices, which may be termed the evolution of personality. The
law of it is that men come to feel toward more things and to feel
toward them more strongly. The world's gray is broken up into
lights and shadows. For instance, during a definite period we
can see the Greek race pass from indifference to the strongest
feelings of admiration or dislike for a work of art. During the
Middle Ages we observe the dawn of that sense of the charm of
woman that was to give birth to romantic love. With the Renais-
sance the feeling for natural beauty develops prodigiously, while
in about a century and a half we have seen the rise of a passion
for absolute self-direction. Now, in the midst of these developments we can discover a growing sense of the charm of persons."[34]

These two laws betray another characteristic of the type of
social laws we are now discussing, namely, their unsystematic
character. Since a "Social Ego" has been formulated in terms of
organization of public opinion (in the last law discussed) we
might expect laws of social control in terms of interests, ideas,
and opinions. Instead, Professor Ross has presented them in
terms of "feeling" and "prestige" which are irrational. These
laws seem to be based on Professor Ward's theory of feeling as
the "social dynamic." It is probable that in the animal world at
large, feeling, especially sexual emotion, forces even the most unsocial animals such as tigers to associate with others, while the
hunger emotion compels even the wolves to hunt in packs. It is

[33] *Social Control*, pp. 78-80.   [34] *Ibid.*, p. 281.

also probable that in the savage world feeling and prestige play a much larger rôle in social control than they do in advanced societies.

The word "prestige" is derived, according to Mr. Leopold, from the Latin "praestigiae"; and in the same language the juggler, dice-player, and rope-walker were called "praestigiator." Latin authors and Medieval writers of glossaries used the word in the sense of "deceptive and juggling tricks."[35] Etymological arguments, of course, require a certain amount of discounting. But the point is that prestige is an illusory element, hence irrational. A certain amount of illusion is probably necessary in social control, due to the clumsiness of human ways. Blind conformity to convention is to a large extent inspired by the illusion of universality: "everybody does, therefore I must!" Even hero-worship is a partial illusion, for no hero is heroic enough to his own valet to be worshipped. At present about half the world seems to be governed by great jugglers, and some of the greatest of them seem to have even forgotten that they are jugglers. But I do not see why this should be so. If democracy has any meaning, it means a move away from jugglery.

As for the law of "the evolution of personality" that "men come to feel toward more things and to feel toward them more strongly," it may also be called a law of the devolution of personality, if it is a law at all. Personality emerges only when the various feelings are organized on a higher level than their own. The mere multiplication and intensification of feelings and desires may lead to a dissociation of personality rather than to a development of it. Multifarious feelings and multitudinous desires are the symptoms of insanity, while a few well-chosen and well-organized desires directed toward some ideal goal may mean a strong and healthy personality.

[35] See Mr. Lewis Leopold's interesting book called *Prestige, A Psychological Study of Social Estimates*, pp. 16, 187, etc.

22. "The volume of social requirement will be greater when social power is concentrated than when it is diffused." The reasons given for this are as follows: "What keeps social commands from multiplying and choking up life, as the rank growth of swamp weed chokes up water courses is, of course, the resistance of the individual. Naturally a man prefers to do as he pleases, and not as society pleases to have him do. The more then that social power dwells in the mass of persons whose necks are galled by social requirement, the more the yoke of the law will be lightened. On the other hand, the more distinct those who apply social pressure from those who must bear it, the more likely is regulation to be laid on lavishly in obedience to some class ideal." Hence the law.[36]

23. "The character of social requirement changes with every shifting of social power." To illustrate: "When the reverend seniors monopolize power, much will be made of filial respect and obedience, infanticide will be a small offense, while parricide will be punished with horrible torments. Let the priests get the upper hand, and chastity, celibacy, humility, unquestioning belief, and scrupulous observance will be the leading virtues. The ascendancy of the military caste shifts the accent to obedience, loyalty, pugnacity, and sensitiveness to personal honor. When the moneyed man holds the baton, we hear much of industriousness, thrift, sobriety, probity, and civility. The mandarins and literati have no moral programme of their own, but they are sure to exalt reverence for order, precedent, and rank. The élite, whatever ideal they champion, will be sure to commend the ordering of one's life according to ideas and principles, rather than according to precedent and tradition. For only by fostering the radical spirit can they hope to lead men into untrodden paths."[37]

Both these laws deal with the relation between social requirement and social power: in particular, the first attempts to de-

[36] E. A. Ross, *Social Control*, p. 84.   [37] *Ibid.*, p. 85.

termine the volume of social requirement, while the second attempts to determine the character of social requirement. Like most empirical observations they contain a large element of truth, but they are too indefinite to be laws. Social power is widely diffused, in theory at least, in a democracy, while it is highly concentrated in an autocracy. Shall we say then that the volume of social requirements in a democracy is smaller than that in an autocracy? The tendency of modern governments has been to emerge from the laissez-faire policy in which the eighteenth century philosophers confined them, and to assume a more and more constructive rôle. Meliorative legislation such as the Volstead Act, the Blue Sky Laws, and the factory-labor regulations, increases the volume of social requirement and directly controverts Professor Ross's law quoted above.

The element of truth, however, contained in Professor Ross's law seems to be that the volume of compulsory and irrational requirement is greater when social power is concentrated in the hands of a class-biased minority or in the hands of superannuated elders as in some oriental villages and in the primitive savage world at large. The primitive and the backward races control their society by means of irrational instruments such as fear, superstition, tradition, and custom. These instruments continually check the natural inclinations of the members of their society; hence, from the psychological point of view they are much less free than a civilized man. The number of things which they are forced to do is disproportionately large in comparison with their free acts; hence the amount of their social requirement seems larger than that of an advanced society.

On the other hand, a gentleman of the present society has to do a great many things which the members of primitive societies do not even think of doing. The late Speaker Thomas Reed was reported to have said that "No gentleman should weigh more than two hundred fifty pounds." A gentleman has to control his gluttony and his lust; he conforms more or less to the etiquette of the élite, the fashions of the "four hundred," and the numerous laws of the State. Objectively measured, the volume of social requirement he has to fulfil is actually greater than that in any primitive society. Still the civilized gentleman is much freer than a member of the primitive society; for his fulfilment of the social requirement is generally voluntary, not compulsory; he generally has a chance to choose between the several alternative requirements. Furthermore, in a democratic society where social power is (in theory at least), widely diffused, the laws and conventions can be changed (again in theory at least) when there are sufficient numbers of persons who favour the change. Hence, their laws, their customs,—their social requirements—are in part their own doing. From the subjective point of view, therefore, their burden is much lighter than that of a savage. So much seems to be the sound element in Professor Ross's law.

With regard to the second law that "the character of social requirement changes with every shifting of social power," this again seems to contain a large element of truth. This is, in fact, what we more or less tacitly assume in sociological reasoning. But it is too indefinite to be much of a law. Take, for example, the perennial upheavals and revolutions in China, Greece, Portugal, and the Central American republics. Does their social requirement change with every revolution, or is it a case merely of tweedle-dum and tweedle-dee? Sometimes it looks one way, sometimes the other. Before the change is brought about, everything is vague; after the change has occurred, all is clear; and the law merely says that changes occur. Some changes, no doubt, occur with every shifting of social power; a tyrant may lose his head and his sycophants be put out of their jobs; but this is not saying much.

24. "The greater the ascendancy of the few, the more possible is it for social control to affect the course of the social movement." The reasons given for this law are as follows: "When the laws, standards, and ideals a man is required to conform to, spring up

among the plain people, they will be ahead of the community, but not very far ahead. But when they originate with the few, they may be very far in advance of the community and so hurrying it forward, or they may be far in the rear and hence holding it back. It is a well-known fact that we never find a legal or moral code pitched high above the natural inclination of a people without signs of minority dominations." Hence the law.[38]

25. "In general, the more distinct, knit together, and self-conscious the influential minority, the more likely is social control to be coloured with class selfishness." The reasons given for this law are as follows: "Classes differ in readiness to twist social control to their own advantage. Elders, élite, or genius have rarely abused their social power. But ecclesiasticism claims exemptions and privileges for the clergy, makes the word of the priest binding even when he is living in open sin, and grants for money indulgences to commit the most horrible crimes. When the fighting caste guides social opinion, it is permissible to mulct the husbandman and the merchant, and to condone the violence and sensuality of the men of the camp. Under the ascendancy of the rich and leisured, property becomes more sacred than person, moral standards vary with pecuniary status, and it is felt that 'God will think twice before He damns a person of quality.' "[39]

These two laws are moderate statements of general tendencies, with, as usual, lucid illustrations. I can only make them a little more plain by paraphrasing them. The first of these laws means that social conditions are affected, either for good or for ill, in proportion to the domination by the few: for good, when the dominating minority are superior like the class of the élite; and for ill, when they are inferior like the ignorant and bigoted reactionaries. A splendid truism! In the second law which reads, "In general, the more distinct, knit together, and self-conscious the influential minority, the more likely is social control to be

[38] *Ibid.*, p. 85.　　　　　[39] *Ibid.*, p. 86.

coloured with class selfishness," a substitution for one word may make it a truism, namely the word "self-conscious." By "self-conscious" Professor Ross here does seem to mean "selfish"; hence, the law may be rephrased to read: "In general, the better organized and the more selfish is the dominating minority, the more likely is the social control to be coloured with class selfishness,"—which is another truism.

26. "All institutions having to do with control change reluctantly, change slowly, change tardily, and change within sooner than without."[40]

I suppose this law needs little explanation, except possibly the last clause which bears a striking resemblance to one of Tarde's Laws of Imitation. All institutions of social control such as custom, convention, law and religion, generally change reluctantly, because a change in them almost always runs against somebody's interest, and therefore invites opposition from those whose interests are at stake. They change slowly because a sudden change undermines their prestige. The Roman Catholic church, the Holy Roman Empire and the Japanese imperial house, all set up claims of supernatural or divine origin because even the length of their mere existence is impressive. The Supreme Court of the United States has often shown courage in rendering decisions which conflicted with its previous decisions and in reversing the judgments of the lower courts, but in doing so it frequently invited criticism and helped to undermine the prestige of the august tribunal. Hence, it is considered a bad policy to change institutions suddenly, and a wise policy to preserve the external identity even when the internal meaning has long since gone to the dust. And since the world is governed most of the time by wise men, institutions of social control change slowly, or at least it looks that way.

The institutions change tardily because the reformers are always in a hurry, while God is not. They change from within

[40] *Ibid.*, p. 192.

sooner than from without (with some exceptions), for the meaning of a custom or a convention changes generally before a
formal change is adopted. One might go on saying in the same
strain that they change faster in a progressive nation than in a
stagnant nation, though not every change is a progress; that their
change is generally more welcome to the "have-nots" than to the
"haves"; that their change is more enthusiastically advocated by
the long-haired men and the short-haired women than by the
high-hatted men and high-toned ladies, and so on and so forth.
But in spite of all this, catastrophic changes do occur, of which
the reforms of Peter the Great, mass conversions to Christianity,
and the Islamic conquests during the seventh and eighth centuries, are a few of the conspicuous examples.

27. "The doing of work by religious beliefs tends to weaken
or deform them."[41] The author's explanation of this law is
rather difficult to present intelligibly in a few sentences. His
meaning seems to be somewhat as follows: There are two
branches of belief which the author styles as "ethical religion" as
distinguished from the "mystical." One of these two branches is
"legal religion," the root of which is the spontaneous feeling of
piety of the primitive man for the head of the patriarchal family;
"a sentiment of mingled awe, respect, and confidence." The
other is "social religion," the root of which is the "feeling of
sympathy with other members of the family." Social religion is
defined as "the conviction that there is a bond of ideal relationship between the members of a society and the feelings that arise
in consequence of this conviction."[42] The root of legal religion
being fear, it promotes ego-centric activities, while the root of
social religion being love, it promotes altruistic interests. "To
put others on an equal footing with self, to love them, to refrain
from using them as instruments to his own schemes, to admit in
them every claim he makes for himself," these are said to be the
ideal of a social religion. But "there is only a fraction, perhaps a

[41] *Ibid.*, p. 209.   [42] *Ibid.*, pp. 198-99.

small fraction, of any population that can be reached and regenerated in this way! For the common run of persons only the nomistic side of belief is effective for control. Hence social religion, though it loathes legal religion, has never been able to shake itself free. The scheme of supernatural rewards and punishments is too useful to be dispensed with, and after every epoch of freshening and purifying of religious emotion, legal religion quietly slips back into her old place and takes up her old tasks.

"In some instances a conviction unlocks great natural stores of ethical-religious energy. But in general, we can say that an improvement of character and conduct by beliefs running counter to natural inclination is a doing of work; and we can lay down the law that the doing of work by religious beliefs tends to weaken or deform them."[43] In other words, "an improvement of character and conduct by beliefs running counter to natural inclination" tends to "weaken and deform" such beliefs. Why weaken and deform them? The reason which the author gives seems to be that the "majority of those whose lives are shaped by social religion must receive constant stimulation, if they are not to lapse into lukewarmness and moral deadness. The life of every church shows a curious wave like alternation of ardor with chill due to the abundance or lack of men gifted in a religious way." With regard to "weakening" and "deforming" the author says that the "most common path of degeneration is from the ethical to the ceremonial. The substitution of worship for right-doing, of outer purity for inner purity, of many scrupulous, God-pleasing observances for the far heavier burden of a brotherly behavior toward the fellow-man, is the inevitable fate of social religion."[44] In other words, the majority of the religious populace need periodic inspiration by great religious leaders. So long as this inspiration lasts, their character and conduct are improved, but as soon as it evaporates they follow their "natural inclination" which is

[43] *Ibid.*, p. 209.   [44] *Ibid.*, pp. 209-10.

presumably bad. Therefore there are mechanical ups and downs in the standard of their character and conduct.

In this discussion the author has made an attempt to analyse the psychological background of religion, and to deduce a law from the common phenomena of religious revivals. It should at once be conceded that there are in religious institutions the tendencies of "weakening" and "deforming" referred to above. These tendencies are so strong that one often finds religious institutions, the spirit of which has long since gone, while mere ritualism, the husk of the spirit, alone remains. From the impressionistic point of view, therefore, there are in the religious spirit of the people mechanical ups with the presence of religious leaders, and mechanical downs with their absence. But behind these "wave like alternations of ardor with chill," and even behind the religious leaders themselves, there are some fundamental "forces" which bring about these changes. As a transient phenomenon, the presence of the hell-fire theologians generally has some effect, but it is ephemeral; and if repeated frequently, the endeavor loses its efficacy. For even the ignorant do not like to be scared twice by the same trick. Further, the phenomenon of alternate ardor and chill is not a mechanical swing, but is rather a dialectical movement. The chilling of the religious zeal and the decay of religious institutions are to some extent the necessary steps toward progress, and in so far as they are necessary, they leave behind them certain elements of their own which grow together with the new, or as a part of the new synthesis.[45]

Independently of Professor Giddings' theories of association, various other alleged laws of association have appeared in sociological literature, of which the following is an example:

28. "Association in equality is the law of progress. Association frees mental power for expenditure in improvement, and equality, or justice, or freedom—for the terms here signify the

---

[45] See discussion on Dialectical Laws, Chapter VIII.

same thing, the recognition of the moral law—prevents the dissipation of this power in fruitless struggles. Here is the law of progress, which will explain all diversities, all advances, all halts, and retrogressions. Men tend to progress just as they come closer together, and by coöperation with each other increase the mental power that may be devoted to improvement, but just as conflict is provoked, or association develops inequality of condition and power, this tendency to progression is lessened, checked, and finally reversed."[46]

That "association in equality," whatever it be, has something to do with progress, may be granted. But to cap it with the high-sounding title the "law of human progress," or to boast that it will explain "all diversities, all advances, all halts and retrogressions," is a rhetorical flourish rather than a scientific statement. The social scientists should look askance at such a law, as honest doctors do at any prescription which is advertised to be the sovereign remedy for all diseases and ailments. There are other factors besides association, which are indispensable to progress, such as rivalry, and even conflict if occasion demands it. As for the questions, what is meant by "human progress" and "association in equality," and in what sense "equality," "justice," and "freedom," all "signify the same thing," to these the author gives no answer.

In opposition to this easy-going view of progress through association, is the following "law of social antagonism":

29. "The social organism comes into existence, and soon the world's surface becomes covered with active specimens of this new creation. As soon as these organisms become really self-conscious, they become self-assertive; and as soon as they become self-assertive, in accordance with nature's established principle, they begin to fight. . . . This is a generalization so universally true of historical and progressive times that its force is in no way

impaired by a few instances that have been discovered of more or less amicable relations between social groups at a certain unprogressive stage of social development."[47]

The author is evidently easy-going in treating exceptions, as well as dogmatic in his assertions. For, unless one is prepared to defend the scandalously loose formula that "the exception proves the rule," how could one say that the validity of this "law" is "in no way impaired by a few instances" of exceptions? Is it not exceptions, if anything, which go to disprove a scientific law? Why is fighting "in accordance with nature's established principle"? Is it because men fight? They fight because it is "in accordance with nature's established principle 'to fight' as soon as they become self-conscious." It is "in accordance with nature's established principle" to fight "as soon as they become self-conscious," because they do fight! A naïve specimen of circular reasoning! It was once said that there was an instinct of war, but nowadays no psychologist of reputation, I suppose, would maintain such a proposition.

After these two violently antithetical laws, one of association and the other of conflict, one might feel relieved to hear that there is a "law of the double aspect of the people." This law, as applied to politics, is said to be as follows:

30. "The people can not grasp all the particulars of a general proposition, though when a single one of these particulars is detached and presented to them for decision, the matter is brought within the compass of their minds and they are able to decide, sometimes wisely, but at any rate, to decide."[48]

The author quotes Machiavelli to support his argument even though Machiavelli himself declares apparently the contrary.[49] The author's meaning seems to be that the judgment of the people can not be relied upon in matters requiring a high degree

[47] Hugh Taylor, *Origin of Government*, pp. 75-76.
[48] George W. Walthew, *The Philosophy of Government*, p. 47.
[49] *Ibid.*, p. 78.

of generalization, and that in such matters they should follow the guidance of their leader whom he elsewhere declares to be "the one best able to interpret the National Soul and carry into effect the ordinary development of the national life."[50]   That there is a certain large element of truth in this law can not be doubted. The people in general, like over-grown children, are fond of concrete particulars which alone seem real to them; their mastery of abstract generalities is a comparatively later development.   But is it not also true that the people are equally helpless in matters requiring a high degree of specialization and technical skill?   The people may all vote for an honest government and efficient public service, but they know little of the technical questions involved in these.   Hence, the people are weak at both ends; they can not be trusted either with too abstract general problems or with too special ones, but only with everyday, common problems.   The law of "the double aspect of the people," as it now stands, is an incomplete analysis of this commonplace observation.

LAWS BASED ON PSYCHOLOGICAL ANALYSES WITH IMITATION AS
THEIR CENTRAL PRINCIPLE

Gabriel Tarde is such an illustrious name in the history of sociology that some detailed treatment of his famous Laws of Imitation seems desirable.   By imitation the author meant "the action at a distance of one mind upon another," and the "action which consists of a quasi-photographic reproduction of a cerebral image upon the sensitive plate of another brain" (or of the same brain, if it is a question of imitation of self).   Again: "By imitation I mean every impression of an inter-psychical photography, so to speak, willed or not willed, passive or active."[51]

Imitation thus defined is said to be one of the three principal forms of universal repetition: undulation in the physical realm, heredity in the biological, and imitation in the social.   Society

[50] Ibid., pp. 108-9, 116.
[51] Laws of Imitation, p. xiv.

itself is declared to be imitation; and imitation, "a kind of somnambulism."[52] Nay, "the whole, the only thing which is of interest to history" is proclaimed to be "the career of imitations." For "there is no truly historic fact outside of those that can be classed in one of the following three categories: (a) the progress or decay of some kind of imitation; (b) the appearance of one of those combinations of different imitations which I call invention, and which come in time to be imitated; (c) the actions either of human beings, or of animal, vegetal or physical forces, which result in the imposition of new conditions upon the spread of certain imitations whose bearing and direction are thereby modified."[53] These three categories Tarde called Imitation, Invention, and Opposition respectively; elsewhere he renamed them Repetition, Adaptation, and Opposition.[54]

Science deals, says Tarde, only with quantities or, in more general terms, with the resemblances and repetitions of phenomena, and all resemblance is due to repetition. All resemblances in the physical world—the dance of atoms, the waves of light, the concentric attraction of heavenly bodies—can be explained solely by periodic and, for the most part, vibratory motions. All resemblances between vital organisms result from hereditary transmission, from either intra- or extra-organic reproduction. All resemblances of social origin are the direct or indirect fruit of the various forms of imitation—custom-imitation, fashion-imitation, sympathy-imitation, obedience-imitation, precept-imitation, education-imitation, naïve-imitation, deliberate imitation.[55] In his later work the author says that the general laws governing imitative repetition are to sociology "what the laws of habit and heredity are to biology, the laws of gravitation to astronomy, and the laws of vibration to physics."[56]

The general laws governing imitative repetition may be stated under nine headings although there is some doubt as to the exact

[52] Ibid., p. 87.
[53] Ibid., p. 139.
[54] Social Laws.
[55] Laws of Imitation, p. 14.
[56] Social Laws, p. 61.

number. Two of them are always associated with the name of Tarde, and four others are more or less frequently quoted, while the remaining three are rarely mentioned. I present them in the order in which the author presented them:

1. "In the absence of interference, imitation spreads in a geometrical progression."

2. "Imitation is refracted by the medium."

These two are commonly known as the "laws of the spread of imitation." The center of imitation is invention which Tarde conceives as a combination of imitations. From this center imitation tends to spread in concentric circles, like the ripples started by a stone dropped into the water; and like the ripples, too, which diminish in size as they recede, imitation grows weaker as it spreads farther. Other things being equal, the denser the medium through which imitation has to pass, the more rapid is its progressions, as is shown by the greater speed with which a fashion is adopted or a craze is imitated in the commercial and industrial centers than in the rural districts. Where the opportunities for contact are many and communication is convenient, where popular education is effective and democratic institutions are rooted, where class conflict is minimized and a certain uniformity of social ideals prevails, the spread of imitation will approximately conform to the first of these laws. But as a matter of fact, such ideal conditions rarely obtain; indeed, the opposite of all these conditions is more normal: hence the second law of imitation, that imitations are stopped, modified or fused with one another as they pass into new environment. This law is typically illustrated in language by Grimm's law of linguistic refraction, in religion by schisms and reformations, in politics by the diverse forms of parliamentary government.[57]

The next and most specific question is why, given a number of inventions conceived all about the same time, a great majority

[57] Tarde, *Laws of Imitation,* pp. 20-33.

of them are dropped, while only a few of them are successfully imitated and surviving? Tarde answers that this is due to two species of social causes, namely, the logical and the extra-logical. By a logical social cause he means the rational cause, such as the preference of one innovation to another because of its greater utility or its greater harmony with some accepted principles. By an extra-logical social cause he means any irrational cause, opposed to the logical. There are, according to Tarde, three logical laws of imitation, to wit:

3. *The Thesis.* Everything which is invented or imitated is an idea, a belief or a desire. An idea which is meagre at first may continue to spread by accretion of or alliance with new ideas of the same sort; the alliance reënforces the original idea so as to spread with greater vigor. In a strongly conservative country and among the ignorant mass, the mere length of survival and the distance traversed are sufficient to clothe the idea with venerableness and prestige, and to cause it to be blindly imitated.

4. *The Antithesis.* But everything has its antithesis, or as Tarde puts it, "everything in history is a logical duel"; and every successful adversary affirms his own thesis at the same time that he denies that of his opponent. A successful adversary never merely denies the thesis of his opponent, but always affirms positive theses of his own. In the face of the antithesis, the contradiction is solved either by suppression of the opponent, or by:

5. *Synthesis,* "the logical union" by means of which the contending parties are reconciled, enabling them both to survive. "There are two ways of imitating, as a matter of fact, namely, to act exactly like one's model, or to do exactly the contrary. Hence the necessity of those divergences which Spencer points out without explaining in his law of progressive differentiation. Nothing can be affirmed without suggesting, no matter how simple the social environment, not only the idea that is affirmed, but the negation of this idea as well. This is the reason why the supernatural, in asserting itself through theologies, suggests natural-

ism, its negation. This is the reason why the affirmation of idealism gives birth to the idea of materialism; why the establishment of monarchy engenders the idea of republicanism. . . . Every positive affirmation, at the same time that it attracts to itself mediocre and sheep-like minds, arouses somewhere or other in a brain that is naturally rebellious,—this does not mean naturally inventive,—a negation that is diametrically opposite and of about equal strength. This reminds one of inductive currents in physics. But both kinds of brains have the same content of ideas and purposes. They are associated, although they are adversaries, or rather, because they are adversaries."[58]

Besides these three logical laws of imitation, there are also four extra-logical laws which, according to Tarde, together with the logical laws determine imitative choices.

6. Imitation spreads from the inner to the outer man; or more precisely, imitation of ideas precedes that of their expression, and imitation of ends that of means. The imitation of the spirit of the age or of the race precedes the imitation of its arts and culture. Submission to religious dogmas precedes the practice of the rites, and loyalty to a great leader the obedience to his commands. Furthermore, even after the spirit which gave rise to imitation has passed away, imitation generally continues much longer. There are many customs, the spirit of which has long since fled and the dead husk alone still lingers; others only partially dead go on living "in a state of self-mutilation and suicide until the moment when some new spirit succeeds them." These tendencies seem to be true when imitation is rational. But there are exceptions in the province of irrational imitation, such as the children's imitation of adult manners without understanding the meaning, or the great masses of Catholics and Buddhists submitting themselves to rituals of mystery without comprehending what they are about.

---

[58] Tarde, *Laws of Imitation*, pp. xvii-xviii, 140-93.

7. Imitation proceeds from the superior to the inferior. The imitation of parents by children, of teachers by disciples, of patricians by plebeians, are the typical examples. The passion to imitate the superior is so great that, when it is arbitrarily restrained, violent reactions are some times precipitated. Every Englishman is said to admire the Lords; and one of the worst grievances of the eighteenth-century French Revolutionists was that they were not allowed to ape the manners of the nobility. Much of hero-worship is probably due to this tendency to imitate superiors. But there are contrary examples to this law. Great religious movements were initiated by persons of humble origin; epoch-making inventions were made usually by some obscure toiler; the European Whites learned to smoke from the American Reds; slang expressions almost always originate in the slum and the disreputable quarters and travel up to high-toned society. Tarde, however, shuts his eyes to these contradictions and says that "in society, the radiation of examples from above to below is the only fact worth consideration, because of the general leveling which it tends to produce in the human world."[59] Elsewhere he says that social superiority does not always consist of political and economic superiority. "The superiority which is imitated is the superiority which is understood; and that which is understood is what is believed or seen to be conducive to benefits which are appreciated because they satisfy certain wants. . . . The qualities which make a man superior in any country and at any period are those which enable him to understand the group of discoveries and to make use of the group of inventions which have already appeared."[60]

8. Imitation proceeds from custom to convention, for example, the imitation of the past precedes that of present. A race sufficient unto itself and completely shut away from outside influence, rigidly adheres to its ancestral traditions; when its eyes and ears

[59] *Ibid.,* p. 215.   [60] *Ibid.,* pp. 233-35.

are opened to foreign culture, first it resists, then half compromises, or is forced to submit to the new order. In any event, the new cultural elements adopted generally fuse with the old, and as time goes on become conventionalized and gain respectability. This law is illustrated in language by the rhythm of the diffusion of idioms; in religion by the progress from exclusivism through proselytism to cosmopolitanism; in politics by the periodic swings from despotism to demogogism and a temporary settlement in some sort of liberalism.

9. Imitation proceeds from the unilateral to the reciprocal. The medieval system of decrees developed into the modern system of contract. The Roman ideals of proper relationship between husband and wife are being replaced by the Lucy Stone League ideals. These are a few of the illustrations of the law. But is there any necessity for these changes? Tarde seems to say, yes, because only in this way can the spread of imitation and invention be made most rapid and progress at its maximum rate be secured. Two small qualifications to this law seem necessary. First, this law could apply only to those acts which require mutuality. Secondly, it could apply fully only where democratic institutions, rather than a caste system, prevail.

I have presented Tarde's laws as fully as I can within a reasonable limit of space. The sweep of Tarde's generalization and the wealth of his illustrations make the laws fit to be ranked with Comte's law of three stages. There can be no doubt that these laws, like Comte's, are great philosophical generalizations. And like all other sweeping generalizations, they have defects. I shall briefly suggest several points of criticism:

(a) *Equivocation.* Tarde recognizes the differences between imitation, opposition and invention. He says, for example, "Only imitation and not invention is subject to laws in the true sense of the word."[61] He points out that statistics can deal only with

[61] *Ibid.,* p. 142.

imitations and their regularity, but not with inventions which must precede imitation, and without which no imitation can exist.[62] But in his eagerness to give prominence to imitation he defines opposition as "a very special kind of repetition," and he defines invention as "combinations of different imitations."[63] The first of these two definitions smacks of the Hegelian logic of identity of contradictories; indeed, the whole chapter on the "Logical Laws of Imitation" strongly savours of Hegelism. As to the second, if we were to say that invention is a combination of different imitations, should we not place emphasis on the word "combination" rather than "imitation"? By shifting the emphasis from "combination" to "imitation" Tarde is guilty of what amounts to a "fallacy of accent." Further: does any one invent any thing of much use by merely combining imitations? It seems more reasonable to say that invention or creative activity always involves some measure of free self-expression. Even mechanical inventions are not a matter of mere combination, but rather some specific kinds of combination such as are fit to yield utility.

(b) *Exaggeration.* Tarde's definition of society as "imitation," and imitation as "a kind of somnambulism," and his statement that "the whole, the only thing which is of interest to history" is "the career of imitation," are a literary man's exaggerations.[64] Imitation can, at the most, assure us continuity; and it is only the backward and stagnant races and the superannuated aristocracy everywhere, to whom social continuity is the only important thing. In fact, if it is true, as Tarde says, that all imitations are refracted by their media, they are doomed to die out sooner or later, and what keeps them alive are inventions and oppositions, which either through compromise or through alliance with imitation form new centers of imitation.

---

[62] *Ibid.*, p. 137.
[63] *Social Laws*, p. 86; *Laws of Imitation*, p. 139.
[64] *Ibid.*, pp. 87, 139, and *passim.*

(c) Geometrical Progression. Since Malthus propounded the geometrical metaphor, various social scientists have tried to make extensive use of it: Tarde is one and Giddings another. But the difference between Malthus' use of the metaphor and Tarde's use of it is great. Malthus was dealing with the question of the number of mouths, and since Socrates had one mouth and Crito had one, the saint has one mouth and the villain also one, so far as the number is concerned, the geometrical metaphor is tolerable. Furthermore, the present day Malthusians do not attach much importance to the geometrical metaphor in Malthus' formula, since they do not wish to be understood to imply any mathematical precision.[65] But Tarde is dealing with social phenomena which are far from being capable of quantitative measurement. In the spread of social phenomena, refraction rather than simple repetition is the more normal occurrence. It is appropriate to use the geometrical metaphor in describing physical phenomena such as the radiation of heat. It is tolerable to us the metaphor in describing biological propagation. But it is very crude to use the metaphor in describing social phenomena.

(d) Exceptions. From the point of view of positivists the last four of the nine laws presented above are of greater interest than the first five which are more sweeping. But unfortunately even these four admit exceptions as indicated already.

(e) No Explanation. Some thirty years ago when psychology was in its infancy, many writers, including William James, thought that there was an "instinct of imitation." But today there is scarcely any psychologist of reputation who would admit such an instinct. We can not explain imitation by imitation: the causal factors beneath the imitative phenomena must be looked for elsewhere. Present-day psychologists recognize only a part of what Tarde called imitation as imitation proper. A considerable part of what Tarde called imitation is properly conditioned cir-

---

[65] See, for example, T. N. Carver, *Principles of National Economy.*

cular response.[66] Another considerable part of what Tarde called imitation is what is nowadays called suggestion or the formation of attitudes and the release or heightening of the psycho-physical tendencies.[67] A third considerable part of what Tarde called imitation is merely the generalized name for the large body of subconscious or automatic habits, our routine devices to economize time and energy. Persons of similar habits generally respond alike, under suitable conditions, to the same stimulus, without imitating one another. It is in this province of automatic and individual responses that the greatest degree of uniformity prevails and lures the positivists into pitfalls. Finally there is a body of behavior which consists in deliberate copying of the model or in deliberate following of the directions. Tarde uses the word imitation loosely. One absorbing problem of social psychologists since the days of Tarde has been to ascertain more carefully what imitation is, and to reformulate more precisely, if possible, the laws of imitation. A great synthesis like Tarde's laws of imitation, of course, has its proper value, but it needs also to be carefully analysed and explained. Causal control of social phenomena is possibly only when one has penetrated beyond their superficial resemblances, and has assigned to each of them its specific cause.

(f) Psychological and Ethical Inadequacy. Psychologically the purer types of imitation are simple linear responses, the stimuli for which proceed always in the same direction.[68] But the linear reactions of the purer types are comparatively rare, such as the relation between a master and his slaves, between Dr. Johnson and Boswell, and between Napoleon and the Imperial Guard; but even Boswell was not a perfect imitator. Few if any people like to be merely ordered about; and most persons prefer the game of give-and-take, which is a circular reaction.

[66] See F. H. Allport, *Social Psychology*, pp. 40, 183.
[67] *Ibid.*, pp. 242-52; see also below, pp. 180f., for Professor Faris's laws.
[68] F. H. Allport, *op. cit.*, pp. 35-41.

Ethically, the ideals of slavish loyalty or blind conformity are now a thing of the past. A slave is one who gives everything and takes nothing in return; a tyrant is one who takes everything and gives nothing in return. All fruitful ethical human relations must involve some measure of reciprocity.

Simultaneously with Tarde, Professor Baldwin formulated a more accurate theory of imitation. While appreciating the importance of imitation, he was free from Tarde's habit of exaggeration. Imitation, according to Professor Baldwin, is simply one of the great socializing functions, instead of being "the whole, the only thing which is of interest to history." It is the medium through which social heredity is transmitted and perpetuated. Of all animals man is least ready-made at birth, least fit to cope with the severities of nature. He is to be very largely remade. Hence, prolongation of infancy is greatest in the human species. After the natural infancy is over, it is extended artificially. Modern education is essentially in the nature of artificial prolongation of infancy, during which the student is left in a state of semi-irresponsibility and of imitation. His personality can grow only by assimilating his social heritage.

But this process of growth is not one of mere imitation in the sense of mechanical repetition; it consists of a cumulative series of self projections,—a conscious process in which one places oneself in others' situations and interprets their meaning, and having discovered their values, makes them his own. Such a new acquisition becomes a part of psychic life, and thenceforth enters as a determining factor of one's value-attitudes, of further processes of growth through self-projection. The whole process is thus cumulative. On the other hand, not every object of perception is *ipso facto* a candidate for assimilation. As a conscious being, the individual continually evaluates the objects of his perception as either good or bad. The former he imitates and makes a part of himself. The latter he criticizes and rejects.

Hence, there is a continual antithesis in the development processes of an individual personality and of society. Hence, Professor Baldwin too has conceived the growth of the individual and of society as a dialectical process.[69]

Another important development of the concept of imitation is that of Professor Cooley. Professor Cooley prefers the word "suggestion" to imitation for the reason that the former is less ambiguous than the latter. He contrasts suggestion with choice. By the former he means a simple mechanical repetition; by the latter a deliberate, and in varying degrees complex, process of creative synthesis. But, he adds, that this distinction is one of degree rather than one of kind: the latter is an extension of the former. "Choice is a central area of light and activity upon which our eyes are fixed; while the unconscious is a dark, illimitable background enveloping this area."[70] This view seems strengthened by both the genetic studies of children and the monistic hypothesis of the identity of the subconscious with the conscious. It is a common mistake to suppose that children mechanically imitate adults; they exert a great deal of effort to understand and to repeat what they see. Further, they rarely repeat exactly what they see, except perhaps by coincidence. It seems, then, that all suggestions and choices involve some exertion of effort. Beneath the surface of apparent mechanicality of suggestion, there lies the substratum of subconscious value-attitudes, by which the stimuli are interpreted and responses thereto are determined. When our attention is heightened, our action is deliberate; when it is lowered, our action is semi-automatic; when we abandon ourselves to pure passivity, our self is lost. In the upper extreme we have creative activity for which no law has yet been discovered; in the lower extreme the discovery of laws is out of question. It is only in the provinces of semi-

[69] J. M. Baldwin, *Social and Ethical Interpretations*, p. 512.
[70] C. H. Cooley, *Human Nature and the Social Order*, p. 67.

automatic behavior that a certain rough and transient uniformity prevails.

Another notable development of the concept is that of Professor McDougall. Professor McDougall thinks that imitation together with suggestion and sympathy constitute the "three forms of mental interaction of fundamental importance for all social life, both of men and animals. . . . When some presentation, idea, or belief of the agent directly induces a similar presentation, idea, or belief in the patient, the process is called one of suggestion; when an affective or emotional excitement of the agent induces a similar affective excitement in the patient, the process is one of sympathy or sympathetic induction of emotion or feeling; when the most prominent result of the process of inter-action is the assimilation of the bodily movements of the patient to those of the agent, we speak of imitation."[71] He has, further, distinguished five varieties of imitation, similar to Professor Allport's distinctions as presented above in my discussion on Tarde's laws. Inasmuch as all scientific inquiries should properly begin with definitive concepts, such distinctions are of value. Recently Professor Faris gave out three definitions of imitation, under the imposing name of "laws of imitation." They are:

10. "Law of immediate, unwitting, imitation: Imitation in crowd behavior is limited to the releases of attitudes or tendencies already existing and which are not new."

11. "Law of the slow, unwitting type of imitation: When in rehearsing the past, emotional situations are re-enacted, taking the rôle of another sometimes gives rise to a new attitude, which is so like the attitude of the person that it is often called imitation."

12. "Law of conscious, volitional, deliberate imitation: When a purpose or ambition appears to be achieved or furthered by

[71] *Social Psychology*, p. 94.

acting like another, the result is the phenomenon known as conscious imitation."[72]

These are admirable definitions of the three types of imitation, stated in behavioristic terms, and are admirable beginnings for the students in search of true social laws.

In imitation of Tarde's laws, Professor Giddings also has formulated the following two "laws of impulsive social action":

13. "Impulsive social action tends to extend and to intensify in a geometrical progression."

14. "Impulsive social action varies inversely with the habit of attaining ends by indirect and complex means."[73]

Professor Giddings contrasts "impulsive social action" with critical and rational. It may be taken to mean emotional, irrational, automatic or semi-automatic behavior such as the behavior of the bird which has flown into a room and which is in vain fluttering round the room to get out. The first of these two laws, since it confines itself within the sphere of irrational and semi-automatic behavior, is a much narrower one than Tarde's first law of imitation; but their kinship in phraseology is recognizable. Various studies of mob-behavior seem to confirm the observation that an excited mob, under suitable conditions, tends to behave approximately according to the geometrical progression described above. As to the second law of "impulsive social action," it is but a tautological statement of what rational behavior presumably is. The behavior of children, of savages, and of men of the muscular-motor type with a violent temper, seem to be governed by their instinctive drives and emotional tendencies. Rationality or intelligence begins only when some effort is made to control the instinctive drives and emotional tendencies by selective reasoning.

Tarde's famous laws not only stimulated theoretical interest in the phenomenon of imitation, but also excited certain persons

[72] "Laws of Imitation," *American Journal of Sociology*, XXXII (No. 3), pp. 367-78.
[73] *Inductive Sociology*, pp. 175-77.

to read in them the justification for certain actual policies of the state. Miss Simon's "laws of social assimilation," based on Tarde's laws, evidently had such a practical end in view. She defines social assimilation as "that process of adjustment or accommodation which occurs between members of two different races, if their contact is prolonged and if the necessary psychic conditions are present." She further intimates that "figuratively speaking, it is the process by which the aggregation of peoples is changed from a mere mechanical mixture to a chemical compound." She then lays down the following five laws of social assimilation:

15. "The greater the number of points of contact between the races, the more rapid will be the assimilation, and conversely."

16. "When the planes of culture differ, the higher element tends to predominate over the lower, even though the higher culture is possessed by the conquered people."

17. "The nearer the planes of culture, the greater will be the interaction."

18. "Other things being the same, the more equal the two elements in mass, the more reciprocal will be their action; hence the effect of assimilating forces varies inversely with the compactness of the passive element."

19. "The more intense its race-consciousness, the greater the resistance of the passive element, and possibly the greater its counter-influence; but this consciousness may be so intense as to prevent all assimilation."[74]

Miss Simon continues with the statement that the obstacles to assimilation are: "(a) lack of vital circulation in society, owing to the difficulty of intercourse; (b) strong barriers of religion or tradition which prevent interclass assimilation and cause monopoly of civilization by the ruling minority; (c) exclusion of a

[74] S. Simon, "Social Assimilation," *American Journal of Sociology*, VI (May, 1901), 807. This discussion is continued in the *American Journal of Sociology* from May, 1901, to January, 1902, inclusive.

majority from participation in military and political life; *(d)* mal-
administration of justice, which grants political and social privileges to some, and imposes corresponding restrictions on others;
(e) predominance of custom over mode imitation; and *(f)* persistence of group feeling in the passive element." The last is said
to be due to "consciousness of belonging to a *Kulturvolk;* a
culture so foreign that there is no common meeting-ground;
segregation, and persistence of the foreign language."[75]

Miss Simon attempts to support these laws by a comprehensive
survey of the various forms of assimilation, racial, religious, etc.,
from the ancient world down to the present. The wealth of her
information relevant to the subject and the lucidity of her illustrations are truly impressive.[76] Although the metaphor of
"chemical compound" and the concept of reciprocity appear both
in the definition of social assimilation and in the illustration of
the laws, these laws are based principally on Tarde's laws of
imitation. She traces the development of the concept of imitation
back to Sir Henry Maine, Bagehot, and other writers before
Tarde; and like Tarde she employs several important concepts
rather uncritically; she could not, perhaps, very well have helped
it, since the publication of these articles antedated the recent
developments in psychology. As far as empirical laws go, these
are good laws, but like all other empirical laws they need critical
analysis and a continued search for causal connections. She
speaks of the "necessary psychic conditions" for assimilation,
"racial consciousness," and "Kulturvolk." She asserts that the
"psychic forces causing the response of the passive element to the
environment are: *(a)* power of appreciation—not apathy; *(b)* ambition—desire to imitate; and *(c)* power to imitate; and that from
these "it is easily seen that the proximate cause of assimilation,
both spontaneous and purposive, is imitation."[77] But these are

[75] *Ibid.*, p. 822.
[76] See "Social Assimilation," *American Journal of Sociology*, VII (No. 5).
[77] "Social Assimilation," *American Journal of Sociology*, VI (No. 6), 817.

literary renderings of the commonplace views. There being no such thing as an "instinct of imitation" or an "instinct of appreciation," if a person is found to be unassimilable, his unassimilability can not be due to the absence of the instincts of imitation and appreciation. We have to look for the causes of unassimilability elsewhere than in the mere fact of unassimilability. As for the concept of "race-consciousness," its status is far from secure, and it can be safely used only as a purely descriptive term for the body of cultural traits acquired after birth.

Miss Simon's fifth law is a case in point. It reads: "The more intense its race-consciousness, the greater the resistance of the passive element, and possibly the greater its counter-influence; but this consciousness may be so intense as to prevent all assimilation." In other words, if the race-consciousness of the active element is very strong, and that of the passive element is very weak, assimilation of the latter by the former might be an easy task. If the race-consciousness of both elements is about equal, assimilation of each element by the other, or interpenetration, is presumably the normal occurrence. If the race-consciousness of the active element is much weaker than that of the passive, there will be presumably a counter-assimilation, as the examples of cultural assimilation of the Germanic invaders by the Romans and of the Mongolian conquerors by the Chinese. But how strong a race-consciousness is a strong enough race-consciousness to assimilate others? And how weak a race-consciousness is weak enough to be assimilated by others?

Miss Simon says: "The Chinese is so utterly out of the sphere of thought of the western man that his non-assimilation to occidental culture seems a well-nigh foregone conclusion. The ideals of the Chinese are diametrically opposed to those of the western man; there are no common culture bonds between the two races; there is no possibility of agreement as to a viewpoint for matters essential to a common life. Hence, since all this precludes the formation of fellowship feeling, there can be no assimilation."[78] Again: "The Chinese may be regarded as practically non-assimilable with western races. The greatest barrier to their assimilation is, perhaps, to be found in the wonderful physical and social unity that exists among them. This unity in race, language, literature, laws, and structure of society has been solid for scores of generations, and the task of overcoming it through contact with western civilization seems hopeless. How far soever he may be from home, the Chinaman always clings to his own land and hopes to go back, for the superstition that he must be buried in the sacred soil of China never leaves him."[79] From these arguments she proceeds to justify Chinese exclusion, and triumphantly concludes: "For the Chinese do not assimilate with the whites. There is no potential resemblance—no consciousness of kind— between the two peoples. Hence sympathy and like-mindedness are impossible. Western civilization makes little impression on the Chinese, for he has no sense of inferiority, and consequently no desire to imitate the life about him. Race-consciousness is so strong among the Chinese, tradition and custom are so binding upon them, that they have no appreciation of a life different from that to which they have been accustomed. Here is an instance in which race-consciousness is so intense as to prevent all assimilation."[80]

This certainly is a remarkable demonstration. But has she proved her point? The substance of her argument appears to be this: The Chinese are not assimilable, because they have too strong a race-consciousness; the Chinese have too strong a race-consciousness, because they never can be assimilated. Is it not a circular argument? The root of the difficulty lies in the misunderstanding of the imitative phenomena. No man is born with a ready-made *race consciousness* any more than with a re-

<hr>

[78] *Ibid.*, p. 799.
[79] "Social Assimilation," *American Journal of Sociology*, VII (No. 4), 539-40.
[80] *Ibid.*, p. 542.

ligious dogma or with a party loyalty. These are all acquired through education and habit-formation.

1. Incomplete Unification. The near-causal laws discussed in the last two chapters, in varying degrees, describe, analyse, and generalize, empirical observations; like all empirical observations they are true within certain limits. Their chief characteristics are that they generally make some attempts to analyse social phenomena in terms of the simpler sciences, such as psychology, or to deduce them from some unitary principles, such as imitation and the consciousness of kind. But such analyses and deductions as are made scarcely go beyond the level of observation, and fail to prove any invariability of the association of the several social phenomena described. They leave the social phenomena they describe relatively isolated from one another, as is shown by the numerous exceptions. This is a characteristic of empirical laws. If they are to be made causal laws, they should be unified on the basis of valid causal psychological laws. For, when the several empirical generalizations within the same science mutually contradict, there is evidently an incomplete unification, a lack of a valid theory by which the contradictions may be reconciled.

2. Tautological Explanations. Professor Giddings has been most painstaking in his attempt to found a system. But some of his laws are hardly more than tautologies. The value of a tautology is to make the reader familiar with the phenomena. It follows immediately that if any tautology fails to make the phenomena more familiar to the reader, its value is nil. But Professor Giddings' tautologies seem to be even worse: instead of rendering the things they are intended to explain more definite, they seem to make them less definite! Many a person may have some idea, however vague, as to what society is or what assimilation means. But few, I think, can readily understand what "social composition," "social constitution," "sympathetic like-mindedness," and such concepts mean. The attempt to explain "society" and "assimilation" in terms of "passion for homogeneity," "sympathetic like-mindedness," and the like, is an attempt to explain the more intelligible in terms of the less intelligible, like the lexicographer's definition of water as "a form, variety, or aspect of the fluid," which hardly gives any idea of water. As has been shown, a large proportion of social laws in the last analysis are circular statements.

3. Circular Statements. A circular statement becomes doubly objectionable when it is contradicted by facts. When it is said, for example, that war is due to an instinct of war, it makes war a preordained phenomenon, about which we can do nothing but fight. Similarly, when it is said that assimilation is due to an instinct of imitation, and that the Chinese are impossible to assimilate because they have no instinct of imitation, it is flatly contradicted by the fact that there are a great many Chinamen who do imitate. A circular statement of this type is bad also from the pragmatic point of view, because the contradictory evidences against it vitiate the controllability of the phenomena described.

4. Possibility of Pluralistic Developments. The foregoing laws are selective representations of social phenomena, and like a work of art, they rest their claim of validity on the judicious selection of examples. Professor Ross's personification of society (discussed above) is an interesting example of poetic imagination wrought into a scientific system. Selective representation varies according to the point of view, and same phenomena may be portrayed from different angles. The propagation of a new faith, for example, may be looked upon as a spread of imitation, or an expansion of the consciousness of kind, a triumph of the superior spiritual forces over the inferior, or a demonstration of its conduciveness to economic productivity. So far as hypothetical social sciences go, all these different points of view may be true. Hence,

the justness of Professor Cooley's remark, "In reading studies of
a particular aspect of life, like M. Tarde's brilliant work, *Les Lois
de l'Imitation,* it is well to remember that there are many such
aspects, any of which, if expounded at length and in an interesting manner, might appear for the time to be of more importance
than any other. I think that other phases of social activity, such,
for instance, as communication, competition, differentiation,
adaptation, idealization, have as good claims as imitation to be
regarded as the social process, and that a book similar in character to M. Tarde's might perhaps be written upon any one of
them. The truth is that the real process is a multiform thing of
which these are glimpses. They are good as long as we recognize
that they are glimpses and use them to help out our perception
of that many-sided whole which life is; but if they become doctrines they are objectionable."[81]

5. *Creative Imagination in Science.* As already intimated, a
scientist is an artist to the extent that in the selection of examples,
he is invariably guided by his creative imagination; the less exact
the science is the more does he rely on his imagination. The
social sciences being the least exact of all sciences, the various
systems are imaginative correlations of facts from different points
of view. The presentation of such a systematic construction often
gains vividness at the expense of accuracy. The vivid impression
which, for example, Tarde's laws of imitation leave on the mind
of the reader is partly due to the author's ignoring of certain
vital aspects in social phenomena such as leadership and opposition. The man of one idea often looks more convincing than
his level-headed antagonist of many ideas; and if he is capable of
rhetorical flourish, he often carries the assembly by storm. And
this is unfortunately the case at present with many a treatise on
social phenomena. The unification of the social sciences will be
achieved only when the several conflicting points of view are
subsumed under some one common point of view.

[81] *Human Nature and the Social Order,* pp. 302-3, footnote.

CHAPTER VIII
DIALECTICAL LAWS AS SYNTHESES

Historically the germ of the dialectical method may be traced to Socrates and Plato, who used a dialectical method of their own, for the purpose of refuting the views of their opponents. As they used it, it consisted of first destroying the thesis of an opponent by pointing out its self-contradictory nature, the antithesis, and then resolving both the thesis and the anti thesis in a synthesis. Kant's method of procedure in demonstrating the antinomies was in part dialectical, while Schelling's treatment of the self as a union of mutually contradicting tendencies was decidedly dialectical. But the philosopher who saw its fundamental importance as a method of investigation and who employed it with consummate skill was Hegel. According to this philosopher, everything in nature, whether high or low in the scale of development, seeks its opposite in order to transcend its own solitary nature. Every natural object is a polarity of mutually opposed tendencies, whose very opposition unites them: the attraction and repulsion of atoms, the polarity of the magnet, the behavior of positive and negative electricity, the active seeking and passive response of the sexes, the ascendant and submissive attitudes in the social behavior of animals as well as of men.

Every entity acquires status by virtue of its relation to its surroundings, by seeking out its opposite, and then by transcending the opposition. But the overcoming of the opposition is not the end, it merely serves as a link to another round of opposition and overcoming: and so the series extends to the Absolute. As applied to the progress of knowledge, this doctrine says that error is a necessary step toward knowledge. Without error, wisdom is impossible. Wisdom consists in conscious observation of one's own unwisdom and in rising above this unwisdom; without such illusion and error, one will forever remain a conceited fool. Furthermore, this swing of the pendulum from error to wisdom, from opposition to reconciliation, is not an accidental phenomenon, but is the very characteristic of our logic of passion, or in Hegel's language, is the "law of heart." For the self is conceived as a synthesis of antithetical tendencies. The synthetic self Hegel calls the Absolute which can manifest itself only in the form of a series of finite truths; and since every finite truth is incomplete, and if pushed far enough is self-contradictory, the Absolute alone can interrelate all finite truths and resolve their self-contradictory character. The life of the world is expressible in a series of finite forms each of which bears dialectical relations to the rest, and all of which can be reconciled in a synthesis on a higher level. The lower forms are necessary because without them the higher is logically impossible. The lower forms even independently persist and preserve their meanings, and when they are assimilated in a higher form, they stamp their indelible marks of individuality upon the organic whole, as is evidenced by the entire phenomenon of evolution.[1]

1. Dialectical Progress in Individual Development. Every man is a subconscious *Weltgeist* incarnate. The child, the savage, or the naïve egoist, is vaguely conscious that he is the Absolute-incarnate, and that the best way in which to establish this presumption is to destroy whomsoever obstructs his way. Hence even head-hunting among savages, fratricidal war among Mexican military adventurers, or the kicking of the stool which a child stumbles over, appears to them necessary,—necessary to their attainment of social consciousness. But sooner or later they find that this method of establishing their sovereignty is too costly. And therefore, instead of destroying their enemy, they enslave him and live on the fruit of his labour, as well as gratify their sense of superiority by giving orders and putting on airs.

---

[1] J. Royce, *Lectures on Modern Idealism*, Lectures III-V.

This is the method of the slave-master. It has many shades and gradations: in its most grotesque forms, the enslavement of women, the subjugation of serfs, the maintenance of a prostitute class, and the peonage of recent times; in its sublimated forms, the American heiress running unabashed after foreign princes and counts.

But sooner or later the slave-master comes to disillusionment: sometimes because he is ashamed of surfeited gluttony and unrestrained lust with their accompanying physical suffering, sometimes because he is seized with superstitious fears from which he can not escape by merely dedicating pyramids to the offended deities and by having the psalmists sing their praise. He may even be ashamed to see his own slaves; for his lawless freedom has led him into bondage, whereas his slaves work out their freedom through servitude. And thus there comes a stage of contrite or monkish consciousness. He may renounce all his worldly possessions and retire into a lonely hermitage, and brood over his sins like Gautama Buddha; or he may rhapsodize like the Hebrew skeptic: vanity, vanity, all is vanity, even his very aloofness is vanity. In either case his effort to free himself by mere renunciation and brooding is doomed to failure, because of the barrenness of all mere renunciation and brooding. He may perish in this vain effort at humility which is but another form of pride. But sometimes he returns to the world, like the persons in William James' *Varieties of Religious Experience,* with renewed zest for life.

Freed from the sickroom atmosphere, and full of enthusiasm for life, he now wishes others to share the same joy of living. And if this wish is strong enough, he imagines that he is inspired, and he sets out on a crusade to free the fettered and shackled. For a while his cause is the holy cause, and he himself is nothing short of a prophet, a knight-errant, or a new Moses. Will this last? Alas, no! This, too, is doomed to pass away. For sooner or later he finds that the world is full of mad

prophets, the Reverends Mike Monday and Elmer Gantry rub-
bing elbows with Jesus and Socrates. Thereupon he breaks
down: he is ashamed to own that he has been an unconscious
humbug. A self-confessed humbug, whither now should he
turn his head? Yet once more the unfailing dialectical swing
returns to the positive, for the satanic process of negation is
powerless to prevent the *Weltgeist* from re-incarnation, enriched
with new wisdom won by hard experience. The social order, it
now appears to him, which he but a little while ago so snobbishly
despised, is the objective manifestation of reason, even his own
reason; and the only sane attitude toward life is to accept the
world as his,—his to live in, his to work with, his to endow with
meaning and dignity. Thus the weary sinner, who has been
estranged from himself, is at last reconciled to the Absolute, the
Holy Ghost of Hegel, through illumination or the forgiveness of
sin. At no time in his career should he have said, "This is the
whole truth, this alone is good." For, as soon as he presumed to
speak thus, he was sure to be brutally disillusioned and severely
rebuked: "Why callest thou me good? there is none good but
one, that is the Absolute." "Our heart is restless till it repose in
Thee."[2]

2. *Dialectical Progress in History.* The goal of historical development, according to Hegel, is the attainment of rational freedom or the Absolute Consciousness. "The East knew that One
is free (the Eternal Being,—on earth the despot); the Greek and
the Roman world knew that some are free, (as in aristocracy or
democracy); and the Germanic world knows that all are free."
Among the savages the individual is nothing and society is every
thing: from birth to death his life is bound by all sorts of taboos
and superstitious fears. Among the Orientals, even down to the
recent years, the emperor alone was free and the people were
treated as persons of nonage: they knew little of such things

---

[2] J. Royce, *op. cit.*, Lectures VIII-IX.

as individuality, they were mere spokes in the wheel of social continuity. From birth to death their first and last and most important concern was how to secure an heir in order to insure social continuity. "Of the three thousand and odd sins" said the sage, "filial impiety is the greatest; and of all forms of filial impiety, to die heirless is the greatest."[8] Children are married often under the age of ten; and as soon as they come to age, reproductive activity is their recognized sacred duty. At forty or thereabouts they are prematurely old, are even proud to be acknowledged as "the old men of such and such families"; their wives are already veritable hags, worn out by child-bearing and household drudgery.

Among the Greeks and the Romans, not the despot alone, but also a few others were recognized as free, while a great many were unfree. Their civilization was founded on slave labour; and women and children were regarded as mere chattels of the husband. A philosopher as wise as Aristotle pronounced that slaves were born slaves; and the balmiest days of the Roman Empire were made glittering on the surface only with the sweat and blood of legions of slaves. Only occasionally here and there a noble slave-philosopher like Epictetus preached the true gospel of freedom. But with the ascendancy of Christianity there dawned upon the human mind the idea of universal freedom: the idea that all men might be free, not merely outwardly by removing social taboos and legal fetters, but inwardly by emancipating the self from its own conflict and bondage. Though this noble idea smoldered through the thousand years of the chaotic Dark Age, it was rekindled at the dawn of the Modern Age, it grew steadily brighter through the periods of the Reformation and the Industrial Revolution, and was in full blaze at the conclusion of the Great War.

The greatest obstacle to the advancement of freedom is not

[8] *The Book of Filial Piety.*

so much institutional fetters as it is the ignorance and inner conflict of men. The former may be abolished by an act of parliament, but not the latter. Men's mental and moral conditions are
the manifestations of their subjective reason, while their social
and religious institutions are the manifestations of their objective
reason: and their freedom consists in a synthesis of the two.
"They that make them are like unto them" is as true of social
ideals as of religious idols. Where men lead a brute existence,
fetishism and shammanism are their religion. Where mere social continuity is their ideal, ancestor-worship, blind obedience to
tradition and consequent centuries of stagnation are the natural
outcome. Where men are overwhelmed by nature and their
only longings are for re-absorption in nature, the Hindoo lethargy
and suicidal striving are normal phenomena. But where men
are endowed with a vigorous physique and a vigorous mind,
where the standard of living is raised above the level of mère
brute existence, where natural forces are subjugated so as to serve
human welfare, where individuality and originality command
respect and admiration, where self-control, frugality and honesty
are rewarded as virtues,—only there is found anything like
rational freedom. Hence Hegel's dictum: *Alles wirkliche ist, ist
vernünftig; alles vernünftig ist, ist wirkliche.* This may sound
rather hard to the ears of some liberals, or may even be turned
into a weapon for the defense of the things as they are. But this
is not what Hegel meant. To him what is "real" is not merely
what is, but what is necessary; whatever is, and yet is not necessary, is simply "accidental." To be sure there is some danger of
circular reasoning; nevertheless, Hegel is not a naïve champion
of conservatism. That he defended the corrupt Prussian monarchy of his day as the visible manifestation of the Absolute is
rather grotesque; but it does not seem altogether improbable that
if he were alive today he might pronounce the visible manifestation of the Absolute to be the League of Nations. Thus the his-

tory of the world is the history of the Spirit's struggle for freedom, which is the true Theodicea.[4]

MARX: THE MATERIALISTIC VERSION OF DIALECTICAL LAW

The contrast between the Hegelian and the Marxian conception may be expressed thus: according to the former, nature exists only as the alienation of the Absolute Idea; according to the latter, Nature is the sole reality, existing independently of all thinkers; according to the former, the Absolute Idea and the logical categories existed before the universe came into being; according to the latter, this very Idea is nothing but the relic of the primitive belief in ghosts, and the categories are merely the reflections of the material world in the human mind which is itself a product, the highest product of nature; according to the former, the historical process of the world is essentially static, timeless, at the most only half-way evolutionary; according to the latter, the historical process is through and through dynamic and evolutionary.[5] The Hegelian conception of the dialectical progress is logical and a priori, while the Marxian conception of it is claimed to be empirical and a posteriori.[6] According to Hegel, the Absolute Idea, existing from eternity to eternity, is the living soul of the material world; and the dialectical progress is nothing but the self-development of the Absolute Idea from itself to itself. The Absolute Idea first projects itself as its object of contemplation; and the object thus projected is nature which begins its career without self-consciousness, goes through further dialectical progress till it becomes conscious in the biological realm, and self-conscious in man himself. This is a topsy-turvy ideology (so complain Marx and Engels), which conceives the pictures of real things as real things, and real things as pictures. Accord-

[4] Hegel, *Philosophy of History*, translated by J. Sibree, Preface and pp. 1-82, 477.
[5] Royce, *op. cit.*, Lecture VII; Fred. Engels, *Feuerbach*, pp. 52-53, 63-67.
[6] Engels, *op. cit.*, pp. 29, 44.

ingly they deemed it their mission to restore Hegel's dialectic to
its proper sphere.[7]

The doctrine developed in accordance with this new dialectical conception is the famous Economic Interpretation of History, which reads: "That in every historical epoch the prevailing
mode of economic production and exchange, and the social organizations necessarily following from it, form the basis upon
which is built up, and from which alone can be explained, the
political and intellectual history of that epoch; that consequently
the whole history of mankind (since the dissolution of primitive
tribal society, holding land in common ownership) has been a
history of class struggles, contests, between exploiting and exploited, ruling and oppressed classes."[8]

CROCE: THREE CRITICISMS OF MARX'S DIALECTICAL LAW

1. Engels understood by dialectical progress the rhythmical
development of things according to their inner laws. He thought
that this rhythmical development is not to be determined by a
priori deduction, but is rather to be gathered a posteriori through
empirical observation and verification. This way of conceiving
the dialectical progress, says Croce, "would have nothing in common with the old Hegelian dialect except the name." And what
is more important, does this natural rhythm of development
exist? Engels indeed appeals to empirical observation; but what
kind of laws are those which we discover by empirical observation? "Can it ever be a law which governs things absolutely, or
is it not one of those which are now called tendencies, or rather
is it not merely a simple and limited generalization?"[9]

Why is the Marxian conception of the dialectic said to have
nothing in common with the Hegelian? Croce seems to say
elsewhere that the inversion of the Hegelian dialectic logically

---

[7] Marx, *Capital,* vol. I, Preface; Engels, *op. cit.,* pp. 94-96, 107.

[8] F. Engels, Introduction to the *Manifesto of the Communist Party.*

[9] B. Croce, *Historical Materialism and the Economics of Karl Marx,* translated by C. M. Meredith, pp. 83-84. Quotations by permission of the Macmillan Co.

leads to the theory that "history is not a process of the Idea, for example, of a rational reality, but a system of forces: to the rational view is opposed the dynamic view." Hence the Marxian dialectic bears only a superficial resemblance to the Hegelian. "Hegel's Ideas— and Marx knew this perfectly well—are not human ideas, and to turn the Hegelian philosophy of history upside down can not give us the statement that ideas arise as reflections of material conditions."[10] To this, Engels, I suppose, might reply: Hegel's Ideas may not be human ideas, but an idea or anything whatsoever can be known only through the mind of some finite knower: even the Absolute can only be known through the human mind, and to this extent the Absolute is a human idea. As for the contention that the turning of the Hegelian philosophy of history upside down can not give the materialistic hypothesis that ideas are reflections of material conditions, it does not matter whether it can or can not give the materialistic hypothesis. Marx and Engels simply prefer this hypothesis because it seems to be a more naïvely empirical view of the matter than the idealistic hypothesis.

2. Croce says that historical materialism has no necessary connection with metaphysical materialism, and that the term "historical materialism" may mean either one of two things,—either a method of interpretation, or a definite conception of life and of the universe.[11] The slogans which the Marxians employ in order to support their historical materialism, such as "the economic factor dominates the other factors of social life," and "the economic factor is fundamental and the others are dependent," are generally vague, for they rarely define what they mean by "economic factor."[12] This I think is a fair criticism. But in justice also to Marx and Engels, it should be said that they evidently recognized that they overstated their case in the *Communist Manifesto*. For Marx says elsewhere: "The Materialistic

[10] Croce, *op. cit.*, pp. 6-7.
[11] Croce, *op. cit.*, p. 92.
[12] *Ibid., pp.* 28-29.

doctrine that men are the products of conditions and education, different men therefore the products of other conditions and changed education, forgets that circumstances may be altered by men and that the educator has himself to be educated."[13] And Engels apologizes: "Marx and I are partly responsible for the fact that the younger men have sometimes laid more stress on the economic side than it deserves. In meeting the attacks of our opponents it was necessary for us to emphasize the dominant principle denied by them, and we did not always have the time, place, or opportunity to let the other factors, which are concerned in the mutual action and reaction, get their deserts." Again: "According to the materialistic view of history, the factor which is, in last instance, decisive in history is the production and reproduction of actual life. More than this neither Marx nor I have ever asserted. But when any one distorts this so as to read that the economic factor is the sole element, he converts the statement into a meaningless, abstract, absurd phrase. The economic condition is the basis, but the various elements of the superstructure, —the political forms of the class-contests, and their results, the constitutions, the legal forms and also all the reflexes of these actual contests in the brains of the participants, the political, legal, philosophical theories, the religious views,—all these exert an influence on the development of the historical struggles, and in many instances determine their form."[14]

3. In what sense is it true that history is a class struggle? Croce answers: "(a) when there are classes; (b) when they have antagonistic interests; (c) when they are aware of this antagonism, which would give us, in the main, the humorous equivalence that history is a class war only when it is a class war."[15] The trouble with this sort of criticism is that it is not so humorous as the critic imagines it is. If we look around us, by far the

[13] Cf. Engels, Feuerbach, p. 130.
[14] Ibid., pp. 25-26; Cf. W. J. Ghent, Mass and Class, pp. 9-36.
[15] Croce, op. cit., p. 85.

largest part of the conflicts that are raging go on without our being aware of them. Somewhere disease germs attack us without our being aware of them. Somewhere competitors are watching us without our being aware of them. Somewhere various anti-social agents lie in wait without our being aware of them. Above all, we have our inner conflicts of slumbering desires and latent ambitions by which we are unconsciously swayed. All these are conflicts, of which we are either only dimly aware or totally unconscious; yet we are not therefore to say that there are no conflicts. Do not some idealists regard the subconscious as the root of the conscious, or even maintain their identity? The fault of the economic determinists' reasoning is not their recognition of class struggles, but their failure to appreciate the interdependence and coöperation of classes which go on side by side with class struggle; not their emphasis on the economic motive, but their inadequate treatment of other, and in many ways, more important motives. Kropotkin's *Mutual Aid* should be read along with the *Communist Manifesto*.

A more adequate conception of class struggle would be based not on strictly economic motives, but these together with some such motives as the advanced notions of decency and the insatiable desire for display. The savages evaluate things in terms of what goes into their bellies. "Good is that which keeps the tribe alive," said an old Indian chief. The notion of value among peasants in the backward countries even today is no better than that implied in the Hebrew saying: "Eat, and drink, and be merry." Hunger and sex are the two poles of the axis around which their universe revolves. Life among them is unconsciously communistic, and yet it is anything but idyllic. Half of their life is spent in the quest of food and sexual satisfaction; the other half in gossiping, loafing, sleeping, and other wasteful ways. If this state of affairs had continued, there never could have been any civilization. Hence the breaking up of the primitive communistic societies, where according to Marx there were no class

distinctions, was not an event to be lamented, but rather one to
be rejoiced at, although the first man who proposed to break up
the primitive communistic societies was probably regarded by his
contemporaries as a Bolshevik rather than a bourgeois. The
subsequent development of private property and the antagonism
between the possessing and the propertyless class was but a necessary move away from the indistinct and homogeneous primitive
savagery. God having created men unequal in native capacity,
it was natural that the strong and the energetic, the frugal and the
farsighted, should make headway with cumulative advantage,
while the weak and the sluggish should sink deeper into misery.

DIALECTICAL SOCIAL LAWS

The dialectical law, as applied to social phenomena, may be
expressed as follows: that in every historical epoch there are antithetical tendencies, owing to the inherent antithetical tendencies
in nature and in man; and that through the consequent striving
to transcend these antitheses a synthesis emerges, in which the
antitheses are reconciled, and which thereby becomes a new thesis
in order to repeat the same process in an infinite series, either on
the same or on different levels. "It is precisely opposition, or
antithesis, which sets things in motion, which is the main spring
of evolution, which calls forth and develops the latent forces and
powers of being. Had the earth as a fiery, gaseous mass remained in that state, without the contradiction, that is, the cool-
ing and condensation, taking place, then no life would have
appeared on it. Had the State remained autocratic, and the
contradictory principle, middle-class freedom, been absent, then
the life of the State would have become rigid, and the bloom of
culture rendered impossible. Had capitalism remained without
its proletarian contradiction, then it would have reverted to an
industrial feudalism."[16]

The question whether the Absolute Idea or Matter existed

[16] Max Beer, *The Life and Teachings of Karl Marx*, pp. xviii-xix.

first is not so important to sociologists of the Positivist School. As long as man's speculative interest persists both hypotheses will find champions. To Marx and Engels the important thing in social study was to trace the concatenations which link the processes of social evolution, to investigate how one stage succeeds another in the dialectical progression. Like their distinguished contemporary, Auguste Comte, they were a little too confident of the prospect of discovering a positive science of society. They repeatedly speak of "laws," and evidently were excited by the "three great discoveries" which Engels repeatedly mentions, the discovery of the cell, the transformation of energy, and Darwin's theory of evolution.[17]

Dialectical thinking circulates under various names, as "law," "method," "view of history," etc. But it is clear that it is not a law in the same sense in which there are laws of physical sciences. It can be made into a law in the Positivist sense only when the dialectical swings are measured, and the resulting synthesis is rendered controllable. No Positivistic law merely says that the pendulum swings, but it rather says what the distances of the swings will be. Moreover, in the domain of human affairs synthesis is exceedingly variable, and prediction is well-nigh impossible. The dialectical progress is a view of life, of history, perhaps a very important view, and a fruitful method of investigation; but it affords by no means the only view of history nor the only method of investigation. The fruitful character of this method may be appreciated when a number of "social laws" enunciated by various social scientists are surveyed. Their authors, to be sure, did not (except Professor Hocking) set them forth as "dialectical laws," but they are nevertheless all dialectical laws in the sense just explained:

1. "Law of Integration. Societies like all other aggregates pass from less coherence to more coherence."[18]

---

[17] Engels, *op. cit.*, pp. 30-31, 99-100.
[18] E. A. Ross, *Foundations of Sociology*, p. 43.

2. "Law of Differentiation. Society passes from the homogeneous to the heterogeneous."[19]

3. "Societies show increasing definiteness of arrangement."[20]

4. "Law of Equilibration. Social evolution tends toward a more perfect equilibrium."[21]

These four "laws" are derived from one single formula, Spencer's law of evolution, that evolution is "a change from an indefinite incoherent homogeneity to a definite coherent heterogeneity, through continuous differentiation and integrations,"— a formula, on which, according to Martineau, Goldwin Smith commented thus: that "the universe may well have heaved a sigh of relief when, through the cerebration of an eminent thinker, it had been delivered of this account of itself."[22] Spencer attempted to demonstrate that this law of evolution applied to social as well as to cosmological and biological evolution. And now Professor Ross takes each of the foregoing "laws" separately and tears them to pieces.[23] Professor Ross's criticism seems to be just when he takes them one by one. But when they are all put together in a single formula, we seem to have an essentially true description of the formal aspect of evolution. Professor Hocking, in his discussion *On the Law of History,* points out the kinship between Spencer's "differentiation" and Hegel's "negation," between Spencer's "integration" and Hegel's "synthesis." He then goes on to comment: "The correspondence is sufficient to show the relative place that a formula like Spencer's would hold in a philosophy of history—how partial a solution of the problem of history any such formula by itself can offer. A better or worse, a ground for preference, a significant goal, can not be found in differentiations and integrations alone. Neither morality nor desire appears interested in the process thus described. Some formula of this sort may, however, have the great merit of being

[19] *Ibid.,* p. 44.   [20] *Ibid.,* p. 45.   [21] *Ibid.,* p. 46.

[22] Spencer, *Data of Ethics,* chap. V, paragraph 24; J. Martineau, *Types of Ethical Theory,* II, 368.

[23] *Op. cit.,* pp. 42-48.

true. And if we add the material, the interest may begin to appear."[24]

5. "Spontaneous progress gives way to telic progress and individual telesis in turn yields relatively to collective telesis."[25] This "law" Professors Blackmar and Gillin call "The law of survival and progress."[26] According to Professor Ross who, as far as I know, first called it a "law," it originated with Ward. This law, together with Ward's three "Principles," of "Sympodial Development," of "Creative Synthesis," and of "Synergy" may be regarded as dialectical laws, though no one, it is rather to be regretted, seems to have called the last three "social laws."[27] Ward's exposition of his "Principle of Synergy" seems to be especially illuminating:—"The true nature of the universal principle of synergy pervading all nature and creating all the different kinds of structure that we observe to exist . . . is a process of equilibration, for example, the several forces are first brought into a state of partial equilibrium. It begins in collision, conflict, antagonism, and opposition, but as no motion can be lost it is transformed, and we have the milder phases of antithesis, competition and interaction, passing next into the *modus vivendi*, or compromise, and ending in collaboration and coöperation. . . . Synergy is the principle that explains all organization and creates all structures."[28]   And elsewhere he says: "it consists in the ultimate union of the opposing elements and their combination and assimilation. Successively higher and higher social structures are thus created by a process of natural synthesis, and society evolves from stage to stage. The struggling groups infuse into each other the most vigorous qualities of each, cross all the hereditary strains, double their social efficiency at each cross, and place each

[24] W. E. Hocking, *On the Law of History*, pp. 58-59.
[25] Ross, *op. cit.*, p. 64.
[26] Blackmar and Gillin, *Outlines of Sociology*, pp. 377-78.
[27] L. F. Ward, *Pure Sociology*, pp. 76-77, 99, 171-75, 184.
[28] *Ibid.*, p. 175.

new product on a higher plane of existence. It is the cross-
fertilization of cultures."[29]

6. "The Law of the Development of Social Structures.
Whenever two societies conjugate, through a process of conquest
of one by the other, a great and rapid evolution of structure
succeeds."[30]

7. "When two or more peoples, or class-conscious groups,
come into contact with each other in one geographical unity,
social structures and institutions will experience rapid development, provided one party struggles to dominate the other."[31]
Both these laws are fragmentary descriptions of the way in which
the "Principle of Synergy," quoted above, presumably works in
concrete cases. The latter of the pair is an attempted improvement upon the former: in restating the original law (of Gumplowicz), Professors Blackmar and Gillin lost sight of the fact
that the more ideal method of development is through some sort
of integration (or assimilation) rather than domination!

8. Similarly, Mr. Taylor's "Law of Conflict of Opposites"
which reads, "The opposition between those who seek to impose
a rule, more or less autocratic, and those who demand, at least
in words, freedom from all restraints, continues perpetually
throughout history," in so far as it is true, is a fragmentary description of the same law of dialectical progress.[32]

9. "The Law of the Alternation of Political Forces: Government by party is the political expression of a universal law. The
universe invariably presents a dual aspect. Everything has its
opposite." "The only government which is ever free from faction
is that of an absolute despotism ruling over an enslaved and
debased people. The freer the institutions of a nation, the more
marked the influence of faction; and this tendency ever gravitates

[29] *Ibid.*, p. 171.
[30] Blackmar and Gillin, *op. cit.*, p. 375. Gumplowicz, *Der Rassenkampf*, secs.,
34-35.
[31] Blackmar and Gillin, *op. cit.*, pp. 376-77.
[32] H. Taylor, *Origin of Government*, pp. 145-46, 230-34, 241.

. . . towards the division of every people into two great opposing camps or parties. This, in turn, tends to the setting up of the form of government intended by the Great Design—which is governed by party."[33] The author goes on to say that the bi-party system is the most desirable system since it is based on these deep seated antithetical tendencies in human nature, and that it is the most effective system of lodging the responsibility for governmental acts.[34] The author emphasizes the alternate swings of political power rather than their common development through opposition and reconciliation. Hence this "law of alternation" can be regarded as only partially dialectical.

10. "The Law of Value: Value is persistently increased through the original extension of power and the consequent acession of power. In this bi-factorial growth, neither variable can be regarded as absolutely prior in time, nor as absolutely independent of the other in time."[35] The dialectical character of this law is explained by the author thus: "Liberty is the state of having digested a meal, of having awakened from asleep. Men must sleep yet again and again. While the Germanic peoples were living in external contact with Rome, between the times of Tacitus and the invasions, they gradually adopted Roman titles of dignity, and aped the habits of authority, and let their ancient liberal customs of election and assembly fall into desuetude. Were they growing in freedom? or were they entering into the shadow of the great bondage from which they were to emerge transformed? They were, even thus, enlarging their souls, and in this sense were becoming more free; but specifically they were entering into the antithesis of freedom. Could we regard freedom in the wider sense as a synthesis of this more specific freedom and its opposite, then we might say with truth that history presents the recurrent dialectic of freedom, as the shape of the process through which the enhancement of values takes place."[36]

[33] G. W. Walthew, *The Philosophy of Government*, p. 120.
[34] *Cf.* H. Taylor, *op. cit.*, pp. 121-48.
[35] W. E. Hocking, *op. cit.*, p. 65.   [36] *Ibid.*, p. 63.

As regards the limitations of this law, the author's own comment seems satisfactory:—"This is not a satisfactory law. No law of indefinite quantitative increase can be satisfactory. We must know more of the nature of the goal to which it tends. Further, it is but a law of tendency, and like all such laws, calls upon our faith in the configuration of things for its actuality: it is a law of history only by the grace of God. And finally, it is not able to explain the concrete forms which history assumes. It is a law of values, and should give some insight into the sense of advance from savagery to statedom through family and village communities, but it can not show the necessity of the family or the village or the State. These shapes stand in simple vivid naturalness, the gift of nature, the despair of our philosophy. Let us not flatter ourselves that we have fathomed even their 'essence.' The value of such an attempt as this may be to show how compatible, with the proper key, are the thoughts of the greater thinkers; and to unite our hopes of further understanding upon that enlightened love of material nature which, as I repeat, is the prerogative of true idealism."[37] To this I may add that Professor Hocking uses the word "power" in a somewhat strained, sublimated sense.

11. The following law enunciated by Professor Giddings may be regarded as belonging to the same variety of law of value as just quoted, except that it strongly savours of Spencer's formula: "Those subjective values will survive which are component parts in a total, or whole, of subjective values that is becoming ever more complex through the inclusion of new interests, and, at the same time, more thoroughly harmonious and coherent."[38] Professor Giddings uses the terms "subjective" and "objective" in the discussion of the law in a way which makes the understanding of the law more difficult. These terms had better be left out altogether.

12. So, too, Professor Giddings' "law of the Social Choice of

[37] *Ibid.*, p. 65.
[38] F. H. Giddings, *Principles of Sociology*, pp. 412, 413-16.

Combinations and of Means," which reads: "A population that has a few interests which, however, are harmoniously combined, will be conservative in its choices. A population that has varied interests which are as yet inharmoniously combined, will be radical in its choices. Only the population that has many, varied, and harmoniously combined interests will be consistently progressive in its choices." Progress can come only through the path of integration and reintegration of values.³⁹

13. "A Law of Interdependence. Looking over the field of history there seems to be a law of interdependence—interdependence of individuals, of classes, of tribes, of nations. The human race seems to be essentially an organism, a unit. As Paul said, we are 'every one members, one of another.' No part of the human race in history has really progressed by the injury of another. We have all risen or fallen together. Conquests of one people by another have always demoralized the conquerors. Success in war has generally introduced lower standards, less individual freedom, less tolerance, less elevation of spirit. The Persians after their conquests in Asia, Athens when she dominated the Delian League, Rome when she was mistress of the world, the Roman Catholic Church when its alliance with the temporal power had given it supremacy, Britain when she ruled over a group of forcibly annexed dependencies, the Allies after the downfall of Napoleon, Germany after 1871, were, according to the judgment of many of their own contemporary and national historians, defeated morally; and who shall say that France and Italy, England and the United States, are freer and better countries since the Great War than before? The fruits of victory in war have often proved to be apples of Sodom, turning to dust in the mouth.

"So it has been with divided races and classes. Dependent races have been the curse of the ruling race. The Helots of Sparta, the Allies of Rome, Ireland under England, have been

³⁹ *Ibid.*, pp. 411-12.

constant sources of weakness to their masters. Slave-holding classes have been forced into cruelty, shaken by vague fears of servile revolt, weakened by exemption from wholesome labour. Slaves and dependents, on the other hand, have been cowardly, deceitful, unenterprising, incapable of progress. The division into two classes have been demoralizing to both. The abolition of slavery and the freeing of the dependents has been a condition precedent to any considerable economic or political or moral advancement for either class."[40]

There is in this law nothing explicitly dialectical, and some of the statements are rather paradoxical. Nevertheless, there are two points to be noticed in this law, which have some important bearing on the dialectical law. One is the idea of interdependence of everything upon everything else, which is the same as Hegel's idea that the very opposition unites the antithesis. The other is that this emphasis on interdependence is a wholesome antidote to Gumplowicz's and Marx's idea of the group or class domination. Both these writers speak of domination as if inevitable; but true synthesis should always be sought in the direction of interdependence, not of domination.[41]

[40] E. P. Cheyney, "Law in History," *American Historical Review*, XXIX, 240.
[41] The following twenty-three "propositions" are given by Mr. B. W. Brown as possible clues to the discovery of true social laws: "In a given state of group equilibrium:

(1) Frequent and close contact within the group increases homogeneity;
(2) Contacts of group members with outside individuals and groups diminish homogeneity;
(3) Contacts between group and group increase homogeneity of each;
(4) The smaller the physical basis, the more direct the contact;
(5) Larger membership requires more contact among the members to maintain homogeneity;
(6) Introduction of new members into the group decreases homogeneity;
(7) Frequency and directness of contact among members are limited by the physical basis;
(8) As contacts become less direct, structure is necessary to maintain contact;
(9) Structure is the product of repeated and habitual contact;
(10) The group dynamic operates through contacts;
(11) Homogeneity is increased by use of the physical basis;

In conclusion I may briefly recapitulate my evaluation of dialectical laws as follows:

1. A View of Life, Not Positive Law. The concept of the dialectical progress is a view of life, of history, and not a law in the positivist sense.

2. Wastefulness of Antithesis. The dialectical laws speak of antithesis and differentiation as inevitable. But what is meant by antithesis is not always clear. It may mean a mere variety which is generally desirable in so far as variety does not necessitate conflict. It may mean incompatibility such as Marx's conception of the antithesis between bourgeoisie and proletariat, which, according to the Marxian orthodoxy, can not be solved except by the

(12) The dynamic adapts the physical basis to its use; the better the adaptation, the more rapid and complete the achievement;

(13) The larger the place basis, the greater the need of structure for contact and homogeneity;

(14) The stronger the homogeneity, the less need of structure;

(15) The stronger the homogeneity, the more quickly and readily the dynamic can function;

(16) Increased structure requires corresponding homogeneity;

(17) Primary structure promotes the group objective at the expense of homogeneity;

(18) Secondary structure promotes the permanent objective at the expense of the immediate dynamic;

(19) Secondary structure maintains and prolongs group existence;

(20) Structure permits larger groups both in number and space;

(21) The larger the membership, the more structure required;

(22) Additions to membership temporarily reduce but permanently increase the dynamic;

(23) Dynamic utilizes and wears out all other elements, but renews each out of the achievement of the group." (B. Warren Brown, Social Groups, pp. 134-135). The language of the author is in true Spencerian style, and these may be regarded as "laws" of the "formal" character in the sense in which Professor Hocking uses the term. Each of these propositions, being an empirical observation, taken separately, may have only a limited validity; but when they are all put together, they make up an interesting description of the way in which the law of differentiation and integration presumably works. Moreover, "propositions" of this kind are of even greater interest to the positivist than are the more daring and sweeping generalizations.

"direct action" of the proletariat. Or it may mean rivalry as in games, which is indispensable for the success of the game; and the more rivalry there is, the better will be the game. Between two suitors for the same woman there is a real incompatibility; either one or the other must inevitably lose. But is the antithesis between bourgeoisie and proletariat of the same nature of incompatibility as that between two suitors for the same woman? Marx speaks of proletarian dictatorship as inevitable; be that as it may, if it is inevitable, the antithesis between bourgeoisie and proletariat is certainly wasteful.

3. Synthesis Not Necessarily Progress. Hegel's version of the law is teleological, while Marx's and Spencer's are mechanistic. Hegel and his followers conceived progress in terms of value, while Spencer conceived it at one time in terms of structural development and at another time in terms of pleasure. Beneath the conception of progress in terms of differentiation and integration there is an implied assumption that structural development is accompanied by a corresponding increase of value. As for Hegel's synthesis there is no reason why synthesis may not be a retrogression to a lower level rather than a rise a level above its own. The marriage of normal people with defectives generally results in the production of defective children rather than normal. The contact of the white colonists with the North American squaws and the West Indian negresses resulted in mongrelization of the races and often demoralization of the white colonists. Devolution and atavism go on side by side with evolution and progress.

4. Logical Construction not Factual. The concept of dialectical progress as developed by Hegel is logical, but a logical construction is not necessarily true in fact. Hegel himself admitted that the successive forms (in his account) which the spirit assumes in its world-conquering career are not all necessary or inevitable, since probably no human being goes through in orderly succession the stages of a savage, a slave-master, a monk, a knight-errant, a revolutionist, etc., as in Hegel's representation of the *Weltgeist*. Marx and Engels, though they complained that Hegel twisted historical facts in order to illustrate his preconceived ideas, are guilty of the same error. They speak of the inevitability of the proletarian dictatorship. But is there such inevitability? It is nearly a century since the inevitable coming of the proletarian dictatorship was proclaimed, but outside of Russia nowhere are the signs of its coming seen, while in America the proletarians themselves are becoming capitalists through the purchase of stocks and are too busy to think about the proletarian dictatorship.

5. *Its Value.* In spite of all these defects there is something romantic and even heroic in Hegel's picture of the *Weltgeist*. The violent ups and downs in its fateful career are suggestive of its capacity to suffer and of its power to overcome its enemies. Likewise the mechanical swing between differentiation and integration in Spencer's conception is awe-inspiring. Dialectical laws give a spaciousness to our own conception of social process and in this way serve as a majestic vestibule to science. Dialectic is a poetic, but merely preliminary, step in the search for social laws.

CHAPTER IX
SOCIAL ARTS

SOCIAL SCIENCE OR SOCIAL ART?

So LONG as there are no social laws of mathematical precision, the social sciences remain a body of empirical generalizations. That such sciences can not be comparable, in point of precision and certainty, with mathematics, or physics, or even physiology, scarcely needs further demonstration. But inexactitude and uncertainty need not hinder the social scientists from considering sociology a science in a broader sense of that term.

A precise scholar like the late President Wilson might frown at such a term as "political science."[1] But there are others who think differently. Medicine is said to have no laws, but is frequently spoken of as "medical science." Etymologically, the word science is derived from the Latin "scientia," meaning knowledge. Webster's New International Dictionary says that, according to the older usage, an "art or skill regarded as the result of knowledge of laws and principles" was called science; an evidence of this usage may be seen in the expression "a player of unusual science." So long, therefore, as the prestige of science is not misused as a cloak for superstition and exaggeration, so long as we mutually understand what we mean by "science," there is no harm in using the term "social sciences."

But it would seem that the more accurate designation for the social studies should be "social art," just as we should properly speak of "medical art" rather than "medical science." By an art we mean the skill or wisdom in performing certain actions, which is acquired through experience and inference. A social art might then be defined as skill or wisdom which is useful to the appreciation of human values, to the improvement of human relations and the accompanying conditions of living.[2] Now,

---

[1] *American Political Science Review*, vol. V (No. 1). [2] See p. 1.

even an art presupposes certain working principles which need not be exact, but which must possess some measure of probability.[3] The medical art, for example, presupposes certain working principles of bio-chemistry. The social laws which we have gathered and discussed are such a body of at least tentative working principles as a social art presupposes.

NECESSITY OF SOCIAL ARTS

Social arts are necessary for the reason that no sociologist would say that, because we have not yet discovered exact social laws, let us keep our hands off, let nature reign, and let us watch and see. Such an attitude would be, to speak accurately, neither reasonable nor possible. It would be unreasonable because every sociologist has a meliorative purpose in view, and therefore to assume the laissez-faire attitude is contrary to his profession. It would not be possible because every sociologist, like everybody else, has certain value-attitudes: he regards certain things as good, and certain others as bad, and he can universalize his values only by persuading others to his view. To this extent every sociologist is a moralist. He can have a science of sociology only when all values have become universalized.

Fundamentally, then, all social problems are problems of human values. Things in themselves have only vicarious worth derived from human nature. The prevention of cruelty to animals is, in reality, a prevention of vicarious cruelty to human beings. Similarly, the prohibition of abuse to natural scenery and to works of art in public places is, in reality, a prohibition of vicarious abuse to human beings. As remarked above, anything whatsoever which is an object of somebody's interest is, by virture of that very fact, invested with value, and may become an object of social value. And everything is capable of becoming an

[3] *Cf.* J. S. Mill's contrast between art and science: "Art in general consists of the truths of science, arranged in the most convenient order for practice, instead of the order which is the most convenient for thought." *Logic*, Book VI, chap. XII.

object of somebody's value as either good or bad; and the only thing which is of no value is the unknown.

It is because we wish to have our interests furthered and our ideals achieved that social problems arise; and it is because, having furthered our interests and achieved our ideals, we wish to have broader interests and higher ideals, that we have ever more social problems, and through our strivings to have all such wishes fulfilled we have progress. If there were certain and precise social laws, the solution of all social problems might be an easy affair, or even a mechanical affair. But in the absence of such social laws, we need to rely partly on empirical generalizations from past experiences and partly on our wishes. We, therefore, often build our expectations on what we wish to happen. And having built so many expectations upon wishes we often mistake wishes for facts and facts for wishes, even as Alice in Wonderland, who in her drowsy moments became so confused about cats and bats that she asked herself alternately: "Do cats eat bats? Do bats eat cats?" What are the social facts? What are the wishes?

METHODOLOGIES OF SOCIAL STUDIES

The problems before sociological students, then, take the following three forms: namely, how to discover what each one of us most centrally desires? how to get what we thus desire? and what is the meaning of these desires? Corresponding to these three problems, there may be said to be three methods of social studies: namely, the historical, the scientific, and the philosophical. History may help us to impersonate the characters of the past and to build our interest, and thereby to become what we are, since we may at any given time be identified with our interest. Science may help us to get what we want, by presenting us with sets of facts. Philosophy may help us to understand the nature of our wants; whether the things we apparently want are the things we really want.

On the other hand, though history may help us to discover our interests through sympathetic imagination, historical characters do not prescribe for us what to do in any given situation. They knew even less about social laws than we now do. *Science gives us a sense of power, but not of duty. For, science is impersonal.* The same knowledge of facts, which enables us to control our environment, we may utilize either for good or for evil. We need therefore a philosophy of value to interpret and unify our experiences, and not merely to describe them as science does. Our philosophies are so many snap-shot views of life, as consistently reasoned out as we can make them. In our most passive moments life appears as a mere stream of consciousness, without head or tail. *To philosophize is to break up systematically such a stream of mere consciousness, and to make some meaning out of it.*

ILLUSTRATIONS OF SOCIAL ARTS

Every social art has its origin in somebody's interest, his interpretation of its meaning, and his knowledge of the technique by which to further it. Since a social art has been defined as skill or wisdom which is useful to the appreciation of human values to the improvement of human relations and the accompanying conditions of living, no art which is based on self-deception can be called social. A band of thieves or a gang of corrupt politicians may get what they want and prosper for a while. But humanity can not be taken as a reincarnation of Ishmael whose hands were against everybody, and everybody's hands were against him. In dealing with criminals and enemies in war, we tolerate deception, but the ethics of spies is questionable. Excluding, therefore, all arts which are either based on deception or which involve deception, I shall present six of the commonest of social arts, namely, the mystic art of self-annihilation, the mystic art of transvaluation, the naturalistic art of domination, the naturalistic art of explosion, the art of separation, and the idealistic art of interpenetration.

1. The Mystic Art of Self-Annihilation. The mystic's method of discovering what he most deeply desires consists in an endless series of abstractions from all that is self-evident and finally in getting rid of all desires. The Oriental mystics, whose favorite method it is, retire into a hermitage and starve themselves, sit on folded legs and control their breathing, and watch the stream of their sensations. From all their sensations and images they attempt to abstract the universal characteristics and thereby to integrate their ego into the abstract. When they have worked themselves up enough, they are said to be enlightened in a flash in one of their most passive moments, and to come out with the assertion: "I am I" or "That art thou!" When asked, what is the nature of the truth they have attained, the mystic answers that it is ineffable, that it can not be put down in ink on paper, and that the trouble with us ignorant mortals is that we are trying to fit Reality into our beggarly logic, whereas Reality can only be directly perceived by being wholly absorbed in it. All these statements may be true; since the Reality which the mystics experience is said to be ineffable, there is no way of verifying their assertions, short of becoming mystics ourselves. What significance have such assertions to us?

It seems to me that the assertion "I am I" is a last desperate assertion of a fast dissociating personality. For, by his self-imposed starvation, his improper manner of sitting which chokes his breath, and his continual introspection, the mystic has imperceptibly narrowed down the field of his emotion, till it is limited to his immediate environment; and as he watches the passage of the transient sensations and images, which gradually become thinner, his ego becomes blurred, falls into a trance, and finally disappears with the last rays of his mental images. He probably fears to be lost forever: hence the desperate assertion, "I am I!" and when he recovers, "That art thou!" both of which assertions look profound on the surface. This interpretation seems to be a rather naïve view of mysticism. Be that as it may:

if one abstracts everything except the universal characteristics from one's desires, sensations and images, the only thing that is likely to be left is his abstract ego, the will to live; hence, the empty tautology, "I am I!" But in carrying out these abstractions, the mystic has killed all desires, and thereupon he has shrunk to an empty shell, "I."

Should such an art be called social? That is doubtful. Oftener the mystics get trapped in the fast shrinking empty shell, "I," and die without making much noise. But once in a great while, some of them like the great Gautama Buddha himself, come out of their shell and lead a strenuous social life to save the "sorrow-drowned" multitude and to bring them consolation. In this latter event, it may be called a social art.

2. *The Mystic Art of Transvaluation.* Another of the mystic arts, which is shared by certain idealists, is transvaluation. To transvaluate is to re-evaluate interests (and with them also their objects) in terms of other-worldliness or of what is supposed to be eternal values. In the literature of mystics amusing self-contradictions are frequent: "the beginning is the end and the end is the beginning," "the long is the short and the short is the long," "the softest is the toughest and the toughest is the softest," and the like.[4] Other-worldliness in varying degrees is probably a frequent occurrence in the lives of a great many people, especially of those who shun the hurly-burly of social life, retire into solitude, and brood over their wrongs.[5] As a method of getting rid of incompatible desires, which threaten to bring about the dissociation of personality, transvaluation may be preferable to repression. There is, of course, a limit to transvaluation, as there is a limit to everything else. The same method, which is used to get rid of incompatible desires, when used to get rid of all desires,

[4] See for further instances of such strange assertions, Lao-Tzû, Tao-Teh Ching; Chunag-Tzû, Nan-Wha Ching; Royce, *The World and the Individual*, vol. I, Lectures III-V.
[5] See W. James, *The Varieties of Religious Experience;* M. P. Montague, *Twenty Minutes of Reality.*

should be regarded as an instrument of self-abnegation rather than of self-defense.

Most persons, I suppose, have had at one time or another illusions and disillusions, and have felt that this life is not by any means the best of all possible lives in the best of all possible worlds, and also that it is irrational to cling to life like a dog in the manger. Things seem to be somewhat different from their appearances; if so, all finite values must ultimately rest on some thing other than their appearances. It does not necessarily follow from this that all finite values are mere illusions. This is the point where one may either go further with the mystics, if one cares, and assert that all finite values are mere illusions; or stay with the idealists in the faith that all finite values, though they may appear as illusions from the temporal point of view, are real from the eternal point of view, as constituent members of the integrated whole, the Absolute.

The satisfaction of any simple interest is good, whatever that interest may be, since life is an organization of interests. But only the satisfaction of an organization of interests is morally good. And since a man may have all sorts of interests of a conflicting nature, an organization of them requires re-evaluation of the conflicting elements, *in terms of the whole system of interests, and not merely each as a simple interest.* When the interests are organized by such a process of re-evaluation, each simple interest finds its fulfilment as a constituent member of the whole organization of interests. Transvaluation in this sense is not merely *idealistic,* but also an every day routine for everybody. The mystic's aim in transvaluation, however, is not the fulfilment of a whole system of interests, but the getting rid of them all. To him all interests are mere illusions. If one chooses to think that the loftiest sentiments are mere illusions, the heart's battles are mere illusions, even life itself a mere illusion, childish play with pebbles on the beach; if one can go on reasoning in this way, one may not be logically assailable; but such a point of view does seem vain.

3. The Naturalistic Art of Domination: (a) Domination over Nature. The art of domination is especially fruitful in dealing with nature and all infra-human species. We take it for granted that nature needs an exacting master in order to tame her and make her fit to serve human wants; and that it is our birth-right to dominate her for this purpose. Whatever purpose she may have we do not know; in fact, we are far from certain that she has any purpose at all. Until the poets have personified the mountains and the rivers, until the mystics have proclaimed the brotherhood of the stars and the winds with man, and until certain metaphysicians have suggested that all nature may be conscious, we were absolutely innocent of such sophisticated views. Our naïve observations convince us that nature is a thoroughly indifferent, wasteful, and unmoral monster, while the same type of observation equally convinces us that we do know something about human wishes and aspirations, and that it is they and not nature which should guide human acts. We live in a social environment which can grow and expand only by displacing, and converting to itself, the natural environment. For, we never have social relations in a vacuum. Our interest must have its object; and anything in the natural environment, which is an object of somebody's interest, has by virtue of that very fact become a part of our social environment. Hence, all true and permanent improvements in social relations must be completed by improving our natural environment.

Domination over nature is a necessity, because it is the only alternative to being dominated by her. Floods and tornadoes in their sport convert into débris the products of our toil. Wolves and snakes pay us unwelcome visitations; birds and insects ever compete with us. Mosquitoes and bacteria have no better opinion of us than of any foodstuff. Extreme heat will suffocate alike saints and villains; and extreme cold will freeze to death heroes and cowards indifferently.

To dominate is to make an object purely a means to human ends, and not to coerce it to act contrary to its own laws of behavior. For instance, we can utilize the land to raise crops; we can also improve it to counteract its own tendency to diminishing returns, but we can not disregard the tendency. The art of domination over nature consists in continually and cumulatively discovering her values to humanity and the laws of her behavior, and in converting her forces into channels productive of human utilities. It is not inconceivable that some day we may discover the value in even such things as flies and mosquitoes; our welfare may then be lessened without them, just as certain ladies nowadays cannot remain fashionable in many quarters without lap dogs and pet monkeys, hats decorated with dyed feathers and necklaces made of rare fish bones, soups of frog's legs and salads of garlic and onion. Every bit of nature may be utilized some day, even tornadoes and floods, wolves and snakes. Since between man and nature the only problem involved is economic, and not moral (except of course for certain Hindoo mystics), the legitimate thing to do is to combine her mechanical and chemical energy according to her own law of proportionality so as to yield a maximum utility.

Perhaps, the most difficult part of nature to dominate is man as a biological organism. In so far as man is a biological organism, he is a part of nature, and is a fit object for domination by, and only by, the specifically human part of the same man. No man has a right to dominate another, but every man should dominate that part of himself which belongs to nature.

(b) Domination over "Backward Races." We also often take it for granted that in dealing with self-willed children, who do not know what is good for them, coercion is the legitimate method for their own good. Indulgent parents often spoil their children and bring ingratitude upon themselves. The exercise of authority over children is, therefore, justifiable, provided, the intention is good and its goodness is substantiated by the result.

On the other hand, it is alleged that there are whole races which are essentially childlike. In such instances, should we justify the methods of a benevolent despot, provided, he is absolutely certain that the end he has in view is intended purely for the good of his subjects, and that there is no alternative method, all other methods he has tried having failed? It was reported that Marshall Feng Yu-Hsiang, the great Chinese soldier-statesman, had advised the women of Northwestern China to abandon the custom of foot-binding. But years went by and the Chinese women still clung to the savage custom which is an emblem of what Professor Carver calls the ignominious "pig trough" class who eat all and do no work. Toward the end of last year he announced that thenceforth the women over thirty years of age, who still bound their feet, were to be fined fifty cents; those between twenty and thirty years of age, a dollar and a half; and those under twenty years of age, three dollars. With this decree he initiated a vigorous anti-foot-binding campaign. Then, and then only, foot-binding rapidly disappeared. He also stopped within the provinces under his dominion, gambling, prostitution, opium-eating, and a great many other vices to which his country-men are peculiarly addicted. A despot like this is a real savior for his race, compared with the democracy-mongers and liberty-hawkers who do nothing but pose as the friends of the "oppressed."

But suppose a certain class of people in the United States clamour for a certain "right" to have themselves thoroughly soaked in alcohol, should they also be dominated because they do not know what is good for them? It should be observed that there are no races which are "backward" in every respect; neither is there any race which is "advanced" in every respect. Every race is "advanced" in some respects, and all races are "backward" in other respects. Those who clamour for a "right" to get drunk are "backward" in that respect at least; and therefore they are perhaps fit objects for domination.

The question of the right to drink alcohol, however, assumes, in concrete situations, a degree of complexity, and is different from the other questions, namely, foot-binding, prostitution, and gambling. For, one may use alcohol to get only half drunk or only enough to stimulate one's vigor and to relieve one's depression. In these last instances, a less than half drunken person is sometimes even more agreeable than an absolutely sober person. But there are no such freaks as half prostitutes, half gamblers, or half foot-binders. One can be either a prostitute or not a prostitute, either a gambler or not a gambler, either a foot-binder or not a foot-binder. Hence, the problem of the right to use alcohol can not be satisfactorily solved by domination. To say that all incorrigible drunkards should be dominated for their own good as well as for others', is different from saying that everybody who uses alcohol should be dominated. The former alone are fit objects for domination.

(c) The Philosophical Background of Domination over Men. Ordinarily, people have recourse to domination, not for the good of the dominated, but for their own selfish purpose. Modern despots are the jugglers who dominate their weaker neighbors on the pretext that domination is good for them. Their method is to hire unprincipled pedants to persuade the people to submit, while they themselves rattle the sword as additional persuasion. When despotism falls into the hands of unscrupulous adventurers, it is nothing short of a fiendish instrument of conquest and exploitation, engendering mutual distrust and hatred. Back of the motive of domination there is a subconscious faith in dogmatic naturalism. For, from the point of view of dogmatic naturalism, life is something imposed upon us: we never asked for it, we merely found it when we had grown old enough to be self-conscious. We are asked to adapt ourselves, willy nilly, the best we can, to the forces of nature. We owe the universe or multiverse, whichever be the case, neither gratitude nor loyalty. We are to get, by hook or crook, all that we want either here and

now or never. The end justifies the means. If the universe should some day exhaust its energy in its meaningless grinding, and betake itself to its downward course, there would be nothing left for humanity but re-absorption into nature. Out of dust we are made, and unto dust shall we return: neither bitterness nor grudge would be of any avail.

4. *The Art of Explosion.* Loving kindness is beautiful, but patience is often painful. The God of infinite love can put up with infinite amount of suffering; but the god in flesh and blood had a limit to his patience. There were times in the life of even the greatest of all prophets when he wished to say, and did actually say: "Woe unto thee, Chorazin! Woe unto thee, Bethsaida! for if the mighty works, which were done in you, had been done in Tyre and Sidon, they would have repented long ago in sackcloth and ashes. But I say unto you, it shall be more tolerable for Tyre and Sidon at the day of judgment, than for you."[6] Ingratitude and treachery are universally loathed, but they are the two fiends one has to face here and there. We find some spontaneous satisfaction in the stories of Cromwell's kicking out the Rump Parliament and of Adam Bede's knocking down Captain Donnithorne. Where words fail and reason is impenetrable, the body seems to be an effective instrument of persuasion.

When the imperial German government declared that she was *compelled* to plunge Europe into war, when the United States asserted that it was her *manifest destiny* to rob Mexico of her territory, when Mussolini announced that Italian population *must* keep on expanding even by imposing taxes on bachelors and that other nations *must* assume responsibility for the excess mouths of Italy, they were all fit objects for moral indignation. Why was it necessary to commit any one of these crimes? Was it not the villainy of their heart, which created the illusion of necessity? All these necessities are born of self-deception. Explosion as a means of breaking up vicious circles in human relations, is an

[6] Matt. 11: 21-22.

effective instrument, is better than living with a perpetual grudge and in mutual hatred; it will probably last through eternity. Nevertheless, the fact remains that, in getting rid of an evil by smashing it, we destroy some good that may lie unsuspected at its root. Probably few evils are pure evils, and when we come to know them all, they may all have some positive values. The absolute good cannot be attained, until all the good that is in apparent evil is penetrated.

5. *The Art of Separation.* There are certain vicious circles in human relations, which arise from real incompatibility of desires. Such a vicious circle sometimes arises from sex-love, and can be avoided only by separation. When, for example, two suitors fight for the same beauty, there is a real conflict; and sex-love being one of the most personal of all human relations, nothing can be substituted for it, nor ought it to be so. For a lover, who is indifferent as to whether his beloved is a Helen or a Hecuba, is not much of a lover. Either one or the other of the two suitors must inevitably lose, and one can only hope that he loses as a sportsman does. There is a vicious circle in this situation in the sense that any solution of the conflict by any better method than separation is impossible.

It is also safe to say that, under the present circumstances, the only satisfactory solution of many racial problems is to be sought through geographical separation together with cultural interpenetration. The knowledge of one's character is a first step toward friendship. But knowledge without sympathy often breeds contempt and hatred. This seems to be a frequent occurrence, owing to the narrowness of our interest, and our poverty of tact, in the mutual unfolding of our purposes, whether in individual relations or in racial intercourse. No one is so perfect as to be admired entirely, much less is there any whole race to be so admired.

There are times when the perception of the meanness of one's neighbor leaves such an ineradicable impression upon one's memory that the mere recall of the event is sufficient to put an end to friendship. In such situations separation without ill-will is a great relief. A half way between personal and impersonal relations is often a safe device to shield others' weakness, to give them an opportunity to improve themselves without being exposed, and to leave a ray of hope for reconciliation in the future. The distinction between vulgar intimacy and friendship may be said to lie in this: that in the former there is a simple abolition of all privacy, while in the latter there is a privacy as well as mutuality. In all true, lasting, and fruitful friendship, there seems to be a residue of unexpressed sentiment. Great historical personages were often lonely souls; not because their nature was unsociable, but probably because they needed self-protection from inquisitive babblers who pry into the nooks and crannies of their heroes' lives and prattle about their findings. So long as human nature will remain imperfect, it may be a good thing for a multitude of people, not to know all about their neighbors, but to grow together with them in some common purpose. This might be an ideal relationship alike between individuals and races.

6. The Idealistic Art of Interpenetration.[7] Interpenetration

---

[7] There are several other concepts in sociological literature, which in some ways resemble the concept of interpenetration. Among these may be mentioned Professor Giddings' "social coördination" (*Principles of Sociology,* pp. 388-90; also Professor C. A. Ellwood, "The Psychological View of Society," *American Journal of Sociology,* vol. XV, No. 5); Professor Davis's "social co-adaptation" (M. M. Davis, *Psychological Interpretation of Society*); Professor Carver's "principle of balance" (*The Present Economic Revolution in the United States*); Kropotkin's "mutual aid" and even our old friends, "coöperation" and "love." Of these the last three have now become rather sentimental and fail to convey the idea that self-assertion is an important element in social progress. "Social coördination" and "social co-adaptation" are highly useful elements in the interpenetrative processes, but need improvement. Perhaps the most serious scientific attempt of them all is Professor Carver's "principle of balance" based upon the law of proportionality in chemistry, an improvement upon Marshall's concept of "equilibrium." A part of it, which deals with our relations with nature, is entirely satisfactory and is embodied in my exposition on the naturalistic art of domination above. It is, however, an impersonal, scientific concept, best applicable to mass movements, mass reactions and adjustments, in the province of economic activities. It touches ethical problems but imperfectly.

may be defined as *(a)* a circular process of *(b)* integrating several conflicting interests and fulfilling them in their organic unity,

The backbone of the "principle of balance" is "redistribution of human talents," as outlined in the tenth chapter of Professor Carver's *Essays in Social Justice*. The underlying idea is that scarcity of skilled labour is a primary cause of low wages and poverty, and their consequent social evils. If we train our young men in economically productive ideals of life, teach them skill by which to earn an honest living, and help them to find their proper places in industry, they will be economically prosperous. And economic prosperity is a fertile ground on which to sow the seeds of morality. All social problems are individual problems, and every social maladjustment is at bottom an individual maladjustment. If each individual takes care of himself, society will take care of itself. And one of the best ways in which a man can take care of himself, is to make himself proficient in the industrial art that will enable him to participate in the productive team-work of society. In a society which is organized on the basis of reward in proportion to mutual service through economic production, those services will be most highly rewarded which are in most demand. It is, therefore, to the interest of the individual as well as of society to supply such services, and an important part of education should consist of equipping young men and young women with the knowledge and morale for such services. The law of demand and supply operating through the self-interest of individuals, will "in the long run" bring about a rough equality among occupations.

Such is the "principle of balance." How soon can such an economic Zion be achieved? Not in a dozen or two of years. The popularization of birth-control alone will take at least a generation or two. By whom can it be brought about? Not by economists alone. From what motive can it be brought about? Not from the "economic motive" alone. Such an ideal can be achieved only through moral regeneration as well as scientific education. The readers of Professor Carver's writings (especially, *The Religion Worth Having*) must have noticed how fervent is his emotional strain. And this emotional appeal is entirely legitimate and necessary. For there are great multitudes who do not care so much for economic prosperity as they do for the silent admiration or applause of their fellow men; and in order to get these, they grow their finger nails long, they have their women's feet bound, they gabble on poetry and art in dirty hovels, they rattle on liberty, humanity, justice.

The view, which I am about to explain, is based on Miss Follett's concept of "interpenetration" (M. P. Follett, *Creative Experience*) and Professor Richard C. Cabot's concept of "circular social process," both of which are familiar enough to the students of present-day psychology, but which have been given ethical interpretations by Miss Follett and Professor Cabot. A successful interpenetrative process should necessarily recognize all the economic principles, embodied in Professor Carver's "principle of balance"—such as the law of proportionality, of marginal productivity, redistribution of human talents, individual inequality of rewards within occupational equality; otherwise, interpenetraton is likely to degenerate into sentimentalism. If men cannot live on bread alone, much less can they live on mere sentimentalism. But in addition to science, there must be some personal touch in order that we may realize a maximum moral economy.

through *(c)* leadership, *(d)* mutual understanding, and *(e)* improvement of the total situation. In order to emphasize their importance, I have separated the five points mentioned in this definition. I shall explain them in the order in which they are mentioned.

(a) *A Circular Process.* Psychologically, a circular reaction is a continuous process in which a response to a given stimulation evokes a further response in the original stimulator. A series of interstimulating actions and reactions, so perfectly carried out that the participants in the process play the rôle of key and lock, to one another, each event resulting in a creative experience, and integrating all the previous experiences, is called interpenetration. It is a personal process as contrasted with impersonal or mechanical processes. Personality is insisted upon, because it is the most concrete organic unit in all social processes. The attempt to typify a person or to identify him with any one of his conspicuous traits invariably results in abstraction, leaving out some vital aspects of his personality. To be impersonal is to pose and play a rôle. To be personal is to come out from behind one's conventional mask and to play the game as man to man.

(b) *An Integrative Process.* Psychologically, again, an integrative process is one which unifies two or more conflicting conative tendencies so as to secure the satisfaction of them all without conflict. For instance, the fondness for tasteful food conflicts with the dislike for obesity. But one need not therefore either avoid all tasteful food or put on many extra pounds. One could so regulate one's food habits as to satisfy both these desires. That is integration.[8] On a lower level, the body is an integration of millions upon millions of neurons and synapses of conflicting tendencies. On a still lower level, the formation and persistence of molecules are integrative processes. Society itself is an integration of conflicting purposes. It should be noted, however, that below the psychological level the sole end of integration

---

[8] See E. B. Holt, *The Freudian Wish.*

seems to be survival through economy of energy. Moral problems arise only above the psychological level. To live is not merely to keep on breathing and breeding, but also to ethicize nature. All true solutions of social problems must be moral as well as economical.

But the emergence of morality makes the integration of interests even more difficult. For instance, the last war cut off several millions of married or marriageable young men, and led to the young women's demand for a certain "right to happiness." The desire to have the sexual and parental instincts normally satisfied in itself could not be condemned. But it conflicted with their desire to preserve their respectability, and with their ideals of equality of the sexes. One way to attack this conflict is to get rid of those particular varieties of emotional drives by suppression. Another way to attack the conflict is to "sublimate" those emotions through tea parties, dancing, or the adoration of actors and clergymen. But a half killed desire may be more tormenting than one not at all repressed. A better way of solving the conflict is, to put all the several conflicting desires together and create a new, broader and higher desire that will subsume them all, such as a strenuous activity in the fields of art, literature, science, and social welfare work, in which one can most freely express oneself and create values. That is integration.

Yet another example. Suppose labor unions demand an advance in wages because the rise of prices has made their present wages inadequate to keep body and soul together; and suppose employers refuse to comply with this demand because the present rate of their profit has already been reduced to a reasonable minimum; both the demand and refusal are entirely legitimate, yet there is an economic conflict. The best solution for this conflict might be to persuade the workmen to increase their production through heartier coöperation, and thereby to enable the employers to advance their wages. An industrial enterprise is not a charitable institution; the conversion of the former to the latter will not only be uneconomical, but also have a degrading effect upon the workmen themselves. Hence, the advance of wages through the increase of production is the most satisfactory solution of the conflict. That is integration.

(c) Through Leadership. The most definite thing that can be said with regard to leadership is that it is relative to the common purpose of the group. There are no leaders in general; and if there are any who pretend to be, they are generally nuisances. All leaders are leaders of some group of men who stand for a more or less definite purpose. And since society is a functional unity of multiple purposes, there might be a leader for each one of them. The ideal system of leadership is the rotation system, by means of which the group can secure the leadership of the best qualified for each common purpose in view. For everybody can be a leader in some things, just as everybody is a potential hero or heroine to somebody. The man who is the most excellent from the point of view of carrying out the immediate common purpose, is the natural leader of the group for the time being. On the other hand, the attempt to wrest leadership from others who are better qualified is an injustice to oneself as well as to others, for few efforts are more ill-rewarded than the attempt to do things which one is ill-qualified to do. As with Cardinal Richelieu's labor to attain his ambition to be known to posterity as a man of letters, the time and the energy one puts in the effort to do things, which one is ill-qualified to do, are disproportionately large, compared with the paltry results one achieves.

The first duty of a leader in an interpenetrative process is to give every participant member a fair chance to express his views. For, only in this way can we know for certain what each one of us wants or can contribute to the formation of a common purpose. A leader must have some sense of humor with which to smooth over the awkward situations in the game of give and take. Humor is the ability to laugh at oneself; it enables one to break down psychological barriers; one who is wholly devoid of humor is a prig. A skilful leader in group discussions is a magician who provides such favorable stimuli for the mutual responses of the members that an observer may see them in the midst of their discussions bare their souls. And in the aftermath of the excitement there is often a general embarrassment. A tactful leader seizes such opportunities and turns the general embarrassment into general good humor, and thereby facilitates the process of integrating. An integration of this type is called the common purpose of the group. And finally, the common purpose thus formed, the leader must carry it out to his best ability with the powers conferred upon him by the voluntary consent of the group. The power over the group should be identical with the power for it. A leader, in the true sense of the word, is such a personality as just described; if not, he is a "boss."

(d) Through Mutual Understanding. Many social evils arise through misunderstandings of one another's motives; and by far the worst of all evils are human rather than natural evils. A fruitful cause of conflict is the essential unsoundness of our assumptions, on which we base our claims. We base our claims upon certain assumptions; but we can neither always state them clearly nor can we always prove them to be valid. They are metaphysical and can best be brought to our full consciousness by the coöperative effort of ascertaining their nature.

The deepest desire of all persons may be said to be, in the most general terms, the desire to amount to something. In the language of the earlier idealists, they are would-be world-builders and world-conquerors. From this fundamental desire, it seems, there arise such freakish phenomena as temperance advocates who denounce intemperance in the most intemperate language; jacks-of-all-trades, who are experts in everybody else's business except their own; patriots and humanitarians who send out their wives and daughters as washerwomen for somebody else, while they themselves orate on liberty, independence, justice, and humanity. Yet these pathetic people are frequently full of kind intentions and generous motives. If they knew that their single sovereign remedies for all social evils are based on wishful assumptions, and that many social evils arise precisely because there are too many freaks like themselves, it is not improbable that they would invest their generous motives and superabundant zeal in more profitable enterprises both for themselves and for others. Interpenetration is a method of finding out what ails such people, and whether the things which they apparently want are the things which they really want. Having found out their real desires, they are prepared to fulfil them as much as they can. Only in this way can we ever hope to succeed in removing the barriers that enclose the lonely builders of the world, each of whom grinds in his own little cosmos, and from whose confinement arise misunderstanding and evils.

(e) *Through Improvement of the Total Situation.* All efforts at mutual understanding presuppose some measure of creative listening. By creative listening I mean the effort to place oneself in others' position and to carry on their train of thought along with them. To converse is not to compete at noise-making like two victrolas set to work side by side, but to respond to thought. In the integrative process by means of which several conflicting interests are brought together face to face, real meanings are determined, and a common path is discovered for them all; such a process is an unfolding of social purpose. This concept is dynamic. For, it demands that every participant in the interpenetrative process move on, in the light of new facts discovered and new possibilities explored. To improve is to evolve better desires and broader interests out of the total situation. And the total situation is the sum of all the claims and counter-claims and their implications, laid bare before each and all of the participant members. The tool of improvement is invention: invention of new methods by which old desires are satisfied, and invention of new desires by which old conflicts are reconciled.

One of the prerequisites for a successful invention is to recognize the presence of a vast scale of conflict in life, internal and external; and having recognized it, to avoid the habit of thinking in terms of pseudo-dilemmas. Conflicts in the sense of real and permanent incompatibilities are relatively few. If every dilemma were as real as that between "either your life or your purse," with a pistol pointed at the chin, there would be real incompatibility. But not all dilemmas are so real; many of them are merely verbal. Even real dilemmas turn out to be illusions when they are solved by invention. Before the invention of the institution of private property, men lived in a continual dilemma between immediate starvation and plundering their neighbor. Before the invention of a system of social distinctions through intellectual and moral achievements, they lived in a continual dilemma between brutal self-assertion and ignominy. To them these and many other dilemmas were real, and therefore the choice of either the one or the other was necessary and inevitable. That which made these conflicts neither necessary nor inevitable is invention. Is not the history of civilization a history of just such inventive turns of the mind?

(f) Not Opposed to All Self-Assertion. Is interpenetration opposed to self-assertion? Yes and no. In the sense in which self-assertion is good, it is not opposed to interpenetration. In the sense in which self-assertion is bad, it is incompatible with interpenetration. The doctrine of interpenetration implies a view of the unity of growing and expanding pluralistic interests. Society is a functional unity of pluralistic interests, somewhat loosely organized compared with the organic unity of one's personality. Both in the growth of personality and in that of society, there are continual antithetical tendencies between the lesser interests and the greater. The assertion of the lesser interests is a self-assertion, and the assertion of the greater interests is also a self-assertion. The assertion of the Serbian peasants during the war that they would not have a bath was a self-assertion; and

the assertion of the American Red Cross nurses that they must have a bath was also a self-assertion. Each one of these claims is called self-assertion; yet the difference between the two sets of claims is great.

Self-assertion, however, is used in common parlance in the sense of the assertion of the lesser interests. Those who glorify self-assertion in this sense affect an overt contempt for those who speak of good will and community of interests. The doctrine of interpenetration is neither sentimental nor "too idealistic." Why should anything be considered sentimental, which is the very thing by which alone a maximum moral economy can be secured? It recognizes that every legitimate claim has a place in the total system of claims; and it demands that every claimant must assert his interest with all the manly vigor he can command; but that his interest must be a member in a coördinate system of interests. A world full of the Nietzschean Supermen is as impossible as a garden of a thousand trees, each one overtopping all the rest. But a system of interests so coördinated that each one of them can be reasonably fulfilled as a member of the whole, is at least a possibility.

(g) *Good Circles and Bad Circles.* It may be remembered that in Chapter II I represented society as a system of circles, with the individual at the center. I do not imply that the individual is the center of the universe, even though he is in every one of those concentric circles,—the family, the educational, recreational, occupational, political, religious, and ideational circles. Nor do I imply that this enumeration is by any means exhaustive: there are a great many other circles which for the sake of simplicity of treatment may be overlooked for the time being. Any one or all of these circles may be somewhat vaguely designated as "society." I have also said that the interpenetrative process is circular in the psychological and ethical senses I have explained, namely, a give and take process in which every participant member should assert his claims, examine with the rest of the members their underlying assumptions, the limits of their validity, and then evolve a common purpose for the whole group.

If I may keep on using the metaphor of circle to indicate a social group, as indeed in common language we speak of an academic circle, an athletic circle, a business circle, etc., a good circle is one which integrates as many interests of its members as there are, with all their variety, and fulfils them all in their organic unity. A bad circle is one which is dominated by some one interest, and which suppresses other interests or drives them out, thereby weakening itself and ultimately bringing about its own destruction. A good circle fruitfully multiplies its own interests by attracting other circles; and as it grows, it spurts off daughter circles, thereby perpetuating itself on progressively higher planes. But a bad circle, such as a gang of robbers, progressively narrows down its interests, and ultimately goes into extinction. In all good circles, there is rotation of leadership; there being no absolute standard of values, any interest whatsoever may come to play the leading rôle, provided, it can integrate all the participating interests and advance them toward fruition in their organic unity. In a bad circle, it is all otherwise.

From this point of view, the good is that which keeps the social group thinking and talking and working in concert, in order that it may have more fruitful thoughts, more reasonable talks and more satisfying works. Progress is the moving on and on of just such a circle, ever enlarging its radius. Happiness is the satisfaction derived from the participation in just such a circular process, in which one finds a chance to assert his claims and discover their meanings, to find his place and work with others for the common good. Economic productivity is the expression of such circular activities in terms of material goods, to meliorate the material environment and to provide an equitable distribution of opportunities for the participant members. Justice is that system of rewards and punishments, by which those who further these circular processes by their merit are enabled to grow and thrive and perpetuate themselves, and those who obstruct these circular processes by their wastefulness and immorality are eliminated. Love is the good will among the participant members in the circles, that helps them go round smoothly. And,—God? God is He who has set these circles in motion, and toward whom they move; and therefore He is seen only in the Common Purpose.

(h) The Extent to Which Interpenetration Works at Present. At present interpenetration works more or less satisfactorily in the family circles; and, in view of the triumph of the institution of monogamy even in such countries as Turkey and China, interpenetration will probably become more and more the normal practice in adjusting family relations. It works somewhat less satisfactorily in the educational and friendly circles, though there are many exceptions, such as the relation between inspiring teachers and their understanding disciples, and between friends like David and Jonathan. It works still less satisfactorily in the industrial circles, in which the motive of gain rather than that of exchange of services predominates. There seems to be no prospect for permanent improvement so long as the present rate of over-supply of unskilled laborers continues. All permanent improvement in industrial relations will come through the change of the present fatalistic attitude toward the multiplication of the human species, and the giving up of the pernicious notions of gentlemanly life. Since, however, such radical changes can not be effected in a year or two, a heartier coöperation between capital and labor will always mitigate the harshness of the operation of the natural tendencies in industrial relations. The adoption of the workmen's representation plan in adjusting the relations between employers and employees, in such places as the Standard Oil Company in New Jersey, is a step toward the ideal solution.

The art of interpenetration works even less satisfactorily in political circles, in which the meanest of human motives are apt to dominate, such as vanity and greed, which usually can be satisfied only at the expense of other people. When one glances at the enormous waste, crime and immorality, which accompany political rivalry in such nations as China, Greece, the numerous Latin-American and Black-American republics, one needs no demonstration to be convinced of the pernicious character of their present political methods. Since political education of the ignorant masses is a time-consuming process, their best chance for immediate political salvation lies in the direction of interpenetration among the few true leaders with whom they are blessed. It is also safe to say that the establishment of the League of Nations, of the Court of International Justice, and the popularity of settling international conflicts by peaceful methods, all tend to promote interpenetration.

The art of interpenetration scarcely works in the various doctrinal circles, such as the dogmatic religious sects. It does not seem to work at all in the circles of self-appointed crusaders and martyrs. If every Irish patriot hated Englishmen less and loved his countrymen more, Ireland would be far happier. And if every communist hated the capitalist less and loved his comrades more, the brawn-and-muscle class would be better off. That which should be important to them is neither what they never had nor what they have lost, but what they have now, together with the will to make the most of it, through a heartier coöperation among themselves.

COMMENTS

I have mentioned six varieties of social arts: self-annihilation, transvaluation, domination, explosion, separation, and interpenetration. I would recommend every one of these arts, except the first. But is there any way of defining the proper scope of their application? Is it self-evident which of these arts one should practice in any concrete situation? Not so, to me at least. For, if it were, we should be already in possession of social laws. It is one thing to construct a scheme of social control and to illustrate it by selected examples. It is another thing to carry out such a scheme. All artistic representations are illusive; concrete situations often defy them. Among these six arts interpenetration is the most desirable in solving human problems. But it is best applicable to small personal groups in which a rough measure of moral and intellectual equality, and community of interest, pre-exist. If the group is unwieldly, heterogeneous, and impersonal, there is little chance for interpenetration. As the size grows larger, the group frequently degenerates from a thinking circle to a talking circle, and as its talk becomes louder, its sense is drowned in its noise.

Transvaluation and domination, explosion and separation, all involve arbitrary limitations in the form of repression of some-body's interests; but interpenetration alone strives to transcend these limitations through invention and good will, and that which depends on one's inventive genius and good will is an unpredictable process. One can only try to make the best use of one's information with the aid of imagination. Failing this, one might try some of the lesser arts in good faith, in the order in which they are mentioned. One is justified by faith. For, this is where science ends and faith begins. But because good faith is such an all-important factor in the unfolding of human destinies, its counterpart, self-deception, is the root of most social evils.

Philosophically, such a view of life may necessitate the postu-late of the existence of a Divine Purposive Being, or even an Absolute Purpose, in whom all finite purposes may find their proper evaluation, each as a separate purpose and as a member of the Absolute. All finite purposes may then be dependent on the Absolute, but the Absolute may also be conceived to depend on the finite, finding its expression only in the finite. "God Himself, in short, may draw vital strength and increase of very being from our fidelity. For my own part, I do not know what the sweat and blood and tragedy of this life mean, if they mean anything short of this."[9] From this point of view, a good purpose is one which is in harmony with the Absolute, and a bad purpose is one which is in conflict with it. But how can we ever know what the Absolute Purpose is? Not by watching the rocks, examining the fossils, and experimenting with chimpanzees. Not by weighing and measuring one's pecuniary earnings. Not by holding oneself in pure passivity, and by falling into a trance. Physical objects obey the laws of physics, and biological organisms the laws of biology; but man is so "fearfully and wonderfully made" that he transcends these laws. The only conceivable law that he may be said invariably to obey is, the law that there should be a law, which may be called the law of the Absolute. It seems to be the destiny of man, not to naturalize humanity, but to humanize nature.

Perhaps in finding out what man is, we may come to know what the Absolute is; and in fulfilling what men want, we may fulfil what the Absolute wants. Thus far the most direct and successful method of discovering what men want is interpenetration. The Holy Spirit promised that whenever two or three gather in His name, He would be in the midst of them.

[9] William James, *The Will to Believe*, p. 61.

CHAPTER X
THE ARGUMENT IN REVIEW

A VALID SCIENTIFIC law may be defined as a description of an invariant pattern of phenomena, explicable by a generally accepted theory, in turn explicable by a plausible hypothesis, thus making the conceptual unification of phenomena complete. A valid scientific social law, then, should be a law of this type, having to do with human nature and social events.

The ambition of the social scientists is to discover true causal laws which will enable them to predict and control social phenomena as physicists predict and control physical phenomena by their knowledge of physical laws. The study of social phenomena thus far, however, has yielded no causal laws so precise or certain as those of physics. Instead we have a mass of empirical generalizations of limited validity, sometimes called "empirical laws." Technically, an "empirical law" is an empirical generalization which lacks a valid theory to explain it. I call these empirical generalizations "near-causal laws" because they are intended to be causal explanations of social phenomena. But some are pseudo-causal laws, others are tautologies, still others are circular statements, while many might be called quasi-causal laws.

In our search for social laws we have found it necessary to distinguish among propositions of different kinds, even though their authors, or some later writer, have claimed each to be a "law." I shall recapitulate very briefly the classifications which we have employed.

1. Methodological Presuppositions. The Austrian sociologist Gumplowicz laid down ten propositions which he called "universal laws, valid for social as well as for physical and mental phenomena," and Ross reduced these ten "laws" to seven propositions.[1] Neither the original nor the reshaped propositions are worth the name "social laws," even though they may be granted as methodological presuppositions for the discovery of true social laws. These propositions are so entirely devoid of any specific content that they are applicable to no particular social phenomena.

2. *Teleological Laws.* The general distinction between a teleological law and a causal law is, that the former describes and evaluates social phenomena in terms of final causes, whereas the latter describes them in terms of efficient causes. Within the class of teleological laws several types are distinguishable,[2] such as, *(a)* Those based on what may be called enlightened hedonism, for example, the "law of social aims" which reads, "The greatest good for the greatest number of social well-being is the aim of social action." *(b)* Those based on evolutionary formulas, for example the "law of survival and progress," which reads, "Institutions flourish or decay according to their adaptation to the circumstances of life surrounding the people which possess them." *(c)* Those based on theological beliefs, for example, the "law of political selection," which reads, "Under the true form of government, the premier will always be precisely the man intended by the Great Design to occupy that exalted place."

Teleological laws are of value in several ways: as expressions of social ideals, of moral aspiration, and frequently of poetic inspiration. They are also of some value insofar as they are preliminary surveys of the problem and may lead to the discovery of causal laws.

3. *Statistical Laws.* Within this class of laws three types may be distinguished,[3] namely, *(a)* economic laws, such as Professor Pearl's "law of population," and Engel's "law of consumption," which disclose a high degree of probability. *(b)* Eugenic laws, such as Galton's "law of ancestral inheritance," which are much

---

[1] See Chapter III.   [2] See Chapter IV.   [3] See Chapter V.

less reliable than economic laws. *(c)* Social psychological laws, which are least reliable.

The reason for this sliding scale of probability is that, since statistics can deal only with quantitative measurements, when it deals with the number of mouths and the amount of commodity expressed in terms of dollars and cents, its findings disclose a high degree of consistency; when it deals with physical traits, its findings are as reliable as the definition of the trait, which unfortunately is variable; but when it deals with such intangible traits as are encountered in psychology, for example, humor, will-power, intelligence, and the like, its findings are difficult indeed to express quantitatively.

4. Near-Causal Laws. For the sake of convenience of examination I have divided the near-causal laws into five classes:[4] *(a)* Those based on inferences from the order of historical sequences, for example, De Greef's "law of the development of exchange," which reads, "Merchandise money gives way to weighed metallic money, this to coined metallic money, this in turn to the bank note, and the bank note to the clearing-house set off." This is a pseudo-causal law, in that it offers a mere catalogue of historical events as a causal explanation of these events. *(b)* Those based on inference from biological analogy, for example, von Lilienfeld's "law of recapitulation," which reads, "The individual in his development from childhood passes through the culture epochs traversed by human society." *(c)* Those based on inference from mechanistic analogy, for example, Spencer's "law of social motion," which reads, "The attraction of cities is directly as the mass and inversely as the distance." This is another pseudo-causal law. *(d)* Those based on psychological analyses with sympathy as their central principle, for example, Professor Giddings' second "law of tradition," which reads "Tradition is authoritative and coercive in proportion as its subject

---

[4] See Chapters VI and VII.

matter consists of belief rather than of critically established
knowledge." This, as I have shown, is tautology; its substance
amounts merely to this: an uncritically accepted belief is authoritative and coercive in proportion as its subject matter is not
critically established knowledge. *(e)* Those based on psychological analyses with imitation as their central principle, for example, Tarde's nine "laws of imitation." I have criticized these
laws on the grounds of equivocation, exaggeration, misuse of the
metaphor of geometrical progression, exceptions, inadequacy of
psychological distinctions, and ethical inadequacy.

5. *Dialectical Laws.* In Chapter VIII, I have presented and
examined a group of philosophical generalizations on history,
made by Hegel, Marx, Spencer, Professor Hocking, and others.
These generalizations circulate as "social laws," "laws of history,"
or simply "laws." The general thought behind dialectical laws
may be expressed thus: In every historical epoch there are antithetical tendencies in nature and in man; through consequent
striving to transcend these antitheses a synthesis emerges, in
which the antitheses are reconciled, and which thereby becomes a
new thesis, in order to repeat the same process in an infinite series.

GENERAL RESULTS

Of social laws, as precise and certain as the laws of physics
and of chemistry, there seem to be none. There are, however,
some laws of a reasonable degree of probability, of which Gresham's law and the Malthusian laws of population are perhaps the
best examples. As long as the institution of private property
persists, Gresham's law will probably continue to operate in varying degrees of approximation; while under the same conditions
the Malthusian laws will be considerably counteracted by human
efforts at the improvement of the conditions of living. Generalized, this would mean that the laws of a reasonable degree of
probability are valid, so long as the conditions which they imply

remain unchanged, but of the persistence of such conditions we have no adequate knowledge.

Because of the inadequacy of our knowledge of the conditions under which the various social tendencies interact on one another, many social laws of even a high degree of probability should properly be called "statements of tendencies" rather than "laws." In economics this difficulty is frankly acknowledged, and careful writers speak of tendencies rather than laws. Marshall defined an economic law as a "statement of economic tendencies" or a set of circumstances which, if not counteracted, may come to pass, but by no means inevitably. The two indispensable companions of all economic laws are the term "other things being equal" and the term "it tends to"; but "other things" are rarely equal, and the various tendencies continually counteract one another. This might be said with even greater propriety of social laws.

The very notion of an exact science presupposes measurement which in turn presupposes the reduction of all data to a quantitative basis. The unit of measurement in the social sciences is sometimes assumed to be pleasure; sometimes, structural development; sometimes, survival, with an additional assumption of a proper standard of living to be expressed in terms of dollars and cents. But, upon close examination, all these assumptions have been found inadequate.

Science is a conceptual unification; the more perfect is the unification, the more certain is the science. The unification of the social sciences can not be accomplished until the multifarious generalizations which in one disguise or another circulate as "social laws" are brought together on the basis of valid social psychological laws. The history of the social sciences is the history of incomplete success of the various attempts at such a unification: some through biology, others through anthropology, some through economics, others through the philosophy of history.[5]

[5] See L. F. Ward, "Contemporary Sociology, *American Journal of Sociology*, vol. II (Nos. 4-6).

At present the psychologists are attracting much attention; some of them, like Professor J. B. Watson, are so optimistic that their utterances remind one of the boasts of the Homeric heroes before going into battle. But behind this optimistic view there is something essentially sound, which is, that the backbone of all the social sciences is psychology and that the laws of human behavior are the fundamental laws of all the social sciences. Thus the ultimate problem to which the study of all social problems can be reduced is the study of man himself. This simplification of the problem makes the study of social laws easier on the surface, but at bottom more complicated. It is at this point that dispute is rife and the result is least satisfactory; for metaphysics and logic, ethics and religion, all have equal claims to attention with those of the purely naturalistic psychology. But it is clear to me that we should either give up the search for efficient causes in social phenomena or follow the lead of the causal psychologists. Causal psychology is at present the best available avenue of approach left for those who aspire to make sociology an exact positive science. As yet, however, its technique of study is too meagre to deal with all social problems in their infinite varieties, nor has it yet accumulated sufficient data from which to deduce valid social laws. Its success will, therefore, be measured by its ability to coöperate with the various other special social sciences, such as anthropology and economics, politics and jurisprudence, metaphysics and logic, ethics and religion.

All social problems are resolvable ultimately into problems about men: what they are, what they want, and how they get it. The study of history may help us to build our interests, and thereby to become what we are, since we may at any given time be identified with our interest. Science may help us to get what we want, by presenting us with sets of facts. And philosophy may help us to discover what is the nature of things we want, or whether the things we apparently want are the things we really want. From the methodological point of view, therefore, there may be said to be, fundamentally, three avenues of approach to social studies. But, thus far the scientific method still remains largely programmatic, and the historical and philosophical methods have yielded many interpretations of life. So long as there are no social laws of mathematical precision, the social sciences remain a body of empirical generalizations of limited validity. That such sciences cannot be compared, in point of precision and certainty, with mathematics, or physics, or even physiology, needs no further demonstration. But inexactitude and uncertainty need not hinder the social scientists from considering sociology a science in a broader sense of that term, just as some people speak of "medical science."

A social art might be defined as skill or wisdom which is useful to the appreciation of human values, to the improvement of human relations and the accompanying conditions of living. I have outlined in the preceding chapter, six of the commonest of the social arts, namely, the mystic arts of self-annihilation and of transvaluation, the naturalistic arts of domination, of explosion, and of separation, and the idealistic art of interpenetration. In dealing with nature, the art of domination is the most fruitful one, since we assume no moral obligations toward nature, and our social environment can grow and improve only by continually displacing the natural environment. And in dealing with human beings, we can realize a maximum moral economy only by the art of interpenetration, which I have defined as a personal process of integrating several conflicting interests and fulfilling them in their unity, through leadership, mutual understanding, and improvement of the total situation.

Transvaluation and domination, explosion and separation, all involve arbitrary limitations in the form of repression of somebody's interests; but interpenetration alone strives to transcend these limitations through invention and good will. And since that which depends on one's inventive genius and good will, is an unpredictable process, one can only try to make the best use of one's knowledge with the aid of imagination. Failing this, one might try some of the lesser arts in good faith—except the mystic art of self-annihilation. For, even domination and explosion are better than falling into a trance, resigning to fate and doing nothing, provided, the motives of domination and explosion are good. One is justified by faith. And because good faith is such an all-important factor in the unfolding of human destinies, its counterpart, self-deception, is the root of most social evils.

Now, even an art presupposes certain working principles which need not be exact, but which must possess some measure of probability. The medical art, for example, presupposes certain working principles of bio-chemistry. The social laws which I have gathered and discussed, are such a body of heuristic working principles as a social art presupposes.

BIBLIOGRAPHY

Alexander, S., *Space, Time, and Deity.* London, 1920.

Allport, F. H., *Social Psychology.* Boston, 1924.

—— "The Present Status of Social Psychology," *Journal of Abnormal Psychology,* vol. XXI, no. 4.

—— "The Group Fallacy in Relation to Social Science," *Journal of Abnormal Psychology,* vol. XIX, no. 2.

Allport, G. W., "Concepts of Trait and Personality," *Psychological Bulletin,* vol. XXIV, no. 5.

Baldwin, J. M., *Social and Ethical Interpretations in Mental Development; A Study in Social Psychology.* New York, 1902.

Barnes, H. E., *The New History and Social Studies.* New York, 1925.

Barth, P., *Die Philosophie der Geschichte als Soziologie.* Leipzig, 1922.

Bascom, J., *Sociology.* New York, 1887.

Beer, M., *Life and Teachings of Karl Marx.* New York, 1924.

Bernard, L. L., "Scientific Method and Social Progress," *American Journal of Sociology,* vol. XXXI, no. 1.

Blackmar, F. W., and Gillin, J. L., *Outlines of Sociology,* (rev. ed.) New York, 1923.

Boodin, J. E., "The Law of Social Participation," *American Journal of Sociology,* vol. XXVII, no. 1.

Branford, V. V., "The Origin and Use of the Word Sociology," *American Journal of Sociology,* vol. IX, no. 2.

Bristol, L. M., *Social Adaptation; A Study in the Development of the Doctrine of Adaptation as a Theory of Social Progress.* Cambridge, Mass., 1915.

Brown, B. W., *Social Groups.* Chicago, 1926.

Bryce, J., *Modern Democracies,* 2 vols. New York, 1921.

Burtt, E. A., "Real Versus Abstract Evolution," *Proceedings of the Sixth International Congress of Philosophy,* 1926.

Bushee, F. A., *Principles of Sociology.* New York, 1923.

Caird, E., *Hegel.* Philadelphia and Edinburgh, 1883, 1886.

Campbell, N. R., *What Is Science?* London, 1921.

Carver, T. N., *Economy of Human Energy.* New York, 1924.

—— *Essays in Social Justice.* Cambridge, Mass., 1915.

—— *Principles of National Economy.* Boston, 1921.

———— *Sociology and Social Progress; A Handbook for Students of Sociology.* Boston, 1905.

Chapin, F. S., "A Theory of Synchronous Cultural Cycles," *Journal of Social Forces,* vol. III, no. 4.

Cheyney, E. P., "Law in History," *American Historical Review,* vol. XIX, no. 2.

Comish, N. H., *The Standard of Living; Elements of Consumption.* New York, 1923.

Comte, A., *Positive Philosophy,* translated by H. Martineau. 3 vols. London, 1853.

Cooley, C. H., *Human Nature and the Social Order.* New York, 1912.

———— *Social Process.* New York, 1920.

Groce, B., *Historical Materialism and the Economics of Karl Marx,* translated by C. M. Meredith. New York, 1914.

Dealey, J. Q. and Ward, L. F., *A Text-Book of Sociology.* New York, 1920.

De Greef, G. J., *Les lois sociologiques.*

———— "Introduction to Sociology," *American Journal of Sociology,* vol. VIII, no. 4.

Ducasse, C. J., "On the Nature and the Observability of the Causal Relation," *Journal of Philosophy,* vol. XXVIII, no. 3.

East, E. M., *Mankind at the Crossroads.* New York, 1923.

Ellwood, C. A., *Sociology in Its Psychological Aspects.* New York.

———— "Marx's Economic Determinism," *American Journal of Sociology,* vol. XVII, no. 1.

———— "Theories of Cultural Evolution," *American Journal of Sociology,* vol. XXIII, no. 6.

Engels, F., *Feuerbach; The Roots of the Socialist Philosophy,* translated by A. Lewis. Chicago, 1903.

———— Introduction to *The Manifesto of the Communist Party.* 1888.

Faris, E., "Laws of Imitation," *American Journal of Sociology,* vol. XXXII, no. 3.

Fling, F. M., "Historical Synthesis," *American Historical Review,* vol. IX, no. 1.

Fogel, F. H., "Metaphysical Elements in Sociology," *American Journal of Sociology,* vol. X, no. 3; vol. XII, no. 6.

Follett, M. P., *Creative Experience,* New York, 1924.

———— *The New State. Group Organization the Solution of Popular Government.* New York, 1918.

Ford, J., *Social Problems and Social Policy; Principles Underlying Treatment and Prevention of Poverty, Defectiveness, and Criminality.* Boston, 1923.

George, H., *The Law of Human Progress.* New York, 1917.

Ghent, W. J., *Mass and Class.* New York, 1904.

Giddings, F. H., *The Elements of Sociology.* New York, 1919.

——— *Inductive Sociology; A Syllabus of Methods, Analyses and Classifications, and Previously Formulated Laws.* New York, 1914.

——— *Principles of Sociology; an Analysis of the Phenomena of Association and of Social Organization.* New York, 1896.

——— *Scientific Study of Human Society.* Chapel Hill, N. C., 1924.

——— *Studies in the Theory of Human Society.* New York, 1922.

Gide, C., and Rist, C., *A History of Economic Doctrines from the Time of the Physiocrats to the Present Day.* London, 1915.

Goldenweiser, A. A., *Early Civilization; an Introduction to Anthropology.* New York, 1922.

Grosse, E., *Die Formen der Familie und die Formen der Wirthschaft.* Leipzig, 1896.

Gumplowicz, L., *The Outlines of Sociology,* translated by F. W. Moore. Philadelphia, 1899.

——— *Der Rassenkampf.* Innsbruck, 1928.

Hall, A. C., *Crime in Its Relation to Social Progress.* New York, 1902.

Hankins, F. H., *The Racial Basis of Civilization; A Critique of the Nordic Doctrine.* New York and London, 1926.

Harrison, F., "Sociology, Its Definition and Its Limits," *Psychological Review,* vol. III, no. 2.

Hayes, E. C., "The Social Forces Error," *American Journal of Sociology,* vol. XVI, no. 5.

Hegel, G. W. F., *Lectures on the Philosophy of History,* translated by J. Sibree. London, 1857.

Hobhouse, L. T., *Social Development, Its Nature and Conditions.* New York, 1924.

Hocking, W. E., "Mind and Near-Mind," *The Proceedings of the Sixth International Congress of Philosophy,* 1926.

——— *Man and the State.* New Haven, 1926.

——— *On the Law of History* (University of California Publications in Philosophy, vol. II, no. 3). Berkeley, 1909.

Holt, E. B., *The Freudian Wish and Its Place in Ethics*. New York, 1915.

Kallen, H. M., "Political Science as Psychology," *American Political Science Review*, vol. XVII, no. 1.

Kroeber, A. L., "The Super-Organic," *American Journal of Sociology*, vol. XXIII, no. 5.

Letourneau, C. J. M., *L'evolution politique dans les diverses races humaines*. Paris, 1890.

Lowell, A. L., "The Physiology of Politics," *American Political Science Review*, vol. IV, no. 1.

McDougall, W., *An Introduction to Social Psychology*. (14th ed.). Boston, 1921.

——— *Outline of Psychology*. New York, 1923.

——— "Instinct and the Unconscious," *British Journal of Psychology*, vol. X, no. 1.

——— "Can Sociology and Social Psychology Dispense with Instincts?" *Journal of Abnormal Psychology*, vol. XIX, no. 1.

McIver, R. M., *Community, A Sociological Study; Being an Attempt to Set Out the Nature and Fundamental Laws of Social Life*. London, 1920.

——— "What is Social Psychology," *British Journal of Psychology*, vol. VI (1913).

Marshall, A., *Principles of Economics; An Introductory Volume*. 8th ed. New York, 1920.

Martineau, J., *Types of Ethical Theory*. 2nd ed. London, 1886.

Marx, K., *Capital; a Critique of Political Economy*. (1885, 1894). Chicago, 1909-10.

——— *The Communist Manifesto*. (1848). Chicago, 1913.

Mayo-Smith, R., *Economics*. Baltimore, 1888.

Mill, J. S., *A System of Logic; Being a Connected View of the Principles of Evidence and the Methods of Scientific Investigation*. 8th ed. New York, 1884.

——— *Principles of Political Economy, with Some of Their Applications to Social Philosophy*. Ashley ed. New York, 1923.

Morgan, Lloyd, *Emergent Evolution*. New York, 1925.

Müller-Lyer, F., *History of Social Development*, translated by E. C. Lake and H. A. Lake. London, 1920.

Novicow, J., "The Mechanism of Human Association," *American Journal of Sociology*, vol. XXIII, no. 3.

Ogburn, W. F., *Social Change with Respect to Culture and Original Nature.* New York, 1922.

Palgrave, R. H. I., *Dictionary of Political Economy,* edited by Henry Higgs. 3 vols. New York, 1926.

Pearl, R., *Studies in Human Biology.* Baltimore, 1924.

Pearson, K., *Grammar of Science.* 2nd ed., London, 1900.

Perry, R. B., *Approach to Philosophy.* New York, 1905.

—— *Present Philosophical Tendencies.* New York, 1912.

——*General Theory of Value; Its Meaning and Basic Principles Construed in Terms of Interest.* New York, 1926.

Popenoe, P., and Johnson, R. H., *Applied Eugenics.* New York, 1920.

Ritchie, A. D., *Scientific Method.* New York, 1923.

Rivers, W. H. R., "Sociology and Psychology," *Psychological Review,* vol. IX, no. 1.

Ross, E. A., *Foundations of Sociology.* New York, 1905.

—— *Principles of Sociology.* New York, 1920.

—— *Social Control; A Survey of the Foundations of Order.* New York, 1904.

—— "Moot Points in Sociology," *American Journal of Sociology,* vol. VIII, no. 6.

—— "Social Laws," *American Journal of Sociology,* vol. IX, no. 1.

Royce, J., *Lectures on Modern Idealism,* edited by J. Loewenberg. New Haven, 1919.

—— *The World and the Individual.* New York, 1900-01.

Russell, B., *Scientific Method in Philosophy.* London, 1915.

Santayana, G., *Scepticism and Animal Faith; an Introduction to a System of Philosophy.* New York, 1923.

Simons, S. E., "Social Assimilation," *American Journal of Sociology,* from vol. VI, no. 6, to vol. VII, no. 4, inclusive.

Slater, G., "The Psychological Basis of Economic Theory," *Psychological Review,* vol. XV, nos. 3-4.

Small, A. W., "The Methodology of the Social Problem," *American Journal of Sociology,* vol. IV, no. 3.

—— "Points of Agreement Among Sociologists," *American Journal of Sociology,* vol. XII, no. 5.

—— "Fifty Years of Sociology in the United States," *American Journal of Sociology,* vol. XXI, no. 6.

Spencer, H., *First Principles.* 6th ed. New York, 1912.

—— *Principles of Sociology.* 3 vols. New York, 1900-1901.

838x

———— *Data of Ethics.* New York, 1879.

Swain, J. M., "What is History," *Journal of Philosophy,* vol. XX, nos. 11-13.

Tarde, G. de, *Laws of Imitation,* translated by Parsons. New York, 1903.

———— *Social Laws,* translated by Warren. New York, 1899.

Taussig, F. W., *Principles of Economics.* 2 vols., 3d ed. New York, 1927.

Taylor, H., *Origin of Government.*

Teggart, F. J., *Theory of History.* New Haven, 1925.

Thomson, J. A., *Introduction to Science.* New York, 1911.

Todd, A. J., *Theories of Social Progress.* New York, 1918.

Walthew, G. W., *The Philosophy of Government.* New York, 1898.

Ward, L. F., *Dynamic Sociology.* 2 vols. New York.

———— *Pure Sociology.* New York, 1903.

————"The Social Forces," *American Journal of Sociology,* vol. II, nos. 1-2.

———— "Contemporary Sociology," *American Journal of Sociology,* vol. VII, nos. 4-6.

White, R. C., "The Human Pairing Season in America," *American Journal of Sociology,* vol. XXXII, no. 5.

Whitehead, A. N., *Enquiry Concerning the Principles of Natural Knowledge.* New York, 1919.

———— *Science and the Modern World.* New York, 1925.

Wilson, W., "The Law and the Facts," *American Political Science Review,* vol. V, no. 1.

Wood, E. B., "Progress as a Sociological Concept," *American Journal of Sociology,* vol. VII, no. 6.

Znaniecki, F., *Laws of Social Psychology.* Chicago, 1925.

INDEX

ABSOLUTE, 189f., 192, 194f., 197, 237f.
Adaptation, 79f.
Adjustment, 226.
Alexander, S., 32.
Allport, F. H., 32, 177.
Allport, G. W., 114.
Analogies, biological, 80, 124-126, 128f.; historical, 115-124; limitations, 128-130; mechanical, 126-130.
Analysis, causal, 32-35; illustrations, 35-41.
Anthropology, 42f.
Antiquity, 139.
Antithesis, 171, 209f.
Apriorisms, 7, 53-77.
Art, social, 10; definition, 212, 245; domination, 219-223, 245; explosion, 223f., 245; interpenetration, 225-236, 245f.; necessity, 213f.; self-annihilation, 216f.; separation, 224f., 245; transvaluation, 217f.
Assimilation, 182-185.
Attention, 179f.
Authority, 138.
Axioms, 54.

BALANCE, principle of, 226.
Baldwin, J. M., 178f.
Bascom, J., 56, 63.
Beer, M., 200.
Belief, 138, 240.
Biological analogy, 80, 124-126, 128f.
Blackmar, F. W., and Gillin, J. L., 3, 9, 57, 58f., 78, 83, 131, 138, 203, 204.
Böhm-Bawerk, E., 21, 77.
Boston Transcript, 47.
Brown, B. W., 5, 208f.
Bryce, J., 6.
Burtt, E. A., 33.
Bushee, F. A., 103, 112.

CABOT, R. C., 226.
Campbell, N. R., 13, 14, 16.

Carver, T. N., 4, 45, 176, 225f.
Causation, 11, 18, 30f., 50, 76; psychological, 35-41.
Cause, efficient and final, 18, 34; social, 171.
Character, 163-165.
Cheyney, E. P., 7, 67-70, 80-82, 85-90, 93, 207f.
Choice, 179.
Christianity, 193.
Circle, social, 233-235.
Circular reaction, 187, 227.
Class, 207f.; distinction, 143; struggle, 196, 198-200.
Coercion, 137f.
Comish, N. H., 55, 64.
Comte, A., 5, 68, 115f., 117f., 122, 201.
Conditioning of behavior, 35.
Conduct, 163-165.
Conflict, 232.
Consciousness of kind, 131-135, 144, 148, 151.
Cooley, C. H., 179f., 188.
Creative imagination, 188.
Croce, B., 196-200.
Crowds, 83.
Culture, 182.

DARWIN, C., 201.
Davis, M. N., 225.
De Greef, G. J., 8, 119, 121, 126, 241.
Democracy, 157, 159, 160.
Desires, 228.
Dialectical law, history, 192-195; individual development, 190-192; list, 200-209; materialistic version, 195-200.
Differentiation, 202.
Diminishing returns, 54f.
Domination, 145, 149, 219-223, 245.
Durkheim, E., 126.

EAST, E. M., 106.
Eaton, R. M., 19f.

[253]

Economic, factor, 196-200; laws defined, 64f.; laws enumerated, 55; man, 53.
Economics, 43-46.
Education, 48.
Ego, social, 152, 154f.
Ellwood, C. H., 225.
Emergence, 32-34, 69.
Engels, F., 110, 195-201, 211, 240.
Equalization, 146, 150.
Ethics, 50.
Evolution, 202, 240.
Explanation, scientific, 16; see also causation.
Exploitation, 143-150.

FACT, scientific, 14f.
Faris, E., 177, 180f.
Follett, M. P., 226.
Freedom, 192-195, 205.
Friendship, 225.

GALTON, F., 112, 113, 240f.
General Mind, 116f., 135f.
Generalization, 26f.
George, H., 109, 166.
Ghent, W. J., 198.
Giddings, F. H., 4, 8, 60, 82f., 131ff., 165, 181, 206f., 225, 241f.
Gide, C., and Rist, C., 9, 55, 56, 63.
Goldenweiser, A. A., 119, 120.
Gregariousness, 133.
Gresham's Law, 54, 242.
Grosse, E., 119.
Groups, 148; morality, 151-155.
Gumplowicz, L., 54, 68, 204, 208, 239.

HABITS, 37, 177.
Haeckel, E., 125.
Hall, A. C., 90f., 104.
Happiness, 234.
Hayes, E. G., 119.
Hedonism, 25, 78ff., 96, 240.
Hegel, G. W. F., 189-197, 208-211.
Historical sequences, 115-124.
History, 47, 214f.; economic interpretation, 196.

Hocking, W. E., 201-203, 205f., 209.
Holt, E. B., 227.
Humor, 229f.
Hypothesis, scientific, 15.

IDEAS, 197.
Illusion 157.
Imitation, definitions, 168, 178. 180f.; instinct, 176; laws, 168-178, 180f.
Individual development, 190-192.
Institutional change, 162f.
Integration, 202, 227-229.
Interdependence, 146, 208.
Interests, 217f.
Interpenetration, 184.
Invention, 170, 174f., 231f.

JAMES, W., 217, 237f.
Justice, 234f.

KALLEN, H. M., 6.
Kant, I., 133f., 189.
Kemal, M., 47.
Kropotkin, P. A., 199, 225.
Kroeber, A. L., 33, 120.

LANGUAGE, 36.
Laws, causal and teleological, 78, 91; dialectical, 8, 190-200; general, 238; nature, 11-14; near-causal, 7f., chs. VI, VII; positivistic, 201.
Laws, scientific, 12f., 15, 239, 243; aesthetic value, 17; discovery, 13; exceptions, 27f.; least assumption, 30; novelties, 28; types, 11-13; utility, 16f.; verbal pitfalls, 29.
Laws, social, adult life, 90; aesthetic development, 119; alternation, 204f.; ancestral inheritance, 112; antagonism, 166f.; apriorisms, 53-77; assimilation, 182-186; association, 165f.; choice, 206f.; choice of ideals, 82; classification, 5f., 25; conflict of opposites, 204; conscious resemblance, 131-135; continuity, 66-71; definition, 20, 21; definiteness of arrange-

ment, 202; democracy, 85-87; derived demand, 64; development of exchange, 119; development of social composition, 135f.; development of social constitution, 136; development of social structures, 204; dialectical, 200-209; differentiation, 202; diffusion, 119; double aspect, 167f.; economic development, 127f.; Engel's, 110; equilibration, 202; evolution, 202; evolution of colonies, 109f.; exploitation, 143-150; family, 90; filial regression, 112; free competition, 63; free consent, 87; imitation, 162, 168-178; impermanence, 80; impulsive social action, 181; individual choice, 56ff.; integration, 201; interdependence, 207f.; least cost, 63f.; liberty, 139-143; malthusian, 104-109; moral progress, 89f.; parsimony, 56; Pearl's equation, 100-103; psychological, 47; recapitulation, 125; selection, basis, 3-5; self-interest, 56, 63; social aims, 78; social control, 151-165; society, 90; spiritual development, 83; substitution, 64; survival and progress, 79; teleological, 6f., 78-94; telesis, 203; three stages, 118; tradition, 137-139; universal, 71-74; value, 205f.

Laws, statistical, 7, 95-114.
Leadership, 229f.
Le Bon, G., 83.
Leopold, L., 157.
Lewis, C. I., 19.
Liberality, 139f.
Liberty, 139-143.
Likemindedness, 140-142.
Lilienfeld, von, P., 125, 421.
Logical Construction, 210f.
Love, 224, 235.

MALTHUS, T., 20, 29, 176, 242.
Marshall, A., 55, 64, 77, 243.
Martin, E. D., 83.
Martineau, J., 202.
Marx, K., 195-201, 208-211.
Materialism, 195-200.
Mayo-Smith, R., 99.

McDougall, W., 133, 134, 180.
Measurement, 25.
Mechanistic analogies, 126-130.
Metaphysics, 32, 49.
Methodological presuppositions, 7, 214f.
Mill, J. S., 12, 14, 26, 29, 63, 65, 66, 96, 213.
Montague, M. P., 217.
Morality, 151-155.
Morgan, L., 69, 121.
Müller-Lyer, F., 5, 127f.
Mutual Understanding, 230f.
Mysticism, 216-218.

NATURAL laws, 91-93.
Nature, 195, 219f.

OGBURN, W. F., 70.

PALGRAVE, R. H. I., 9, 55, 64.
Pareto, V., 23.
Pearl, R., 100, 102, 240.
Pearson, K., 12, 112.
Perry, R. B., 20.
Personality, 39, 156f., 227.
Philosophy, 214f.
Plato, 189.
Politics, 46, 235f.
Popenoe, P., and Johnson, R. H., 112.
Population, 29, 100-109.
Power, social, 155f., 158-160.
Prestige, 155-157.
Presuppositions, 7, 53ff., 214f., 239f.
Primary data of sociology, 23.
Primitive societies, 199f.
Progress, 50f., 165f., 203, 210, 234.
Prohibition, 221f.
Psychology, 244; and social laws, 47; and sociology, 40f.; assumptions, 30; causal, 31, 35-41, 51.
Publicity, 145f.
Purpose, 238.

RACE, 207f.
Race consciousness, 182-186.
Reason, 194.
Religion, 50, 163-165.

Repetition, 169.
Results, 9f., 242-246.
Ricardo, D., 77.
Rights, 221f.
Ritchie, A. D., 11, 13, 16, 92.
Ross, E. A., 5, 8, 9, 61, 74f., 109, 118f., 125, 126, 127, 143-165, 201-203, 239f.
Royce, J., 190, 192, 195, 217.
Russell, B., 15.

SANTAYANA, G., 17.
Science, 16, 212, 214f.; limitations, 18; social, 41-51.
Secondary data of sociology, 24.
Secondary qualities, 19.
Self-assertion, 232f.
Self-consciousness, 39f.; of group, 144, 148, 154, 161.
Selfishness, class, 161.
Self-projection, 178f.
Simon, S., 182-186.
Small, A. W., 3f.
Smart, W., 21.
Smith, A., 29, 131.
Smith, G., 202.
Social Art, see Art, Social.
Social constitution, 136.
Social control, laws, 151-165.
Social fact, 22, 23.
Social laws, see Laws, Social.
Social Mind, 116f., 135f.
Socialization, 178.
Sociology, and history, 47; and politics, 46; as synthetic science, 42, 51; hypothetical science, 23; methodological assumptions, 31.
Socrates, 189.

Spencer, H., 25, 61, 66, 76, 103, 124f., 126, 202, 210, 241.
Statistical Laws, see Laws, statistical.
Streightoff, F. H., 110.
Suggestion, 177, 179f.
Sympathy, 131-168.
Synergy, 203f.
Synthesis, 171f., 202f., 210.

TARDE, G., 8, 29, 162, 168-178, 188, 242.
Taussig, F. W., 137.
Tautology, 186f.
Taylor, H., 167, 204f.
Teleological laws, see Laws, teleological.
Teleology, 18, 34f.
Tertiary data of sociology, 24, 41.
Theory, scientific, 15.
Thompson, A. J., 15.
Tradition, 138.
Types, psychological, 142.

UNIFICATION, 186.

VALUE, 213f.

WALTHEW, G. W., 84f., 167, 205.
War, 207f.
Ward, L. F., 56, 57, 125f., 133, 156, 203, 243.
Watson, J. B., 60.
Weltgeist, 190, 192, 211.
Whitehead, A. N,. 22, 71.
Wilson, W., 212.

ZNANIECKI, F., 14.

THE UNIVERSITY OF NORTH CAROLINA
SOCIAL STUDY SERIES

UNDER THE GENERAL EDITORSHIP OF HOWARD W. ODUM. BOOKS MARKED WITH *
PUBLISHED IN COÖPERATION WITH THE INSTITUTE FOR RESEARCH IN SOCIAL SCIENCE

BECKWITH: *Black Roadways: A study of Folk Life in Jamaica*............ 3.00
BRANSON: *Farm Life Abroad*... 2.00
*BREARLEY: *Homicide in South Carolina*.......................*In preparation*
*BROWN: *Public Poor Relief in North Carolina*....................... 2.00
*BROWN: *State Highway System of North Carolina*..............*In preparation*
*BROWN: *State Movement in Railroad Development*.................... 5.00
CARTER: *Social Theories of L. T. Hobhouse*........................... 1.50
CROOK: *General Strike, The*.. 6.50
FLEMING: *Freedmen's Savings Bank, The*............................. 2.00
GEE: *Country Life in America*....................................... 2.50
*GREEN: *Constitutional Development in the South Atlantic States, 1776-1860*..$4.00
GREEN: *Negro in Contemporary American Literature, The*............... 1.00
*GRISSOM: *Negro Sings a New Heaven, The*........................... 2.50
HAR: *Social Laws*... 4.00
*HEER: *Income and Wages in the South*.............................. 1.00
*HERRING: *History of the Textile Industry in the South*...........*In preparation*
*HERRING: *Welfare Work in Mill Villages*............................. 5.00
HOBBS: *North Carolina: Economic and Social*........................ 3.50
*JOHNSON: *Folk Culture on St. Helena Island*........................ 3.00
*JOHNSON: *John Henry: Tracking Down a Negro Legend*................. 2.00
*JOHNSON: *Social History of the Sea Islands*........................ 3.00
JORDAN: *Children's Interests in Reading*............................ 1.50
KNIGHT: *Among the Danes*... 2.50
LOU: *Juvenile Courts in the United States*........................... 3.00
*METFESSEL: *Phonophotography in Folk Music*....................... 3.00
MILLER: *Town and Country*... 2.00
*MITCHELL: *William Gregg: Factory Master of the Old South*.......... 3.00
*MURCHISON: *King Cotton is Sick*.................................. 2.00
NORTH: *Social Differentiation*..................................... 2.50
ODUM: *Approach to Public Welfare and Social Work, An*............... 1.50
*ODUM (Ed.): *Southern Pioneers*................................... 2.00
*ODUM and WILLARD: *Systems of Public Welfare*..................... 2.00
*ODUM and JOHNSON: *Negro and His Songs, The,*.................... 3.00
*ODUM and JOHNSON: *Negro Workaday Songs*........................ 3.00
POUND: *Law and Morals*... 2.00
*PUCKETT: *Folk Beliefs of the Southern Negro*...................... 5.00
*RHYNE: *Some Southern Cotton Mill Workers and Their Villages*........ 2.50
ROSS: *Roads to Social Peace*....................................... 1.50
SALE: *Tree Named John, The*....................................... 2.00
SCHWENNING (Ed.): *Management Problems*.......................... 2.00
SHERRILL: *Criminal Procedure in North Carolina*.................... 3.00
*STEINER and BROWN: *North Carolina Chain Gang, The*.............. 2.00
*VANCE: *Human Factors in Cotton Culture*.......................... 3.00
*WAGER: *County Government and Administration in North Carolina*...... 5.00
WALKER: *Social Work and the Training of Social Workers*............. 2.00
WHITE: *Some Cycles of Cathay*..................................... 1.50
WILLEY: *Country Newspaper, The*.................................. 1.50
WINSTON: *Illiteracy in the United States*........................... 3.50

*The University of North Carolina Press, Chapel Hill, N. C.; The
Baker and Taylor Co., New York; Oxford University
Press, London; The Maruzen Company, Tokyo;
Edward Evans & Sons, Ltd., Shanghai.*